Inclusive Instruction

WHAT WORKS FOR SPECIAL-NEEDS LEARNERS

Karen R. Harris and Steve Graham
Editors

Vocabulary Instruction for Struggling Students
Patricia F. Vadasy and J. Ron Nelson

Preparing Effective Special Education Teachers
Nancy Mamlin

RTI for Reading at the Secondary Level:
Recommended Literacy Practices and Remaining Questions
Deborah K. Reed, Jade Wexler, and Sharon Vaughn

Inclusive Instruction:
Evidence-Based Practices for Teaching Students with Disabilities
Mary T. Brownell, Sean J. Smith, Jean B. Crockett, and Cynthia C. Griffin

Inclusive Instruction

Evidence-Based Practices for Teaching Students with Disabilities

Mary T. Brownell
Sean J. Smith
Jean B. Crockett
Cynthia C. Griffin

THE GUILFORD PRESS
New York   London

KH

Library of Congress Cataloging-in-Publication Data

Inclusive instruction: evidence-based practices for teaching students with disabilities/
Mary T. Brownell . . . [et al.].
  p. cm. — (What works for special-needs learners)
  Includes bibliographical references and index.
  ISBN 978-1-4625-0388-9 (pbk.) — ISBN 978-1-4625-0402-2 (hard cover)
  1. Inclusive education.   2. Learning disabled children—Education.   I. Brownell,
Mary T.   II. Title.
  LC1200.I545 2012
  371.9′046—dc23

                                                                        2011049677

11/26/12

To Colin and Nolan,
who continue to be a driving force in our work
to ensure that all students with disabilities
receive the instruction they need

About the Authors

Mary T. Brownell, PhD, is the Irving and Rose Fien Endowed Professor of Education and Director of the National Center to Inform Policy and Practice in Special Education Professional Development at the University of Florida. Over the course of her career, Dr. Brownell has focused her work on special education teacher quality and retention, teacher development through collaboration and Reading First coaching, education for teachers working with students with disabilities and other high-risk learners, and professional development in literacy for teachers of high-risk learners. She has published over 50 book chapters and articles in some of special education's most prestigious journals, including *Exceptional Children, Journal of Special Education*, and *Learning Disability Quarterly*. Dr. Brownell has been recognized by the University of Florida with two teaching and research awards.

Sean J. Smith, PhD, is Associate Professor of Special Education at the University of Kansas in Lawrence. Dr. Smith's background is in the area of special education and technology, and he has authored and presented a number of articles on the subject. He is also a project director for several U.S. Department of Education program initiatives on the integration of technology components into teacher preparation programs and classroom instruction for students with disabilities and on the development of a virtual social skills training experience for students with autism. Dr. Smith is an associate editor of *Teaching Exceptional Children* and has served as an associate editor of the *Journal of Special Education Technology*.

Jean B. Crockett, PhD, is Professor and Director of the School of Special Education, School Psychology, and Early Childhood Studies at the University of Florida. Before earning her doctorate she served as a teacher, building principal, and special education administrator in New York. Dr. Crockett's research interests address the relationship between policy reform initiatives and the instruction of exceptional

learners. She is the author of more than 40 publications on instructional programming and placement issues for students with disabilities; the conceptual, historical,
and legal foundations of special education; and frameworks for conducting special
education in contemporary schools. She also is a frequent speaker at both national
and international conferences and serves on numerous editorial and advisory
boards for professional organizations. Dr. Crockett is a past president of the Division for Research of the Council for Exceptional Children and the special education
editor for the *Journal of Law and Education*.

Cynthia C. Griffin, PhD, is Professor in the School of Special Education, School
Psychology, and Early Childhood Studies at the University of Florida. Dr. Griffin's
early research focused on intervention studies in reading for students in inclusive
elementary classrooms. She also coordinated internship programs in special education and studied novice special education teachers. She subsequently pursued
intervention research focused on elementary school mathematics for students with
disabilities. Dr. Griffin is studying teachers' knowledge of mathematics, their classroom practices, and the influence these factors have on student achievement in
math. She has received U.S. Department of Education grants to support her work,
is published widely in both special and general education journals, and was recognized as one of the 2011 University of Florida Research Professors.

Preface

Making the Case for Using Evidence and Collaborative Inquiry in Inclusive Classrooms

This is a book about becoming an accomplished teacher in order to help students with high-incidence disabilities (i.e., those with specific learning disabilities, behavior disorders, mild mental retardation, and high-functioning autism) become more accomplished learners in the competitive and inclusive context of contemporary schools. In response to recent legislation and social preference, most students who struggle to learn are taught in general education classes for all or part of the school day, where they are expected to be successful in mastering challenging material alongside more proficient classmates. Struggling learners, including most students with high-incidence disabilities, are expected to engage in authentic problem-solving activities and to integrate thinking skills within subject areas such as history and science. Their teachers are expected to provide high-quality instruction that results in access to the general curriculum and mastery of state-level academic standards. For students with high-incidence disabilities to have opportunities to learn appropriately in inclusive classrooms, teachers must recognize their individual learning needs and respond quickly with practices that "work " for improving academic learning and social growth.

APPROACH

This book is intended to help both general and special educators become more adept at recognizing and responding to the needs of students with high-incidence disabilities by using powerful evidence-based practices in inclusive elementary instruction.

We encourage teachers to observe the skills and abilities of their more accomplished learners as they think about ways that learning and behavioral difficulties challenge the development of a struggling student's expertise. We have grounded our approach to this book in the concept of *accomplishment* and what would be required to help these students become more accomplished learners. We use the term *accomplishment* to mean the achievement of abilities or skills acquired through intensive instruction and practice, as well as accommodation of learning struggles. Throughout the book we address two questions that provide its central theme:

1. What kinds of learning opportunities help students with high-incidence disabilities become more accomplished learners?
2. What instructional approaches and technology supports help educators become more accomplished teachers of students with high-incidence disabilities?

We have structured the book to reflect the dual themes of *recognition* (identifying students' needs and monitoring progress) and *response* (using research-based instructional approaches and technology supports) (see Coleman, Buysee, & Neitzel, 2006). Our approach is also based on the principle that special and general education teachers must work together to analyze and interpret assessment data if instruction is to be both responsive and powerful. Recognizing and responding to students' needs with effective instructional practices depends on *collaborative inquiry,* which we define as the work of professionals reflecting collectively on student progress to design and evaluate instruction. In each chapter we use case studies to illustrate the work of special and general education teachers who are accomplished at problem solving collaboratively and implementing a hierarchy of increasingly intensive interventions to support struggling learners.

The theme of *recognition* frames Part I. Chapters 1–4 are designed to help you recognize your professional responsibilities as well as the varied needs of your students. Inclusive instruction requires teachers who keenly observe the ways in which each student with disabilities learns and who precisely describe those learning needs to other professionals. Spotting learning problems early and communicating effectively with colleagues depend on:

- Recognizing your responsibility for teaching students with high-incidence disabilities.
- Recognizing the learning needs of students with high-incidence disabilities.
- Recognizing the attributes of effective inclusive teachers.
- Recognizing the power of assessment data in guiding effective instruction.

The theme of *response* frames Part II. Chapters 5–10 are intended to provide you with strategies to respond effectively to the complex needs of students with high-incidence disabilities in the following ways:

- Planning effective classroom instruction.
- Fostering concept development across content areas.
- Creating strategic learners.
- Building fluent skills use.
- Managing inclusive classrooms.
- Establishing a culture of inquiry and evidence-based practice.

CONTENT AND ORGANIZATION

Chapter 1 introduces the ethical and legal commitments that special and general educators have to students with high-incidence disabilities and how these responsibilities require increasing sophistication in the type of instruction provided. In creating inclusive classroom ecologies special and general education teachers need to be aware of the general curriculum, evidence-based practices for teaching curricular content, techniques for making challenging content more accessible, and ways to facilitate positive interactions with students and colleagues. Engaging in sophisticated planning and instructional delivery requires intensive collaboration, and teachers need to have the skills to engage in such collaboration and the administrative support to do so.

Chapter 2 details the types of problems most students with high-incidence disabilities are likely to have when accessing the general education curriculum and how these issues may be addressed when designing instruction and classroom management plans. This chapter describes the typical literacy and numeracy needs of these students, as well as the behavioral and social problems they might display. The challenges that their diverse learning needs pose to standardized ways of delivering instruction are discussed, as well as the flexible type of instruction that is required for success.

Chapter 3 discusses the beliefs, attitudes, and practices of effective teachers of students with high-incidence disabilities. This chapter explains how effective inclusion teachers hold more interventionist beliefs about students with these disabilities. That is, these teachers believe they can engage in instruction that will facilitate the learning of students with high-incidence disabilities, even though they realize that these students are disadvantaged by their disabilities in certain ways. This chapter also illustrates the practices of effective general and special education teachers who work with these students and how a strong focus on professional development is essential to becoming an accomplished teacher.

Chapter 4 focuses on assessing the educational progress of special-needs learners in order to design instruction that is both tailored to those needs and sufficiently powerful to support them in becoming more proficient. This chapter articulates why the assessment process is so essential in planning for instruction and in determining if instruction is responsive to the needs of students who struggle the most in the general education classroom. Specific information about types of assessments and the information they generate is provided. Additionally, special and general education teachers will acquire information about techniques for organizing assessment data and using technology to support the assessment process. Emphasis is also placed on how teachers can communicate with parents about their students' ongoing educational progress and how they can assist parents in becoming stronger advocates in the assessment process.

Chapter 5 focuses on planning a universally designed curriculum that meets the needs of all learners in inclusive classrooms and also addresses the needs of students with high-incidence disabilities. Specifically, the chapter is designed to help you articulate (1) what the big ideas of the curriculum are; (2) what types of concepts, skills, and strategies you expect all students to have; (3) what levels of acquisition you expect students with high-incidence disabilities to have for various skills, strategies, and concepts; (4) what aspects of the curriculum will present problems for students; and (5) how you will minimize these problems in the curriculum through remediation of skills deficits or circumvent them through teaching strategies and the use of technology. It also discusses how to balance providing remediation with providing access to higher-order skills and strategies in the curriculum, as well as the roles that special and general education teachers play in planning together.

Chapter 6 addresses the instructional principles and strategies needed to make curricular concepts accessible to students with high-incidence disabilities. The introduction emphasizes the acquisition of curricular concepts as the goal of school learning. The chapter identifies the types of curricular concepts that students need to acquire across content areas, the challenges that might be encountered in helping students learn these concepts, and research-based strategies for helping students with concept acquisition. Sample content-enhancement routines and graphic organizers for learning social studies and science concepts, as well as techniques for using concrete manipulative materials combined with direct instruction routines for teaching mathematics, are provided. Various technology applications that enable students to acquire content are interwoven throughout the chapter.

Chapter 7 focuses on ways to help students with high-incidence disabilities become strategic learners in acquiring content and achieving important outcomes more independently in both literacy and mathematics. Specifically, this chapter targets what it means to be a strategic learner, the problems students with these disabilities might encounter in becoming strategic learners, and the type of instructional routines and technologies that can support the development of students' strategic abilities in reading, writing, and mathematics.

Chapter 8 addresses fluent skills use in literacy and mathematics and why rapid, fluent decoding is important to reading, why spelling and handwriting fluency are important to writing, and why fluency in basic math facts is important to learning mathematics. The instructional procedures needed to develop students' fluency are described, along with technology for fostering fluent skills use in students who continue to struggle in these content areas.

Chapter 9 discusses structuring an inclusive classroom to maximize responsiveness to the learning and behavioral needs of your students. It describes strategies for maximizing intervention, such as classwide peer tutoring and structuring small-group and individualized instruction. Strategies are also included for decreasing behavioral disruptions in the classroom and for increasing behavioral supports (e.g., behavioral contracts, cognitive-behavioral interventions) to help students who need more intensive assistance.

Chapter 10 offers strategies for effective collaboration that are essential for successfully crafting the type of instruction needed for students with high-incidence disabilities. This chapter addresses (1) the collaborative process and the role of a general and special education teacher in that process; (2) what struggles might be encountered in the collaborative process; (3) how ideas can be made more accessible to a teaching partner; (4) how language can be used to raise issues and communicate ideas effectively; and (5) how conflicts over ideas and instructional strategies can be negotiated. In conclusion, it identifies the workplace structures that should be in place to support successful collaboration, as well as how teachers might work with building administrators to secure such supports.

Written with the tenets of the Individuals with Disabilities Education Act (IDEA) and the No Child Left Behind Act (NCLB) in mind, this book should have broad appeal for university courses and for professional development with teachers in inclusive schools. We have attempted to explain and illustrate systematic instruction grounded in research evidence and in collaborative inquiry for teaching curricular concepts, strategies, and skills successfully to students with learning and behavior difficulties. Research-based applications of instructional technology that are effective in providing universal access to the general curriculum are embedded throughout this instructional framework. Given the conceptual guidance and practical strategies offered in each chapter, this book should be especially useful to teachers and to school-based professional learning communities, as well as to scholars who work with graduate students in both special and regular education. Table 1 provides a list of inclusive instructional practices adapted by accomplished educators and the chapters in which they are discussed throughout the book.

TABLE 1. Inclusive Instructional Practices of Accomplished Educators

Practices of accomplished inclusive educators	Importance	Chapter
Recognizing ethical, legal, and collaborative responsibilities to special-needs learners	Recognizing students' individual needs in order to design instruction that enables students to access challenging curricular content	Chapter 1
Identifying students' individual learning needs	Recognizing why some students struggle to become more accomplished learners	Chapter 2
Identifying the qualities of accomplished inclusive educators	Crafting instruction that is responsive to students' learning needs and helps them become more proficient	Chapter 3
Assessing and communicating student progress	Acquiring techniques for organizing assessment data and using technology in the assessment process	Chapter 4
Planning effective instruction	Planning a universally designed curriculum to meet the needs of learners in inclusive classrooms	Chapter 5
Teaching curricular concepts	Strengthening the concept development of struggling learners	Chapter 6
Developing strategic and independent learners	Helping students achieve outcomes more independently in literacy and mathematics	Chapter 7
Building students' fluency skills	Implementing effective routines that foster fluency in reading, writing, and mathematics	Chapter 8
Managing positive learning environments	Using evidence-based classroom management strategies that promote social and emotional learning	Chapter 9
Building a culture of evidence and collaborative inquiry	Solving problems successfully with colleagues, parents, and school administrators	Chapter 10

Contents

RECOGNIZING OUR PROFESSIONAL RESPONSIBILITIES TO STUDENTS AND UNDERSTANDING THEIR NEEDS

CHAPTER 1

Recognizing Professional Responsibilities to Students with Disabilities in Inclusive Classrooms

Study Guide Questions

- What is inclusive instruction?
- Who are students with high-incidence disabilities?
- What is special education?
- What are my responsibilities to students with disabilities?
- What principles should guide inclusive instruction?

Close to 6 million students with disabilities receive special education in the United States. Ninety-six percent of these students in kindergarten through 12th grade are included for all or for part of their school day in general education classrooms where they are expected to participate in social activities and to learn challenging academic content (U.S. Department of Education, 2010). The purpose of this chapter is to provide background information about the foundations of inclusive instruction for students with disabilities so that general and special educators might recognize and fulfill their professional responsibilities.

INCLUDING STUDENTS WITH LEARNING AND BEHAVIOR PROBLEMS

THE CASE OF NOLAN

Six-year-old Nolan Patrick Smith is a student at Sunflower Elementary School in Kansas. Nolan has a broad range of cognitive abilities that cannot be summed up in a single test score. He loves to sing and he remembers the names of his classmates, but he gets easily distracted and finds it hard to remember academic information. With frequent and systematic prompts he has better recall and pays closer attention to his teachers.

Nolan receives special education in an inclusive kindergarten where his classroom teacher, Joanne, collaborates with other team members to implement his individualized education program (IEP). His annual goals indicate that Nolan learns well through repetition and he needs extra time to practice new skills. Suzanne, a special education teacher, works with him daily, reinforcing what he has learned or teaching him new skills. Counting is hard for Nolan, so Suzanne assesses his progress daily and gives him stickers to earn a weekly prize. Along with his classmates Nolan practices putting sounds together to make words, but this task is also hard for him, and he needs much more practice than his classmates to master these goals. His immature social skills are addressed in the classroom and on the playground, and speech therapists help him to communicate his thoughts so that others can understand him.

Nolan is very much a part of the school community. His teachers provide him with instruction that meets his unique needs in a classroom that is centered on learners and focused on content, assessment, and community membership. Nolan's parents work closely with local service agencies and college students who provide him with additional support outside of school. For now, Nolan is making progress in this inclusive kindergarten where his teachers are committed to using evidence and collaborative inquiry to recognize and respond effectively to his disability-related needs.

In this case Nolan is a student with disabilities who is included for instruction in a general education kindergarten class. His parents and his teachers agree that he needs to learn practical academic and social skills that will help him now and in the future. The reality is that Nolan's instructional goals might be the same as his classmates in some areas and very different in other areas, so his instruction needs to be carefully planned. To help him meet his goals his teachers work collaboratively to analyze data about his performance and to implement research-based curriculum, instruction, and interventions. By using evidence and collaborative inquiry in their inclusive classroom they are meeting their professional responsibility to provide Nolan with an appropriate public education in what for him is the least restrictive learning environment.

What Is Inclusive Instruction?

The term *inclusion* has many different meanings. As a social philosophy inclusion means fostering acceptance, belonging, and community in schools and other social institutions for a diversity of students, families, educators, and community members (Salend, 2008). Adopting an inclusive philosophy might be thought of as the first step in providing effective instruction to students with wide-ranging needs who come increasingly from different cultural and linguistic backgrounds. In schools across the United States, nearly one of every three students now claims an ethnic heritage that is African American, Hispanic, Asian American, or Native American, and in cities such as New York and Chicago close to half of the students entering kindergarten are English language learners (Lerner & Johns, 2009). Some of these students have disability-related needs and require special education to become more accomplished learners.

As an educational practice, inclusion for students with disabilities typically means attending a neighborhood school and participating as much as possible in the general curriculum and other school activities alongside students of the same age who do not have disabilities (Smith, 2007). When students with disabilities are included in general education classes, they can receive the specialized services required by their IEPs within the general class, or in another setting, such as a resource room, for a portion of the day when important goals cannot be achieved in the classroom environment (Mastropieri & Scruggs, 2007; Vaughn & Bos, 2009).

Inclusive instruction differs from *mainstreaming*, an earlier practice that required special-needs learners to be able to achieve near grade level without significant support before they could be taught in a general education class. Although inclusion and mainstreaming are similar concepts, the critical difference of inclusion for students with disabilities is:

- The general classroom is considered to be the primary placement.
- The general education teacher is regarded as the primary instructor.

Inclusive instruction transfers the primary responsibility for teaching students with disabilities to general educators. Special education and related services are provided as ancillary supports to basic instruction in meeting students' disability-related needs and ensuring their appropriate access to the general curriculum (Mastropierri & Scruggs, 2007).

Students with disabilities have diverse needs and their right to be educated appropriately is guided by a formal set of procedures. Whether a special-needs learner receives inclusive instruction is an individually based decision made by a team of the student's parents or guardians, general education teachers, special education teachers, and other professionals familiar with evaluating the student's performance.

- First, the student's IEP is written to reflect the goals recommended by the team and the specialized services to be provided by the school district.
- Next, the team considers how the student's social and educational needs described in the IEP could be met appropriately in the general education classroom or in another more specialized instructional setting (Bateman & Linden, 2006).

Research does not support the position that all children should be educated all the time in general education classrooms. Thus, there are justifiable reasons for teaching students certain skills in other settings. For example, some students need to learn skills not covered in the general curriculum such as Braille or sign language. Some students shy away from unwanted special attention in the presence of more accomplished classmates, but master challenging material with more privacy, time, and intensive intervention (see Elbaum, 2002). Although parents and educators might agree to instruction provided outside the general class, it is important to note that students with disabilities should never be removed from classes because teachers or school administrators simply refuse to accommodate their specialized learning needs. Providing effective inclusive instruction that meets students' needs requires general and special educators to be sensitive to and accepting of individual differences that result not only from cultural and linguistic diversity, but also from disability.

Who Are Students with Special Needs or Disabilities?

Disability is another term with multiple meanings. The way professionals think about disabilities can influence how they interact with students included in their classrooms. For example, some teachers hold negative attitudes toward students who look like everyone else but whose serious learning or behavioral disorders interfere with classroom instruction. They assume students are lazy or unwilling to learn because they cannot visually observe the impact of the disability on learning and they think it is unfair to provide them with special treatment. It is not unusual for students with disabilities to be held either to low or to unreasonably high expectations, which can have negative long-term results, when teachers misunderstand the meaningful differences between their needs and those of their nondisabled classmates (Cook, 2001). Recognizing when a student needs to learn something different from other classmates or to learn the same thing through highly specialized and intensive special education instruction is an important responsibility (Zigmond, 2003).

In this book we use the terms *special-needs learners* and *students with disabilities* interchangeably, and we use the term *disability* to mean an inability to do something that most others of the same age, and with similar opportunities and instruction, can do (Kauffman & Hallahan, 2005). All children have special needs, but only some children require special assistance because of chronic physical or mental conditions that interfere with their ability to learn.

Not every student with a disability is eligible to receive special education and related services. Some students only need an extra boost from environmental accommodations such as preferential seating or extended time on tests to access learning appropriately and as adequately as their classmates without disabilities. Special education is only for those students whose disability interferes with their ability to participate and progress in the general curriculum without intensive, goal-directed, and specially designed instruction.

When thinking about special-needs learners it is important to remember three things:

1. *Most students who receive special education have mild disabilities; relatively few students have severe cognitive or physical disabilities.* These students struggle for a variety of reasons and their struggles arise from one or a combination of difficulties in thinking, learning academic content, paying attention, behaving in class, and communicating with others (Kauffman & Hallahan, 2005). Most special-needs learners have mild or moderate difficulties. Fewer students have multiple or complex needs that occur infrequently.

2. *The most frequently identified disabilities among special education students are specific learning disabilities, speech–language disorders, mild intellectual disabilities, and emotional disturbance* (U.S. Department of Education, 2010). Approximately 96% of all school-age students with disabilities receive instruction in regular classrooms for some portion of the school day. Students with frequently occurring, "high-incidence" disabilities are taught most often in inclusive classrooms, although they can receive instruction across a range of learning environments. To have meaningful inclusive opportunities to learn, these students require well-designed, collaborative instruction from general and special education teachers. The common learning and behavioral characteristics of these students are illustrated in Table 1.1..

3. *Students differ widely in how they learn, and it is important to recognize that not every inability to do something is the result of a disability.* The majority of struggling students do not have disabilities. Most students with learning and behavior problems receive supplemental support from reading and math specialists, counselors, or classroom assistants as part of a sound, basic general education. Supplemental interventions and careful progress monitoring can help many struggling students achieve expected performance goals. Such students are unlikely to be classified as disabled because they are able to profit from moderate changes to instruction. Sometimes, though, basic instruction and small-group interventions are not enough. Students who have more serious learning and behavior problems often need to have academic and social tasks broken down into smaller, more achievable steps in order to be successful. These students could have disabilities that merit the intensive support of special education.

What Is the Goal of Special Education?

From an inclusive perspective, the goal of special education is "to minimize the impact of disability and maximize the opportunities for children with disabilities to participate in general education in their natural community" (Hehir, 2005, p. 49). Students with disabilities cannot profit from a general education curriculum without teachers acknowledging their special learning and behavior needs. Thus, to minimize the impact of a student's disability, teachers must attend to key tenets of the Individuals with Disabilities Education Act (IDEA), the federal statute that protects the rights of students with disabilities and funds intensive services associated with educating them. The purpose of the IDEA is to ensure that

TABLE 1.1. Common Learning Characteristics of Students with High-Incidence Disabilities

Characteristics	Description
Disorders of attention	The student does not focus when a lesson is presented; has short attention span, is easily distracted, displays poor concentration; may exhibit hyperactivity.
Poor motor abilities	The student has difficulty with gross motor abilities and fine motor coordination (exhibits general awkwardness and clumsiness).
Psychological processing differences	The student has problems in processing auditory or visual information (difficulty interpreting visual or auditory stimuli).
Poor cognitive strategies for learning	The student does not know how to go about the task of learning and studying, lacks organizational skills, has a passive learning style (does not direct his or her their own learning).
Oral language difficulties	The student has underlying language disorders (problems in language development, listening, speaking, and vocabulary).
Reading difficulties	The student has problems in learning to decode words, basic word recognition skills, or reading comprehension.
Writing difficulties	The student performs poorly on tasks requiring written expression, spelling, and handwriting.
Mathematics difficulties	The student has difficulty with quantitative thinking, arithmetic, time, space, and calculation facts.
Poor social skills	The student does not know how to act and talk in social situations, and has difficulty with establishing satisfying social relationships and friendships.

Note. Adapted from *Learning Disabilities and Related Mild Disabilities*, 11th edition, by J. Lerner and B. Johns (2009, p. 8). Copyright 2009 by Wadsworth, a part of Cengage Learning, Inc. Reproduced by permission. *www.cengage.com/permissions.*

children with disabilities have available to them a free appropriate public education that emphasizes special education and related services designed to meet their unique needs, and prepare them for further education, employment and independent living. (20 U.S.C. § 1400[d][1][A]

Special education is defined in the IDEA as *specially designed instruction*, which means that teachers have the responsibility to adapt the content, methodology, or delivery of instruction to meet a student's disability-related needs, and to ensure his or her access to the general curriculum and school activities. In practice special education differs from general education not so much in kind as in degree across a number of dimensions including pacing or rate, intensity, relentlessness, structure, reinforcement, pupil–teacher ratio, curriculum in some cases, and monitoring and assessment (Kauffman & Hallahan, 2005). Special education is intended to provide instruction that is individually planned, specialized, intensive, goal directed, research based, and guided by student performance (Heward, 2009). These defining features of special education are illustrated in Table 1.2.

RECOGNIZING RESPONSIBILITIES TO SPECIAL EDUCATION STUDENTS IN INCLUSIVE ENVIRONMENTS

Little more than 30 years ago most children with disabilities were excluded from attending public schools, and many children with more significant disabilities received no education at all. Other children and youth with mild or moderate learning problems often received inappropriate instruction that failed to meet their needs, or they were taught in schools that were more restrictive or more separate from their home communities than necessary. Over time, parents across the United States advocated powerfully for their children to receive special education in schools instead of institutions, and, within the last 20 years or so, to be included more fully in general education classrooms. To ensure that students receive the specially

TABLE 1.2. Features of Special Education

Individually planned instruction

Goals, methods, materials, and setting of instruction are selected or adapted on the basis of what a student needs to learn.

Specialized instruction

Incorporates a variety of materials and adapted instruction, including related services and assistive technologies not usually part of the general education curriculum, to help students target learning goals.

Intensive instruction

Instruction is presented with attention to detail, precision, structure, clarity, and opportunities for learning skills and strategies through repeated practice.

Goal-directed instruction

Instruction is purposeful and targets goals for personal self-sufficiency and success.

Research-based instruction

Effective teaching methods and materials are selected on the basis of research support.

Instruction guided by student performance

Learning is frequently assessed to evaluate effectiveness of instruction and to make adjustments if necessary.

Note. Adapted from *Exceptional Children: An Introduction to Special Education,* 1st edition, by W. L. Heward (2009, p. 42). Copyright 2009. Adapted by permission of Pearson Education, Inc., Upper Saddle River, NJ.

designed instruction they need in a general education environment (at least to the greatest extent possible), the IDEA guarantees three key educational rights:

1. The right to receive a free appropriate public education emphasizing special education and related services to meet their unique learning needs.
2. The right to be taught appropriately in the most integrated and least restrictive social environment.
3. The right to be taught by qualified teachers that use state-of-the-art instructional approaches and technology (Crockett & Kauffman, 1999).

Ensuring a Free Appropriate Public Education

The IDEA requires schools to provide a free appropriate public education (FAPE) to students with disabilities and to develop written documentation in the form of an IEP to protect the rights of each student who needs the intensive support of special education. The IEP is the centerpiece of the IDEA; it is intended to outline a plan that addresses students' individual needs. The primary responsibility of special and general educators in the IEP process is to engage with parents in planning a program of special education and related services, including accommodations and modifications to be used in the general classroom, so the student can benefit from his or her education (see Bateman & Linden, 2006, for an extended discussion).

Providing Instruction in the Least Restrictive Environment

The IDEA does not guarantee inclusion but uses the legal principle of the least restrictive environment (LRE) to guide placement decisions so that students are never placed in schools or classrooms based upon their disability label or category. The LRE principle requires that special education students, to the maximum extent appropriate to their needs, be taught in general education classes. Special and general education teachers have the responsibility for doing their best to first restructure the general education environment to serve students with disabilities and only consider other settings when the IEP team determines that satisfactory progress cannot be made inclusively even with the support of specialized aids and services.[1]

Using Effective Instructional Practices

Teachers are responsible for providing special-needs learners with an appropriate education in the LRE, and for using effective instructional practices in the process.

---

[1] Although the IDEA presumes that all students will be educated together, the presumption can be overcome when a student's learning or behavioral needs suggest otherwise (see Yell, 2010). As a result, school districts are legally required to make a full continuum of alternative learning environments available that range from general classes, special classes, separate schools, residential facilities, hospitals, and home settings so that students might receive a meaningful and appropriate public education.

The right to be taught effectively shifts the focus from *where* students learn to *how* their instruction is actually provided. The IDEA requires that students' IEPs be aligned with state curriculum, standards, and that professional development is made available to teachers and administrators so they might use practices proven to be effective with special-needs learners. The IDEA's instructional provisions are not new, but they have taken on greater significance in recent years with related policies of accountability and school reform.

The Elementary and Secondary Education Act, reauthorized as The No Child Left Behind Act of 2001 (NCLB), requires all students, including students with disabilities, to learn the general curriculum, to participate in state and local assessments, and to make gains in achievement toward the goal of making adequate yearly academic progress. The IDEA is now aligned with the NCLB, and both laws require teachers to be highly qualified and to use practices based on scientific research to strengthen both basic and specially designed instruction. The NCLB has important implications for special education. When groups of students with disabilities fail to make adequate yearly progress toward achieving 100% proficiency in reading and math their schools face punitive accountability measures. As a result many schools are turning toward inclusion as a means to provide students with greater access to the challenging content of the general education curriculum. However, inclusion alone without the use of effective, intensive, and specific teaching practices will not help students with disabilities gain access to learning or achieve appropriate outcomes (Crockett, 2004; Salend, 2008; Zigmond, 2003).

As pressures have risen to provide positive results for students with disabilities, so have opportunities for teachers to turn to practices with a record of success, particularly in the area of reading. For over three decades, researchers have tested academic and social interventions to see "what works" for special-needs learners. As a result a growing body of knowledge based on well-conducted research syntheses supports the use of instructional practices, such as small, interactive groups, directed questioning, and carefully controlled task difficulty that are predictive of positive outcomes for students across content areas (Swanson, 2000). Teachers are now in a better position to combine these evidence-based practices with their own practical knowledge to make effective instructional decisions (see Cook, Landrum, Cook, & Tankersley, 2008).

MAKING CLASSROOMS CONDUCIVE TO LEARNING

How teachers deliver instruction has changed over the past 30 years, and so has the scientific basis that explains how people learn. Research on human cognition is now guiding teachers as they help struggling learners understand complex subject matter, and transfer what they have learned to new situations and settings (Bransford, Brown, & Cocking, 2000). The goals of schooling have also changed. Special-needs learners are now expected to engage in higher order thinking and authentic problem solving, and their teachers are expected to provide high-quality instruction that supports their success. What can be said with confidence is that inclusive classrooms will only succeed if general and special education teachers can work together to create classrooms that foster positive interactions among students and teachers; design challenging curriculum; employ high-quality instruction; and carefully manage the learning environment. These four classroom factors exert the most powerful influence on student learning (Bransford et al., 2000; Speece & Keogh, 1996; Vaughn & Bos, 2009).

Changes in the IDEA 2004 acknowledge that effective inclusive instruction now depends on the quality of a school's basic educational program as well as the quality of a student's specially designed instruction (Swanson & Deshler, 2003; Vaughn & Boss, 2009). As a result, general education and special education teachers have new responsibilities to become more proficient themselves in helping struggling students become more accomplished learners in classrooms that are student-centered, content-focused, assessment-driven, and community-oriented (Bransford et al., 2000). The following principles provide a framework of prevention, collaboration, and effective instruction to guide teachers' inclusive responsibilities:

1. Strengthening basic instruction so that academic and social problems might be prevented in the first place.
2. Fostering collaborative relationships and building a sense of community to support students' academic learning and social growth.
3. Recognizing and responding to students' individual learning needs by assessing and monitoring progress and intervening with powerful and effective instructional approaches.

Strengthening Basic Instruction

Classroom teachers have the responsibility to provide all students with well-paced, research-based instruction, and to actively monitor their progress in learning the general curriculum (Bradley, Danielson, & Doolittle, 2007). Inclusive instruction begins with the premise that all students are learners who deserve access to challenging, meaningful, and quality general education in classrooms conducive to learning. Most students start school without any additional help whether they later need assistance because of disability, disadvantage, or cultural and linguistic differences. The activities involved in preventing the development of serious learning and behavior problems—such as universal screening, effective and differentiated instruction, and progress monitoring—are the fundamental responsibility of general education teachers.

Early intervention in general classrooms is a high priority for students from diverse backgrounds who have not been identified as needing special education, but who need additional support to learn the core curriculum. The IDEA now funds early intervening services, including coaching and training for classroom teachers, that may reduce the need for struggling students to receive special education. Preventing the overidentification of disabilities and inappropriate referrals to special education especially among students from cultural and ethnic minority groups is another inclusive concern. The IDEA now permits teachers to consider a student's response to scientifically based interventions in the process of distinguishing students with suspected learning disabilities who need special education, from students with learning problems who progress when they receive more effective basic instruction (Bateman & Linden, 2006).

In many schools teachers are now responsible for implementing response-to-intervention (RTI) procedures and systems of schoolwide positive behavior support (PBS). Both of these practices employ screenings and increasingly intensive interventions in general education before referral to special education. These prevention models frequently utilize three or more levels of increasingly intensive interventions.

- At Tier 1 all students are provided with primary prevention, or core instructional efforts, to keep problems from developing (Division for Learning Disabilities, 2007).
- At Tier 2 teachers use supplemental interventions with small groups of struggling students, in addition to core instruction, to correct problems before they get worse (Division for Learning Disabilities, 2007). Special education teachers can be helpful at this level by consulting with classroom teachers and serving on decision-making teams, but their primary responsibility is providing specially designed instruction to students already identified with disabilities.
- At Tier 3 teachers individualize instruction and progress monitoring to treat problems very aggressively and reduce their negative consequences (Division for Learning Disabilities, 2007). Tier 3 often represents the most intensive level of academic and behavioral interventions. Some students with or without disabilities might need this level of highly intensive teaching for only brief periods of time before returning to lower tiers of support depending on their measured response to intervention. Special education can also be provided as tertiary prevention, but a comprehensive evaluation must determine a student's eligibility to receive services.

Tiered levels of intervention hold promise for minimizing students' disabilities while maximizing their opportunities to learn in the general classroom, but issues critical to their implementation, teacher support, and student achievement remain unresolved. Much more needs to be learned about using these approaches as components of inclusive school reform (Fuchs & Deshler, 2007). The basic concept of assessing an individual student's responsiveness to intervention is not new, however. Years of research suggest that when teachers emphasize well-accepted instructional principles that are based on data and grounded in scientific research, more students achieve benchmarks and fewer students lag significantly behind their classmates with learning delays that require special education (Batsche, 2007; Nelson, Benner, & Mooney, 2008; Torgeson, 2007). Although tiered models of prevention and intervention are currently promising practices rather than proven approaches, it is likely that schools will increasingly use these collaborative models to make classrooms more conducive to learning for students with wide-ranging abilities (Boardman & Vaughn, 2007; Nelson et al., 2008).

Fostering Collaborative Relationships

Teaching students with disabilities in general education classrooms requires the commitment to create collaborative learning environments where instruction is planned carefully, proactive, and effective (Stichter, Conroy, & Kauffman, 2008). In addition to teaching academic content well, classroom teachers must also be skillful, knowledgeable, and willing to work with special-needs learners (Lerner & Johns, 2009). Collaboration is considered to be an essential ingredient of inclusive instruction and research suggests that it is most likely to be beneficial when collaborators (1) each have something to contribute, (2) share mutual goals, (3) work together voluntarily, (4) contribute equally, and (5) share responsibility for making decisions and achieving student outcomes (Friend & Cook, 2010).

In the ideal inclusive classroom, general and special educators share teaching responsibilities in a variety of ways. In some cases the special educator might play the role of a consultant by providing learning materials for the classroom teacher to use with selected students. At other times the special educator might serve in a co-teaching role by actually providing intensive and personalized instruction within the classroom setting. Throughout this book we use examples from our own research on student-centered and content-focused preventive instruction. We share many examples of classroom teachers using effective basic instruction, and we feature case studies of special education teachers collaborating with colleagues in using evidence-based practices and technology supports that offer special-needs learners more individualized and intensive instruction.

Recognizing and Responding to Students' Individual Learning Needs

In inclusive classrooms general and special education teachers share the responsibility for recognizing students' learning needs and using objective data to guide their instructional decisions. The IDEA is now aligned with standards-based reforms and the IEP for each special education student must now stipulate how teachers will provide access to general education curriculum standards and other school activities available to students without disabilities. In order to provide inclusive instruction in line with a student's IEP, teachers need to work together to gather data and monitor progress, with the general education teacher being primarily responsible for detailing the knowledge, skills, and strategies needed to be successful in the general education curriculum and special education teachers being primarily responsible for determining if strategies are working and if special-needs learners are making progress toward meeting the measurable annual goals in their IEPs. In Chapter 4 we provide an in-depth discussion of ways in which accomplished inclusive teachers use classroom-based assessments.

In responding to students' learning needs, all teachers have a responsibility to understand and properly implement educational practices based on the latest research. Special education is intended to deliver meaningful benefit to special-needs learners, and it is unlikely that this level of benefit will be realized if ineffective, unproven strategies are used (Crockett & Yell, 2008). In responding to the needs of students in inclusive classrooms special and general education teachers need to be aware of the general curriculum, evidence-based practices for teaching curricular content, techniques for making challenging content more accessible, and ways to facilitate positive interactions with students and colleagues. Each of these topics is covered in depth in subsequent chapters of this book.

FINAL THOUGHTS

Effective inclusive instruction for special-needs learners requires teachers to be (1) committed to the philosophical goals of inclusion; (2) responsive to the academic and social needs of struggling learners; (3) diligent in fulfilling their collaborative responsibilities to special education students; (4) skillful in basing instruction on evidence and collaborative inquiry; (5) committed to acquiring the knowledge, skills, and strategies needed to teach special education students; (6) engaged in ongoing professional development; and (7) supported with adequate resources to work together and develop professionally (Crockett, 2002; Lerner & Johns, 2009). These components form the foundation for achieving more accomplished teaching and more accomplished learning in classrooms that welcome an increasing diversity of children and youth.

CHAPTER 2

Recognizing the Individual Needs of Students with High-Incidence Disabilities

Study Guide Questions

- What is an accomplished learner?
- What are the essential abilities of an accomplished learner?
- What struggles do students with serious learning and behavior problems encounter, and how do these struggles create hurdles to becoming accomplished learners?
- What role does the accomplished inclusion teacher play in recognizing the academic and social needs of students with learning and behavior problems?

Including students with disabilities successfully into the general education classroom requires teachers to be able to recognize their specific needs and respond to them in ways that help these students become more accomplished learners. We begin this chapter with two essential questions: What makes a student an accomplished learner? What struggles do students with learning and behavior problems have that make it harder for them to develop the skills, knowledge, and dispositions of an accomplished learner? These questions form the foundation for how teachers can respond to help students with learning and behavior problems develop into more accomplished learners.

RECOGNIZING INDIVIDUAL NEEDS

THE CASE OF COLIN

Colin is a seventh-grade student who has excellent oral language abilities and strong background knowledge for science and social studies. Since he was a small boy, he enjoyed listening to his parents read books, especially books with information. He has traveled extensively with his parents, visited museums, and been an avid consumer of the History and Discovery channels. His teachers are often surprised by his background knowledge and ability to talk about complex ideas. At the same time, they often do not understand the degree to which his learning disability derails him. Colin has enormous difficulties with spelling and handwriting. He also struggles to memorize very specific information and processes, such as calculating basic facts. Colin's learning issues make it challenging for him to take notes during class, write down assignments, solve math problems without error, and recall detailed facts on exams. His struggles are most pronounced when teachers do not use course websites that keep track of assignments and topics to be covered in class or provide worksheets and study guides to structure the information he is supposed to learn. For instance, his science teacher rarely updates his website and expects that students acquire all their knowledge from class activities and lectures. Colin, however, does not understand what he is expected to learn from the activities and his struggles to take clear, readable notes only make matters worse. When the test comes around, Colin is expected to recall information, particularly specific facts and scientific names, that were discussed in class. He has failed his last few quizzes. When it comes to studying for his final, he feels completely defeated and overwhelmed by the information; he does not even know how to start.

Colin's struggles raise questions about the supports he needs to become an accomplished learner. In some aspects of the curriculum, he is an accomplished learner, but the learning issues created by his disability derail him in others. What skills, knowledge, and strategies does Colin need to work independently and persist on independent tasks? And what role do his teachers play in recognizing the skills, knowledge, and strategies he needs?

To help students become accomplished learners, teachers have to recognize the qualities of accomplished learners, understand the struggles a particular student is having, and do what they can to help the student become more accomplished. For instance, a teacher must be able to ask what help Colin needs to become accomplished in his life science class or as a student more generally and then determine what instructional supports can be put in place.

WHAT MAKES A STUDENT AN ACCOMPLISHED LEARNER?

To become accomplished in a content area, such as mathematics or writing, students need organized knowledge about the content, strategies for approaching tasks and problems within that particular content area, essential language skills, the motivation and focus to persist when the task becomes challenging, and an internal locus of control (Alexander & Judy, 1988).

Accomplished Learners Organize Content Knowledge

Accomplished learners *know* a lot about the subject they are studying and what they know is well organized. Their understanding of a particular subject is similar to a well-organized file cabinet; there are sections devoted to the big ideas, files representing related concepts, and the information in each file contains the supporting details. That is, accomplished learners know the big concepts or ideas of a particular subject and how they fit together. They also know how facts support these big ideas. Cognitive psychologists would describe these accomplished learners as having a strong schema for organizing information they have already acquired or for learning new information (Alexander, 2003). For instance, in mathematics, students know that ratios, proportions, and fractions are related to each other and that each represents a comparison. They also know that because fractions are proportions, one cannot change one portion of the fraction (numerator or denominator) without changing the other portion in the same increment. Thus, if students want to change ¾ to a fraction with 12 as the denominator, they must multiply both the top and the bottom by 3. Such fundamental knowledge allows them to compute equivalent fractions.

Accomplished Learners Use Effective Learning Strategies

Accomplished learners employ effective *strategies* for learning information, either through lecture, demonstration, or reading a text (Reid & Lienemann, 2006). To store information effectively, students actively work with the auditory or visual information they encounter in classrooms. They might rehearse information from their class notes, highlight important ideas in their notes that the teacher emphasized, or think about how the information is similar to other things they know. When reading a text, they might write down the main ideas from the text and use them to organize key details into an outline. They also have strategies for tackling tasks, such as solving a word problem or generating written text.

Accomplished Learners Have Essential Language Skills

Accomplished learners have the necessary language and reading skills to learn. Early on, accomplished learners demonstrate fundamental language abilities that enable them to read later on. They are able to hear the sounds (phonemes) and interpret the symbols of spoken and written language, providing them with the knowledge they need to decode words. They have sufficient knowledge of syntax (knowledge of grammar and sentence complexity) and semantics (knowledge of word meanings, morphemes such as prefixes and root words, word combinations, complex sentences, and text) to read and understand what is being said (Catts, Fey, Thomblin, & Zhang, 2002; O'Connor, 2007; Vaughn, Bos, & Schumm, 2007) as well as to generate organized and sophisticated written text. Accomplished learners also understand the pragmatics of language. They know when to use humor appropriately, how to engage in conversations with friends and teachers, how to use language to resolve conflicts, and how to formulate questions to seek more information or craft responses to questions that are posed inside or out of class (Vaughn et al., 2007). Proficiency with the pragmatics of language allows them to engage with their peers and teachers in ways that are considered socially appropriate.

Accomplished Learners Are Fluent

Accomplished learners are able to fluently use many subskills and strategies to tackle more complex tasks in a content area (Binder, Haughton, & Batemen, 2002). They have automatized many of the skills and abilities we have discussed thus far, enabling them to read and write fluently as well as solve mathematical problems fluently. As an illustration, one of the subskills students must automatize is the recognition of rimes (or word chunks, such as -*at* and -*oat*). The ability to accurately and rapidly recognize rimes ultimately leads students to recognize individual words quickly. Automatic word recognition combined with the ability to rapidly retrieve the meaning of words from memory leads to fluent reading of connected text. Such fluent reading is essential because it enables students to comprehend what they are reading, as they are not spending enormous amounts of cognitive energy on decoding and understanding individual words in the text (Perfetti, 1985). Similarly, in writing and math, the ability to spell words quickly and solve basic math facts rapidly affects students' ability to generate text and solve more complex mathematics problems.

Accomplished Learners Are Confident, Focused, and Motivated

Accomplished learners also have academic behaviors that allow them to acquire knowledge, skills, and strategies successfully. These learners have the *focus* and *motivation* to persist on a task, especially when the going gets rough. Such students realize when they need to devote more attention to a task (and are able to do so) because they do not yet have a command of the information or skills needed to complete it. They also have the ability to focus their attention and regulate their behavior in ways that allow them to consume information and work hard. These learners are what researchers would term "self-efficacious." They have acquired confidence in their ability to complete academic tasks as a result of their previous successes in doing so and are more motivated to persist in learning difficult tasks. Such self-efficacy is essential to becoming an independent learner (Seo, 2006; Wentzel, 1996).

WHY DO SOME STUDENTS STRUGGLE
TO BECOME ACCOMPLISHED LEARNERS?

Teachers must recognize the various learning and behavioral challenges struggling students face, be able to assess those problems accurately, and use what they learn through assessment to respond appropriately to students. To enable students who struggle academically and behaviorally to become accomplished learners, special and general education teachers must recognize the strengths a child has to succeed and identify the specific issues that are standing in their way. Recognizing accurately and precisely how the learning process is breaking down for a student enables teachers to respond in educationally powerful ways.

As every teacher knows, students struggle in school for a variety of reasons. Sometimes they have not had sufficient opportunities outside and inside of school to acquire the background knowledge and strategies they need to be successful. Other times, students have second language issues that make it harder for them to learn in English. About 11–12% of the school-age population have cognitive, language, and behavioral disabilities that present stumbling blocks to learning and to successful socialization into schools. In some cases, these students have disabilities that limit certain aspects of their learning. For example, Colin's inability to spell well affects his ability to take notes in class, but when learning material does not demand such skills, he is capable of learning information easily, particularly major concepts. Other students with disabilities can demonstrate more pervasive struggles. Table 2.1 illustrates major areas of difficulties for students with learning and behavior problems as well as questions teachers can ask as they collaborate in assessing students to determine how to plan for and deliver instruction.

CHALLENGES FOR STRUGGLING STUDENTS

What teachers can be certain of is that struggling students will have a variety of learning and behavioral needs. In order to respond successfully, teachers must understand the various struggles students have and what they can do to either limit the impact of their struggles or to circumvent them. In the sections that follow, we describe challenges students with learning and behavioral difficulties can experience.

Insufficient Prior Experience

From infancy to kindergarten, children have the potential to learn an enormous amount of information about the world and the language we use. Yet children's exposure to information and language can be quite different depending on their family's background. Children living in poverty, particularly those living with caregivers whose educational background is limited, often do not have the same exposure to books or language opportunities that children from more affluent homes

TABLE 2.1. Challenges for Struggling Students

Challenges for struggling students	Some questions to ask
Insufficient prior experience	1. What do you know about the student's home environment? • Does the student have access to different types of reading materials at home? • Does the student have access to many different types of experiences (e.g., does he or she talk about visiting different places)? 2. Does the student lack background knowledge but acquire new information easily when it is presented in concrete ways?
Information-processing problems	1. Does the student have difficulty tackling more complex ideas even when they are presented in concrete ways (e.g., through demonstration of how the concept works or by using concrete manipulatives)? 2. Does the student need more extended work with concepts to facilitate understanding than seems typical for other class members? 3. Does the student remember concepts and make linkages, but have difficulty remembering specific details or facts? 4. Is the student focused during instruction, or does poor attention affect the student's ability to acquire information?
Delayed language development	1. Does the student speak using sentence structure that is appropriate for his or her age (e.g., in the early elementary school years, students should be able to use complex sentences that involve a dependent and an independent clause)? 2. Does the student use age-appropriate vocabulary when speaking (i.e., expressive vocabulary)? 3. Does the student use vocabulary words appropriately in different contexts? 4. Does the student seem to understand figurative language (e.g., does he or she understand certain expressions, such as "It feels like a sauna outside" referring to hot, humid weather.)? 5. Does the student understand age-appropriate vocabulary when listening (i.e., receptive vocabulary)? 6. Does the student use pronouns and verbs correctly when speaking (e.g., "She is going to the store" vs. "Her go to the store")? 7. Does the student understand how to use language to initiate and maintain a conversation? 8. Does the student provide enough information about a topic when speaking so that the listener can understand?
Fluency problems	1. Does the student read words easily but lack expression and fail to stop for punctuation? 2. Does the student read in a halting manner? 3. Does the student continue to count on fingers when calculating math problems, even though other students do not? 4. Does the student seem to make many calculation and algorithmic (fail to use the appropriate step while solving the problem) errors when solving problems?

(cont.)

TABLE 2.1. *(cont.)*

Challenges for struggling students	Some questions to ask
Fluency problems *(cont.)*	5. Does the student form letters correctly and easily when writing in class? 6. Does the student spell words easily when writing and are those words generally correct? 7. Can the student rapidly retrieve information to solve a problem?
Poor motivation and learned helplessness	1. Does the student give up easily when the task is somewhat difficult or refuse to engage in the task? 2. Does the student become distracted easily when the task is difficult? 3. Does the student seem to need constant assistance to complete a task? 4. Does the student make negative comments about his or her ability to learn something? (e.g., A student might say that he or she cannot do something because he or she is stupid.) 5. Does the student race through his or her work and refuse to check it?

have (Hart & Risley, 1995). These experiences and opportunities make a difference in what students understand about the world they live in and the development of key academic concepts prior to attending school. Consequently, students from different socioeconomic backgrounds often come to school with rather significant variations in their prior knowledge (Marzano, 2004). Many teachers may not be fully aware of the extent to which students vary in their background knowledge and the degree to which the lack of background knowledge negatively affects students' comprehension of new material. They may proceed instructionally without accounting for these differences or attempting to build background knowledge before beginning instruction on a particular topic.

Information-Processing Deficits

Students can also struggle to learn concepts in a content area because they have difficulty processing incoming information. These difficulties can be related to students' abilities to attend to a task or their ability to manipulate information in order to store and retrieve it when needed (Owens, 2004; Swanson, 1999). Difficulties attending to, processing, storing, or retrieving information can stand in students' way of acquiring well-developed schemas for different concepts or strategies needed to learn new information.

When information enters the brain through the senses, the learner first must determine what information requires attention. Once students attend to the appropriate information, they must hold the information in their working memory in order to manipulate it and store it. Working memory involves the ability to hold onto information while simultaneously doing another task. For instance, a student can spell and write words while listening to information in a class lecture. Once information enters working memory, it must be processed so that it can be effectively stored for retrieval from long-term memory. Thus, students must have effective cognitive strategies that they can deploy to organize the learning process. For example, they are able to state the main ideas in their social studies text and effectively rehearse the main ideas and important details when studying for a test. When students can determine how much to study and select the appropriate cognitive strategies, they are said to have the executive functioning abilities necessary to guide their learning. Finally, students with effective information-processing skills are able to apply what they know to new learning situations; in other words, they can transfer or generalize their knowledge.

Deficits in information processing can be either pervasive or specific. When students have difficulty with every aspect of the information-processing system, they have problems selectively attending to relevant information, learning concepts, making connections between them, automatizing information (to be discussed next), and employing strategies for solving problems or effectively completing tasks. Additionally, these students might struggle to connect concrete understandings with more abstract understandings. When students have pervasive information-processing problems, they find it difficult to move to higher levels of conceptual learning. They need repeated exposure to and concrete examples of concepts and strategies for them to be taught systematically. They also will need to be taught directly how to generalize their knowledge in new settings, so they can recognize the different situations in which they will be required to use and employ it.

In contrast, students with specific information-processing deficits struggle with particular skills and strategies, but do not have more comprehensive processing deficits. They can have difficulty attending to an academic task and ignoring extraneous information occurring in a classroom (e.g., the noise of students shuffling papers). Others experience working memory problems that affect their ability to manipulate information and store it for fast retrieval, such as the fast retrieval of letter names or letter-sound patterns (e.g., *oa* and *ea*) necessary for decoding. Additionally, students may struggle with executive functioning tasks that involve planning, selecting the appropriate cognitive strategy for attacking a task, and evaluating its success. For instance, they may not employ appropriate executive strategies, such as recognizing when comprehension is breaking down and finding a strategy to remediate the problem, such as rereading or self-questioning themselves about the major points of the text.

It is important to recognize that specific problems processing information are either the result of a student's disability, the result of insufficient instruction in the use of strategies, or insufficient background knowledge. For instance, students may have memory problems that make it difficult for them to learn and employ certain strategies. Other students may not have been taught such strategies as finding main ideas and details or summarizing text, or they may have difficulty employing them because they do not have the background knowledge or vocabulary to understand the text. Even though specific deficits are not as devastating to the learning process as more pervasive deficits, they can still have a significant impact on a student's ability to experience success in school unless systematically addressed through instruction.

Delayed Language Development

Language, both written and oral, is the major vehicle for teaching ideas and concepts in schools; thus problems with language have a major impact on a student's ability to learn. As students enter more advanced grades, they acquire knowledge and skills by listening to class lectures and demonstrations and recording notes. Additionally, they acquire a tremendous amount of information from reading texts. Such content demands create real problems for students who have language differences due to culture or disability. In order to help students become accomplished academically, teachers must recognize the different language struggles students encounter, the role they play in instruction, and how to respond instructionally.

Students with disabilities and students with language differences that are the result of culture and poverty often do not develop the English language skills necessary for academic learning. Regardless of the underlying cause, language difference or disability, these students can experience difficulties acquiring the following language skills necessary for academic learning and social interactions: (1) semantic knowledge, (2) phonological awareness or knowledge of words' sound structure, (3) morphological awareness or understanding of the meaning units, (4) orthographic awareness or knowledge of how words are spelled, (5) knowledge of syntax or sentence structure, and (6) knowledge of pragmatics.

Semantic knowledge is necessary for comprehending text and participating in academic lectures (Rayner, Foorman, Perfetti, Pesetsky, & Seidenberg, 2001). As children grow older they encounter more complex words, sentences, and text in both spoken and written language. Their ability to comprehend such complexity is essential to further learning. In their early years, many children living in poverty have fewer opportunities to acquire vocabulary and have less exposure to more complex language interactions than their more affluent peers. Researchers found that, by age 4, children living in homes of professional parents were exposed to 40 million more words than those living with parents receiving welfare; further, professional parents used more complex sentences when speaking with their children and were more responsive to their attempts to talk (Hart & Risley, 1995). Obviously, such differences in learning opportunities impact language development.

Some students have genuine language delays that are due to information-processing deficits or to learning a second language. These students may face all or some of the following challenges: they acquire language later, have word-finding problems, struggle to acquire varied meanings for words, or fail to understand metaphors and idioms when used. Additionally, they might find it difficult to learn the underlying structure of language. For instance, they have difficulty acquiring knowledge of syntax and/or phonological, orthographic, and morphological awareness. Regardless of the reason for language differences, these students will need effective language instruction in order to achieve academically.

Text comprehension in the upper grades is largely dependent on students' knowledge of vocabulary plus their knowledge of syntax or grammar (McGregor, 2004; Scott; 2004). Academic text becomes increasingly important once students enter upper elementary school, and the syntactic complexity of the reading material creates problems for some students. Compared to more accomplished learners, students with language and reading problems produce fewer complex sentences when writing, struggle more to comprehend complex sentences, and display less knowledge of correct grammatical structures (Scott, 2004). Though differences in syntactic abilities can result from specific information-processing deficits, they can also result from language differences due to culture or learning a second language. Regardless of the underlying cause, students need help requiring more sophisticated understanding of syntax and vocabulary as the two are correlated highly with later reading comprehension abilities.

Problems with language's phonology and orthography present different types of hurdles for students in school (Carlisle, 2004; Troia, 2004). In the case of Colin, specific phonological and orthographic problems created his primary struggles in spelling and his inability to take notes in class. Although he had some phonological awareness ability, he struggled to represent the vowel sounds in words correctly, exhibiting extreme difficulties representing short sounds, as he could not discriminate between these phonemes and their written representation. He also failed to recognize morphemes in words, such as *oct-* in *octagon*, even though he understood that an octopus had eight legs. Likely, his difficulties with the orthography of written language (i.e., how words are spelled) stood in the way of his identifying the common morphemes in words. Students who are not phonologically aware demonstrate difficulties rhyming, segmenting the sounds in a word (e.g., they know that *cat* has three sounds), blending sounds together to make a word (e.g., they can blend /c//a//t/) to say *cat*), and manipulating sounds. For instance, if asked to replace the /c/ sound in *cat* with /b/, they would be unable to say *bat*. Such abilities are fundamental to becoming a proficient decoder and speller, as they allow students to shift their attention away from sounding out individual words when reading or writing and focus on understanding the text or generating it.

When students lack morphological awareness, they can demonstrate problems decoding, spelling, and comprehending. For instance, they may not recognize that *re* in *redo, remake,* and *reinstate* means to do something again. Or, like Colin, they may understand the meaning of a word but lack orthographic awareness. They know what the word *please* means, but do not realize that the root word *please* is spelled consistently in *pleasing, pleasurable,* and *pleasant,* even though each word sounds different. Such morphological and orthographic deficits become increasingly problematic with more complicated words. Words with prefixes and suffixes outnumber single-morpheme words (e.g., *please* and *state*) four to one in texts. Without morphological awareness, it is difficult to comprehend and generate text.

If students have difficulties understanding language and struggle to process incoming social information, such as when someone is angry or confused, inevitably they will experience difficulties with the pragmatics of language. For instance, when speaking to the class, they may not present enough information for listeners to understand the topic of their presentation. Additionally, they may not be able to use language to negotiate successful social relationships with their peers. Such problems impair students' abilities to do well in school. They may be socially ostracized, struggle to secure information they need from teachers and peers, or struggle to express the knowledge they do have during instruction.

Fluency Problems

Efficient academic learning requires fluent skill use and rapid retrieval of knowledge. In order to do well in school, students must have the ability to read and write fluently. As mentioned previously, academic texts are the primary vehicle for learning in schools. To comprehend what one is reading, a student must be able to read text fluently, accurately, and with prosody or expression. Fluent readers read text effortlessly, but struggling readers often do not. Struggling readers can have difficulty rapidly retrieving the letter-sound-pattern knowledge (or grapheme–phoneme knowledge), vocabulary knowledge, and syntactic knowledge needed to read fluently (Ehri & Snowling, 2004; Wolf, Miller, & Donnelly, 2000). For instance, if a student was reading the sentence "The man walked down the street to the store," he or she might read "The man work down the stairs in the store." In this case, the student also had to stop and decode the words *walked* and *street*, even though they did so incorrectly. The student also failed to recognize that work requires an inflected ending (e.g., an *s* or an *ed*). In this example you can see how knowledge of decoding and syntax is disrupting the student's ability to read fluently.

Ability to read text fluently is important because it decreases the demands placed on working memory and frees up cognitive space for students to comprehend text. Some students struggle to read fluently because of language development issues (Ehri & Snowling, 2004). Their struggles present enormous barriers in school. Typically, they must read simpler text; thus, they have fewer opportunities to acquire more sophisticated vocabulary and syntactic knowledge or comprehension strategies. These students find reading difficult and often choose not to participate in it, further decreasing their opportunities to develop their language and comprehension skills. Ultimately, they do not gain the skills to read grade-level texts, creating a hurdle for them to overcome in accessing the general education curriculum.

As students progress through the grades, some struggle to keep up with the writing demands inherent in content-area classes. They must write more extended papers and rely increasingly on their ability to take notes during lectures and class demonstrations. Some of their struggles involve the ability to plan, develop, and revise academic texts, problems reflective of possible deficits in executive functioning processes or background knowledge (described earlier). Some of their struggles, however, are due to poor handwriting and spelling fluency. To generate text easily or take notes successfully, students must be able to write fluently; otherwise they spend too much cognitive energy trying to spell words or form letters, leaving less attention for generating ideas or understanding what is being said during class lectures and demonstrations (Graham & Harris, 2000). Deficits, however, in the information-processing system can make it difficult for students to automatize subskills involved in spelling and writing fluently. Colin is the perfect example of a student who despite his extensive background, vocabulary, and syntactic knowledge, lacks the phonological, orthographic, and handwriting skills needed to take notes, and you can see how it disables him in an academic environment.

Finally, students must have fluency with certain math concepts and skills to develop proficiency in mathematics (National Mathematics Advisory Panel, 2008). When students spend too much time counting on their fingers to calculate basic facts or do not have certain mathematical procedures routinized (e.g., the algorithm involved in subtraction with regrouping), they may find it more difficult to solve problems with minimal errors and follow teachers as they are explaining and modeling how to solve novel problems. Additionally, poor automatic retrieval of basic facts affects students' development of number sense and their ability to easily estimate solutions when adding, subtracting, multiplying, or dividing. Insufficient exposure to number concepts prior to entering school, instruction that does not promote automatic retrieval of basic facts and mathematical procedures, or information-processing deficits can interfere with students' ability to develop fluency.

Inappropriate Behavioral and Social Skills

In order to learn effectively, students need to be able to attend to the learning situation and cooperate with teachers and peers. After all, school learning is primarily a social activity. Thus, problems with self-control, interpersonal problems or struggles getting along with others, and intrapersonal problems, such as anxiety or depression, can interfere with a student's ability to focus and cooperate with teachers and peers on academic tasks (Vaughn et al., 2007). Students may display off-task behaviors in the classroom because they are hyperactive and struggle with impulse control, or they experience problems cooperating with peers that interfere with their ability to work alone or with others to complete academic tasks. Students may have difficulty channeling their attention also because of poor impulse control or feelings of anxiety and depression. Students with interpersonal problems can be off-task because negative interactions with peers and teachers disrupt their attention. Rather than paying attention to their work, they are instead complaining about or harassing another student.

Being able to cooperate in a classroom is also essential to learning. Students have to work with their teachers and peers to complete academic tasks and appropriately seek needed assistance. Students who argue with their peers or who have low impulse control cannot work productively on a task. Further, these students disrupt the learning climate of the classroom. They make it difficult for all students in the class to stay focused and be productive.

Students may also lack the social skills necessary for working productively with others. They may not comprehend social situations well and respond to peers inappropriately. Other students demonstrate immaturity in social situations. These students can seem overly dependent on parents or caretakers and may have difficulty being responsible members of a group. Since learning is a social endeavor and working with peers becomes increasingly important in school environments, social problems with peers can stand in the way of these students' ability to learn.

Poor Motivation and Learned Helplessness

When students realize that regardless of their efforts to learn they will fail, they lose motivation to persist on academic tasks and begin to avoid them (Reid & Lienemann, 2006). No one wants to engage in tasks that are difficult and beyond one's capabilities. We all avoid tasks that make us look incompetent, and the students we teach are no different. The repeated failures that students with behavior and learning problems encounter slowly chip away at their motivation. They begin to attribute academic success to being smart or lucky and fail to understand that personal effort and effective strategies can improve their success in school. These students begin to adopt an external locus of control rather than the internal control they will need to become an independent learner, sometimes needing considerable validation and encouragement to persist on academic tasks. They learn to be dependent on others to assist them with academic tasks and fail to develop the strategies they need to work independently and persist with difficult demands. They acquire a certain learned helplessness that if not addressed can interfere with their ability to take charge of their learning in school (Pintrich, Anderman, & Klobucar, 1994). Their sense of frustration and failure can also lead to many of the inappropriate behavior and social problems teachers note, as students who struggle are often seeking to avoid challenging academic tasks and situations.

Inappropriate and Insufficient Instruction

Students can struggle in school because the instruction they receive is insufficient to meet their needs. Sometimes instruction is not well organized or explicit enough for certain students. For instance, about 40% of students have trouble acquiring phonics rules and applying them during reading. When these students receive explicit instruction in helping them "crack the code" of the English language, many of them can make rather dramatic progress. Other times teachers may fail to recognize that many students in their class do not have sufficient background knowledge for the lesson and do not incorporate opportunities to develop that knowledge before forging ahead with instruction. Some students may just need extra practice to learn a skill or strategy or more examples to strengthen their concept acquisition. Failure to recognize their needs, however, will lead to instruction that is not responsive. In Chapter 3, we describe how teachers can use classroom-based assessments to become more responsive to the struggles students can exhibit in schools.

ACCOMPLISHED INCLUSION TEACHERS RECOGNIZE THE SPECIAL NEEDS OF LEARNERS

Designing responsive instruction depends on teachers' ability to recognize the various ways students struggle and how these struggles impact their learning. General education teachers glean much information from observation, work samples, and other types of classroom-based assessments to understand students' needs. Additionally, they can rely on other professionals, such as their special education colleagues, to collect more specific and additional information to help plan and evaluate their efforts to create responsive instruction.

Teachers can acquire a better understanding of the ways in which students are struggling just by becoming careful "kid watchers." They can jot down specific notes in a log or journal about how students approach a task, the tasks they seem to enjoy or avoid doing, and what they seem to accomplish easily versus what they struggle with. Such information can help teachers draw conclusions about a student. For instance, in Colin's case, careful observation would reveal a strong use of oral language when responding to questions about an educational video or passage in a text, but a tendency to shut down or become distracted during activities requiring considerable note taking or writing. Noting changes in his academic behaviors when different instructional demands are present can help general education teachers recognize his strengths and weaknesses. The special education teacher, in collaboration with the general education teacher, can take a closer look at Colin's performance. She can analyze his writing samples carefully to determine how well he is able to spell. She can develop a structured guide for taking notes to determine if that support provides the incentive he needs to take notes in class. Careful examination of Colin's response to different supports will help general and special education teachers determine how to design instruction that enables him to function more like an accomplished learner.

By considering what it takes to be an accomplished learner and identifying the challenges students with serious behavior and learning problems face in becoming accomplished learners, general and special teachers can work together to design instruction that enables these students to function at a greater level of accomplishment in the general education curriculum. Table 2.1 provides a series of questions that teachers might ask themselves to begin the process of understanding challenges faced by struggling learners. Teachers should recognize, however, that responses to these questions do not always indicate the presence of a disability. They might indicate insufficient education experiences in the home environment or instruction that was inadequate in some way. The reason for students' challenges is not the issue. The important point is to collect information that will help general and special education teachers provide stronger, inclusive instruction. By considering the questions in Table 2.1 and using the assessment process to answer them (see Chapter 4), teachers can acquire information about how far students with disabilities (or other struggling learners, for that matter) have progressed in terms of developing as accomplished learners and then use this information to plan for instruction. This information will then allow them to develop research-based instruction that is responsive to student needs, the type of instruction presented in the second part of this book.

CHAPTER 3

Recognizing the Qualities of Successful Inclusive Teachers

Study Guide Questions

- What beliefs do inclusive teachers hold about teaching students with disabilities that allow them to persevere in teaching them?
- What do inclusive teachers need to know to develop instruction that enables students with disabilities to access the general education curriculum?
- What practices can inclusive teachers use to engage students with disabilities in academic instruction and to foster effective outcomes?

In successful inclusion efforts general and special education teachers are the professionals who make learning happen for students. Through their individual expertise and collaborative efforts, they craft instruction that is responsive to students' needs and enables students to become more accomplished learners. In this chapter, we discuss the qualities of accomplished inclusive teachers.

THE CASE OF DESERA AND KRISTI

Desera and Kristi are the type of inclusive teachers that every parent wants for their child who is struggling and every principal dreams of having in their school. Both are accomplished teachers who believe in their abilities to help students. They never stop learning and thinking about how to make instruction better for all of the students they teach. Desera attends every professional workshop she can and participates actively in a collaborative professional development effort in her school. Kristi already has a master's degree in special education and is working hard to acquire a reading endorsement because she knows that she needs all the knowledge she can obtain to meet the significant reading needs of her students with disabilities. She too participates actively in the collaborative professional development effort in their school.

Desera and Kristi always keep the needs of individual students at the forefront of their thinking and push themselves to meet those needs. After learning about the importance of oral reading fluency in their collaborative professional development group, Kristi and Desera decided they needed to secure more information about the skills of their struggling readers. They collected assessment data and decided to use two strategies. First, they worked together to implement classwide peer tutoring to improve the oral reading fluency of all their students. They also decided to regroup some students in the class for more intensive instruction with Kristi; this instruction would focus on specific decoding strategies. To determine if classwide peer tutoring and the small-group intensive instruction were working, Kristi kept continuous records of oral reading fluency rates and updated a checklist of core phonics skills periodically.

Kristi and Desera were also cognizant of their students' background knowledge and the role it played in what they learned. Working in a poor, urban school, they realized that their students might not have the experiences to help them learn new information, so they took care to help them acquire prior knowledge. In a lesson on pre-Revolutionary War history, Desera engaged students in some of the daily tasks of American colonists, such as quilting, making ink, and writing with quills. Students also read trade books about the colonists and used the information they gained from books and various activities to write essays with their peers. Prior to engaging students in a group writing assignment about this experience, Kristi worked with a few struggling students to review what they had learned and arranged the material in a graphic organizer. The students could use this organizer when they worked with their peers on the writing assignment.

BELIEFS, KNOWLEDGE, AND CLASSROOM PRACTICE
OF ACCOMPLISHED INCLUSIVE TEACHERS

Krista and Desera, like other accomplished inclusive teachers, believe that what they do to assist students with disabilities matters (Jordan & Stanovich, 2003). Although they are aware of their students' strengths and limitations, they also believe that through carefully crafted, evidence-based instruction they can make a difference, and they are relentless in their efforts to do so (Bishop et al., 2010). Effective inclusive teachers also understand curriculum; they understand what it takes to be accomplished in the curriculum, and what students with disabilities will need to do to become more accomplished. To determine the exact point in the curriculum where students might struggle, accomplished inclusive teachers use classroom-based measurement to improve their understanding of students' strengths and needs. These teachers then employ effective instructional strategies to enact the curriculum for students with disabilities (Brownell et al., 2009).

Accomplished teachers understand that classroom practices such as direct instruction and other research-based strategies are essential to providing students with disabilities successful access to the general education curriculum (Swanson, Hoskyn, & Lee, 1999). Accomplished teachers also know that measuring their impact through classroom assessments and responding to information from those assessments is essential to meeting student needs. Moreover, they understand that if instruction is going to be effective, it must be motivating to students with disabilities; otherwise, these students will not be engaged. Thus, these teachers seek multiple ways to make instruction more student-friendly and engaging (Seo, 2006). Finally, accomplished inclusive teachers know that it will take knowledge of both special and general education to accommodate students with disabilities (Interstate New Teacher Assessment and Support Consortium, 2001). They understand that working together as general and special educators is essential to delivering the more intensive, direct instruction these students need and if they are to best serve their students, then they must take every opportunity to learn from their partners and secure more information through multiple professional development activities.

Beliefs of Accomplished Inclusive Teachers

Accomplished inclusive teachers are also self-efficacious, relentless, resourceful, and reflective (Bishop et al., 2010). They believe a difference can be made in students' outcomes if solid instruction (i.e., explicit, interactive, and intensive) and classroom management strategies are provided. They believe in their ability to help students learn, even though they realize the challenges many students bring to the classroom (Seo, 2006). These teachers are self-efficacious in that they believe they have the knowledge and skills to work successfully with students with disabilities (Jordan & Stanovich, 2003). As such, they are resourceful and relentless (Bishop et al., 2010). They do not give up on students, but instead find ways to identify strategies and materials will help them. They persevere even when the going gets tough!

Effective inclusive teachers are reflective about the needs of their class and individual students (Brownell, Adams, Sindelar, Waldron, & vanHoover, 2006). These teachers first consider what students need to become more proficient; then they consider the range of individual needs they must address. Such reflective teachers value the use of informal classroom assessment in determining students' needs (a topic we will address more thoroughly in Chapter 4), mostly because of their relentless efforts to help individual students as well as their entire class (see Box 3.1).

BOX 3.1. Accomplished Teachers Are Self-Efficacious, Resourceful, and Relentless

Kristi, the special educator in our case study illustration, would never just provide students with answers. Instead, she asks different questions to help students access their knowledge, or she remodels a strategy or skill when students are struggling, persisting until students understand. Desera admires her for continuously seeking different techniques to foster student success and asks her for advice on how she can present information in more structured ways to minimize students' need for help. Desera describes the content objectives she wants to address in her curriculum, and together they brainstorm structured strategies for helping all students gain access to these objectives.

Together Kristi and Desera design graphic organizers to help the class acquire some of the science concepts Desera is teaching and identify science trade books appropriate for the varying reading levels in the class. When Kristi and Desera discover that Sam, a student with a significant learning disability, is not able to comprehend the text he is reading, they scan the text into the computer and highlight key words that Sam can click on to retrieve definitions. They pose questions for Sam throughout the text to assist him with his comprehension. Kristi and Desera's willingness to respond to Sam's comprehension problems demonstrates just how relentless and reflective they are.

Knowledge of Accomplished Inclusive Teachers

Accomplished teachers have a wealth of knowledge about the content they are teaching, and know how to enact that content using curriculum and interventions, how students are processing the content, and how to keep students engaged in learning. Teachers who teach well, in both general and special education, have a solid grasp of how to teach content and how students learn it (Brownell, Sindelar, Kiely, & Danielson, 2010). Their knowledge enables them to identify what is important to teach and what can be ignored. For instance, effective elementary and secondary general education teachers know mathematical concepts and the connections between them, the types of misconceptions students can have when solving math problems, and how to go about teaching mathematical concepts to students (Hill et al., 2008). More accomplished general education teachers are also more capable of determining and focusing on curriculum's big ideas during instruction. These teachers have a master plan in mind that drives their instruction.

More accomplished special education teachers know a good deal about how to teach reading, writing, and math, specifically numeracy, and they are able to enact that knowledge in the classroom (Brownell et al., 2007; Griffin, Jitendra, & League, 2009). They also know about effective interventions for struggling students that they can bring to bear in assisting general education colleagues to make the curriculum more accessible. They can generate multiple ways to model and practice skills and strategies. They also seem to have a deeper understanding of students' individual needs (Stough & Palmer, 2003).

Knowing how to integrate their respective knowledge bases is also important for designing inclusive instruction. When planning, accomplished inclusive teachers and special education integrate their knowledge bases by focusing on student struggles and how to address them. Kristi and Desera provide an example of how this can be done in Box 3.2.

Classroom Practice of Accomplished Inclusive Teachers

The instruction of accomplished inclusion teachers is explicit, cohesive, intensive, engaging, responsive to student needs, and focused on the big ideas of a curriculum (Brownell et al., 2006; Brownell et al., 2007; Jordan & Stanovich, 2003; Seo, Brownell, Bishop, & Dingle, 2008). Table 3.1 provides a summary of the main features of accomplished classroom practice.

Accomplished inclusive teachers provide explicit instruction that enables students to understand important concepts, skills, and strategies. Explicit instruction is the foundation of any inclusive instruction, since students with disabilities and those who struggle to learn have difficulty mastering content if not taught explicitly.

BOX 3.2. Accomplished Teachers Are Knowledgeable

Our observations of Desera indicated that she had considerable knowledge of the elementary mathematics curriculum. She could identify important concepts to be taught in math and create the type of concrete instruction that helped students acquire those concepts. Her knowledge of the "big picture" in the mathematics curriculum was useful to special educator Kristi, who could then determine where students' learning was breaking down in mathematics, and organize the type of small-group instruction that would help students access broader curricular goals. As an example, Desera noticed that students were not using zero as a place holder when they moved to multiplying with numbers in the 10's and 100's columns. Desera knew that this mistake was commonly associated with an incomplete understanding of place value. Thus, she and Kristi designed some small-group instruction where Kristi used concrete manipulatives to show how place value was working in long multiplication problems. Kristi knew that the students would need considerable practice with these problems to be fluent and that they would feel resistant to engaging in repeated practice, so she found a website where students used computer-generated manipulatives to solve problems. Kristi used this website to create self-directed activities students could complete during learning center time.

TABLE 3.1. Components of Accomplished Classroom Practice

Components	Description	Example
Explicit	Explicit instruction is clear and systematic instruction. It contains many subcomponents (see Table 3.2) designed to help a student master and apply knowledge, skills, and strategies to novel problems. The teacher uses clear language in his or her explanations.	The teacher shows students the steps involved in summarizing a section of a social studies text; uses think-alouds to demonstrate the thought processes behind the steps of summarization; and provides practice using steps until students master the summarization routine.
Focused on big ideas	The teacher concentrates instruction on those curricular concepts, strategies, and skills that enable a student to become accomplished.	The big ideas of geography are place, location, movement, human–environment interaction, and regions. Human–environment interaction and movement might be used to help students understand the migration of Irish immigrants to America.
Intensive	The teacher's instruction is purposeful and focused. He or she always has a goal for the lesson and the goal is obvious to students. The pace is rapid, but not so quick that students are lost. Little time is wasted during instruction; all activities tap important skills and transitions between activities are quick and smooth.	To ensure that students are attending to individual sounds in short-vowel words involving blends, the teacher might ask students to stretch words that follow a specific decoding pattern into their individual sounds. The students might do this activity chorally. Then the teacher moves quickly to asking students to provide individual sounds in targeted words by representing each sound using letter manipulatives. The teacher moves students through examples quickly, but still allows students time to think and respond.
Cohesive	The teacher's lesson moves in a systematic and cohesive fashion where the objective of the lesson and individual activities are clearly linked. He or she relates the current lesson with past or future learning.	Prior to starting a lesson on fractions, the teacher asks students to divide two bags of candy evenly between the total number of students in the class. He or she then shows how the total number of students represent the denominator in a fraction and how the amount of candy each friend receives represents the numerator. She uses the candy demonstration to explain the difference between the numerator and the denominator. The teacher then asks the students to develop fractions to represent number statements (e.g., "You have 12 cattle that you must distribute equally to 2 farmers. Write a fraction representing how many cows each farmer will receive").

(cont.)

TABLE 3.1. *(cont.)*

Components	Description	Example
Engaging	Students are actively engaged in instruction 80% of the time or more. They seem motivated and interested to participate in the instruction. The teacher uses multiple techniques for getting students to respond and redirects students who are off-task quickly and in a positive manner.	In the above lesson on fractions, students work in pairs to determine how to divide the candy. The teacher circulates through the room to make sure they are engaged. The teacher then has all students writing fractions to represent number statements but randomly calls on students to provide responses. Then students work in pairs to write fractions for additional number statements while the teacher circulates to ensure that students understand the task and to foster student engagement.
Responsive	The teacher organizes instruction so that there are multiple opportunities to evaluate student learning. The teacher also helps the student understand what he or she did correctly and incorrectly. Instruction is adjusted based on student need or accommodations are made to allow a student to access the curriculum.	In working with a sixth-grade boy, the general education teacher noticed his essays were slightly disjointed. Some sentences did not always follow from the main idea and his poor spelling seemed to be interfering with his ability to generate ideas. So the teacher worked on two strategies simultaneously. First, she helped him to see how specific sentences did not always support the main idea. Second, she asked the special education teacher if technology could help. The special education teacher identified word prediction software that might alleviate some of his spelling issues. The special educator also provided the student with intensive spelling instruction for about 20 minutes a day to alleviate some of the problems the boy was having.

Explicit instruction involves building a rationale for learning a concept, strategy or skill; modeling how to use the strategy or skill or showing examples; giving clear explanations of concepts and connections between concepts; and practicing with students until they understand a concept and how to apply it or use a strategy or skill with novel tasks. Each phase of instruction is highly interactive. Table 3.2 outlines the components of explicit instruction and provides an explanation and examples of each one.

Explicit instruction, however, is not sufficient if it focuses on a small part of the concepts, strategies, or skills that students must learn to become proficient in a content area. Inclusive teachers must also provide instruction that is comprehensive, including big ideas of a subject area, as well as developing facility with key strategies and skills. For example, a national panel of mathematics researchers identified the type of comprehensive classroom instruction that is most likely to make a

TABLE 3.2. Components of Explicit instruction

Subcomponents	Description and examples
Building a rationale	The teacher helps students understand how learning a particular strategy, concept, or skill will help them in school and their daily life. For instance, the teacher helps students understand how learning to summarize text can help them understand what they are reading.
Explanation	The teacher describes a concept by using clear language and focusing on the features of the concept. For instance, a teacher might explain how the circulatory system is similar to a mass transportation system. Explanations also involve providing clear directions for how to complete a task.
Modeling	The teacher shows students the steps involved in solving a problem or using a strategy (e.g., summarizing text) by demonstrating the thought processes and steps involved in doing so. The teacher achieves this by thinking aloud while using the steps of the strategy. For instance, the teacher might describe how they look for ideas that are repeated in the text and make a statement that captures those ideas in order to create a summary. Additionally, the teacher models using multiple examples to ensure that students are ready for the next step: practice.
Practice	The teacher moves from guided to independent practice by initially giving considerable support to apply strategies, concepts, or skills to novel examples or problems. Once the student is able to apply his or her knowledge easily, the teacher withdraws support. For instance, the teacher might provide students multiple opportunities as a class to solve word problems using fractions before asking students to work in pairs to solve the problems. It is obvious that the teacher is using practice to help students develop mastery.
Generalization	The teacher provides students with multiple opportunities to solve problems or use strategies under new conditions. For instance, after teaching students to summarize expository text, the teacher helps students to see how they can use summarization to organize information they have been collecting for a research project into key ideas.

difference in student learning (National Mathematics Advisory Panel, 2008). They suggested that to be effective mathematics instruction must:

1. Focus on key concepts and their connections, such as the connections between fractions, percent, ratios, and proportions.
2. Simultaneously help students develop conceptual understanding, procedural fluency, and automatic recall of basic calculation skills.

The same is true for reading. Studies of accomplished general and special education teachers indicate that they provide comprehensive reading instruction that fosters improved student achievement, and addresses the main processes underlying reading success: phonological awareness, decoding, fluency, oral language development, and comprehension (Baker, Gersten, Haager, & Dingle, 2006; Seo et al., 2008; Taylor, Pearson, Peterson, & Rodriquez, 2005), and they use explicit instruction that is highly interactive to teach these processes.

These teachers also make sure to connect big ideas during instruction while at the same time intensifying instruction in key areas for their most high-risk learners. Instruction is intensive, in part, because it is well-organized and engaging, with little time being wasted on noninstructional activities. Accomplished teachers have well-established routines for passing out materials and completing activities, and students definitely are aware of those routines. They have smooth and seamless transitions from one activity to the next, and students are engaged in appropriate content for more than 80% of the time. Additionally, students are cognitively engaged in the instruction; they are not just simply responding. Instead, they are willing and even excited to participate with their teachers. They watch the instruction with interest, ask questions, offer a response, and think carefully about what they are being asked to do.

Responsiveness is another key feature of effective instructional practice in inclusive classrooms. Since accomplished teachers know their students well through observation, work samples, and other types of assessments, they realize what students require to support their learning and can craft instruction appropriately. Such teachers also understand their students' learning profiles within the broader parameters of a curricular area.

Accomplished teachers also recognize that those students who are struggling the most in inclusive classrooms will need instruction that is more intensive and responsive than that of their peers. As such, these teachers work together to determine key areas for intensive intervention, such as building oral reading fluency or developing place value knowledge. They also look carefully at how instruction is arranged to ensure that these students can receive small-group, intensive instruction as well as more individualized practice to support learning in these key areas. To ensure that such instruction is responsive to students' needs, they continuously collect assessment data to determine if they should continue intensive instruction in an area, adapt instruction, or just monitor maintainance of student learning.

Desera and Kristi are perfect illustrations of teachers who engage in accomplished classroom practice. In the following example, Desera and Kristi demonstrate a lesson that embraces the following qualities of accomplished classroom practice. The instruction is explicit, engaging, cohesive, intensive, and responsive (see Box 3.3).

Focus on Student Motivation

Accomplished inclusive teachers demonstrate a keen awareness of the role motivation plays in a student's learning. They realize that many students who struggle academically lose motivation after repeatedly experiencing failure (Seo, 2006). They

---

BOX 3.3. Inclusive Teachers Engage in Accomplished Classroom Practice

When watching Desera provide instruction in cause and effect, an important comprehension skill, we noted that she employed concrete techniques for teaching students how cause and effect were related and how one could identify a cause and its effect when reading. For instance, she first shouted "underpants" and the students yelled "yuck." Then she turned out the lights quickly, and it caused students to wonder aloud about what was going on. From there, she explained how what she was doing was causing them to respond in certain ways, so her behavior was the cause and their response was the effect. At that point, she provided the class with several causes, such as eating too much, and helped them generate effects. This large-group instruction, designed to explain cause and effect by using clear examples, was followed by a practice activity. Half the class was provided a cause and the other half an effect; students then had to match the appropriate cause and effect. She called on certain students to explain their answers. The students were engaged in the instruction and excitedly offered responses to Desera's questions.

After the class activity, she asked students to work independently on identifying cause-and-effect relationships in a worksheet she had created based on several stories the students read in class. After Desera and Kristi graded the worksheets, they noticed that three of the students with comprehension problems were continuing to struggle. So Kristi designed several follow-up lessons to help these students when other students were participating in their learning centers. Kristi found that she had to provide these students with multiple hands-on examples of cause and effect before they were able to understand.

---

know that crafting motivating instruction is key to engaging students in the learning process, and that such instruction depends on knowledge of their students' strengths, needs, and interests both inside and outside of school. Plus, these teachers feel that even when the odds are stacked against students, they can still be motivated to do well academically, especially when they receive the help they need to do well. They also know that although some students have real learning challenges and may not always have parents who can help them, as teachers they can overcome some of these challenges by incorporating what they know about effective instruction, providing meaningful activities and tasks, building on student success, creating a learning community, and promoting student choice during instruction (Seo, 2006). In the instructional practices of Desera and Kristi, one can see how they use a combination of interesting and engaging activities combined with more intensive instruction and peer tutoring to create an environment in which students who struggle want to learn. In such supportive environments, even those students who struggle most feel that if they try hard enough they can experience success and therefore become more motivated to try.

Commitment to Collaboration

Accomplished inclusive teachers are committed to working with each other to meet an important goal: including students with disabilities and other struggling learners successfully into classroom instruction (Flesner, 2007). General education teachers often realize that their special education counterparts have considerable knowledge of intervention strategies, accommodations, and classroom management techniques. Special education teachers realize that general education teachers are more familiar with how to teach content and the scope and sequence of grade-level curriculum. Their respect for each other's knowledge base and how it can enhance instruction is an essential ingredient of their work together. Because they value each other's knowledge and skill, accomplished inclusive teachers work to achieve parity in their relationship, integrate their knowledge and skills into cohesive lessons, and negotiate goals and ways of working together.

Kristi and Desera were well aware of the skills and knowledge that their partner brought to the table. Desera brings a knowledge of the content area and curriculum used to support it and the bigger picture of the general education curriculum. Kristi, in contrast, understands how learning can break down for students with disabilities and has learned many evidence-based strategies for addressing student problems. Kristi also understands that she needs to deliver these strategies using intensive, small-group instruction. The illustrations of Kristi and Desera working together make it obvious that they have found ways to draw on each other's knowledge and negotiate ways of working together that meet the needs of the different students in their classrooms.

THE PATH TO BECOMING AN ACCOMPLISHED INCLUSIVE TEACHER

Becoming an accomplished inclusive teacher takes time and requires a commitment to learning that spans one's career in the classroom. Teaching students, particularly those with learning and behavior challenges, is a complex job requiring considerable knowledge and skill. Accomplished teachers realize that regardless of how much they know there is always more to learn. Because of their commitment to ongoing learning, they constantly seek resources and educational opportunities that can improve their knowledge about students with disabilities and how to best instruct them. They are sponges for learning and believe they can always do things better. To become more accomplished, however, inclusive teachers need to know what resources are available, particularly those that can help them develop better instruction collaboratively.

Finally, accomplished inclusive teachers need to recognize how they can work with their colleagues to learn from one another. Planning together, developing concept maps of the big ideas in the curriculum, brainstorming strategies, looking up information, and asking questions of other teachers will enable general and special education teachers to learn from each other. Additionally, general and special education teachers need to recognize when their collaborators may not have the skills and knowledge to implement new ideas and provide greater support in terms of explanation, modeling, and coaching. They may need to begin by introducing less complex ideas and supporting teachers in planning to execute them. In the remaining chapters of this book, we detail strategies teachers can discuss together and ways they can determine their curricular and lesson goals. By incorporating outside resources into their collaborative efforts, general and special education teachers can enhance their efforts to become accomplished inclusive teachers.

CHAPTER 4

Recognizing the Need for Collecting Meaningful Data

Study Guide Questions

- Why do we engage in the assessment process?
- What types of assessment tools can general and special education teachers use to learn more about their students and how they are responding to instruction?
- What can special and general educators learn from these various assessment tools?
- How can special and general educators use technology to make the assessment process more efficient and improve communication with parents?
- How can special and general education teachers work together to organize the assessment process?
- How can they involve parents in the assessment process?

THE CASE OF ANGELA

Angela is a student in Kristi and Desera's second-grade inclusion mathematics class. Angela came to the United States from Nicaragua with her mother 2 years ago and entered kindergarten at Martinville Elementary where Kristi and Desera teach. Upon entering kindergarten, Angela was placed in a kindergarten classroom where the teacher received support from a teacher with a certification in Teaching English to Speakers of Other Languages (TESOL).

As a consequence, Angela received a fairly rich language and early literacy experience, including vocabulary instruction that was concrete and fostered dialogue in both Spanish and English. She engaged in shared reading of picture books in order to foster her understanding of stories and the English language. She also received rather explicit instruction in phonological awareness and alphabetic skills.

As a result, Angela seemed to gain literacy skills and acquired oral language skills in English. By second grade, however, Angela was demonstrating some major difficulties in reading. Kristi and Desera decided that they needed to find a way to assist Angela and do so quickly. As a first step, they knew they should engage Angela's mother in a conversation about her progress in school, but they knew that meeting with her mother, Isabella, would be difficult. Isabella had a smaller child at home and found transportation to school difficult, plus she had limited proficiency with the English language. Thus, Kristi and Desera decided to work with the TESOL teacher, who could speak Spanish fluently, to arrange a meeting with Isabella that would be convenient given her family circumstances.

In the meantime, Kristi and Desera decided they needed to collect some assessment data that would pinpoint the difficulties Angela was having. The three teachers had already examined data collected schoolwide to monitor the progress of students in reading. They noticed that although Angela had command of consonant and short-vowel sounds and many of the long-vowel sounds, she was not very fluent when reading passages in English, nor did she seem able to tell teachers much about what she read. The teachers wondered why she labored during oral reading, so they decided to review Angela's prior assessment and determine how quickly she was able to blend sounds together in nonsense words. Additionally, Kristi and Desera asked the TESOL teacher for help. The TESOL teacher decided to engage her in shared book reading in both Spanish and English so she could tap how Angela's background and vocabulary knowledge might be affecting her comprehension of text. Kristi, Desera, and the TESOL teacher knew they had to better understand the source of Angela's reading problems in order to figure out how to serve her best or determine if she needed additional educational services, such as those provided in special education.

ASSESSMENT IN SCHOOLS:
WHAT CLASSROOM TEACHERS NEED TO KNOW

In order to design responsive instruction, teachers must be able to recognize students' strengths within a curriculum as well as the various ways they struggle and how their struggles impact learning. Thus, accomplished inclusive teachers are those who use assessment data frequently to make decisions about how to design and evaluate instruction. In this chapter, we provide information about what teachers should know about assessment, how it can be used, and how parents can be involved in the assessment process to better serve students in inclusive classrooms.

Kristi, Desira, and the TESOL teacher were collecting assessment data to better understand how to educate Angela and provide the services she needs to make progress in the general education curriculum. These teachers were using what is considered classroom-based or informal assessments, as such assessments are designed to understand the individual student's strengths and needs in an academic-content area and understand his or her progress in the curriculum. Classroom-based assessments are essential to designing and evaluating instruction that is responsive to the needs of struggling students. Teachers and other school professionals must be able to carefully document that they have provided adequate interventions and accommodations prior to referring a student to be evaluated for special education services. Such attention to assessment-driven instruction ensures that students entering the referral process are not curriculum casualties but students whose educational needs require more than the supports and services typically provided in general education. Finally, informal assessment data are needed to provide the ongoing intensive, carefully crafted instruction that students with disabilities will need once they are identified for special education. Without the guidance provided by such data, inclusive teachers will be unable to determine if their curriculum and instructional strategies are helping students make adequate yearly progress on state content standards and become accomplished learners. Likewise, ongoing progress monitoring should lead to effective instruction and/or behavioral interventions, thus addressing the unique needs of the student, and thereby reducing the number of students referred for assessment and identified as individuals with disabilities. We should note that regular assessment combined with evidence-based instruction will not prevent disabilities; however, it should enhance the struggling child's instructional and behavioral supports, thereby reducing the need for specialized education.

Assessment of Classroom Environment

The classroom environment is the first place to start when examining why a particular student might be struggling. Perhaps a student is failing because he or she is participating in instruction that is not well designed or the classroom environment is not conducive to learning. By having a peer conduct an ecological or environmental assessment, teachers can determine how to first change their instruction or classroom management approach before intervening with a particular student. Ecological assessments can target areas such as (1) physical environment and how the students are arranged in the classroom, (2) classroom management procedures, (3) instructional behaviors, (4) teacher–student interactions, (5) teacher interactions with struggling students, (6) academic structures available, and (7) extended learning opportunities. An example of a classroom environment assessment by Overton (2004) is in Figure 4.1. Other commercially made environmental assessments are also available.

Name of Student _____   Date: _____

Class: _____

Duration of observation: _____ minutes.

Check all that are observed during this observational period.

Physical Environmental Factors

____ Seating: Individual student desks

____ Seating: Group tables

____ Seating: Student desks grouped in pairs or groups of four

____ Material organized for quick student access and use

____ Target student's materials organized

Classroom Behavioral Structure

____ Classroom expectations (rules) posted

____ Verbal praise for effort of students

____ Verbal praise for target student

____ Quiet redirection for target student when needed

____ Inconsequential minor behaviors are ignored

____ Transitions were smooth

____ Time lapse to begin task less than 3 minutes (for class)

____ Time lapse to begin task less than 3 minutes (for target student)

____ Time lapse to begin task 5 minutes or more (for class)

____ Time lapse to begin task 5 minutes or more (for target student)

____ Noise level consistent with task demands

____ Classwide behavior plan used

Classroom Teacher's Instructional Behaviors

____ Task expectations explained verbally

____ Task expectations explained visually (on board, etc.)

____ Task modeled by teacher

____ Cognitive strategies modeled by teacher first (thinking aloud)

Teacher–Students Interactions

____ Academic behavior/responses shaped by teacher for all students

____ Teacher used proximity as a monitoring technique for all students

____ Teacher used proximity for reinforcement technique for all students

____ Teacher used one-on-one instruction to clarify task for all students

(cont.)

FIGURE 4.1. Assessment of academic environment. From Overton (2004). Copyright 2004 by the Hammill Institute on Disabilities. Reprinted with permission from Sage Publications.

Teacher–Target Student Interactions

____ Academic behavior/responses shaped by teacher for target student

____ Teacher used proximity as a monitoring technique for target student

____ Teacher used proximity for reinforcement technique for target student

____ Teacher used one-on-one instruction to clarify for target student

Classroom Academic Structure

____ Anticipatory set for lesson/activity

____ Task completed by group first before individuals are expected to complete task

____ Academic behavior/responses modeled/assisted by peers

____ Expected response or task made by pairs, groups, or teams

____ Expected response made by individual students

____ Tasks, instructions were structured and clear to students

____ Tasks, instructions were unclear to target student

____ A variety of teaching methods (direct instruction, media, manipulatives) used

____ Advanced organizers used; cues, prompts, presented to class

Extended Learning Experiences

____ Homework assignment appropriate (at independent level, not emerging skill level)

____ Homework instructions are clear

____ Homework assignment is displayed in consistent place in room (board, etc.)

____ Students use daily planner or other technique for homework/classwork

____ Homework assignment is planned for reinforcement of skill rather than extension of work not completed during class

Other Concerns of Academic Environment:

FIGURE 4.1. *(cont.)*

Curriculum-Based Assessments

Teachers have many different types of assessments available to assist them in better understanding their students' progress in the curriculum. Some assessments are published, and others draw on systematic ways of collecting information from activities that teachers use daily. In the following sections, we describe some of the assessment techniques general and special education teachers can use to improve their understanding of individual students' strengths and needs in the curriculum and evaluate the effectiveness of their instruction. Some of the assessment tools have considerable research data to support them and others do not; yet all of these tools contain useful information for teachers if collected in a systematic and comprehensive way. Systematic and comprehensive data collection depends on teachers' knowledge of what it takes to be accomplished in a particular content area. Referring to state benchmarks for content performance can help teachers attend to the knowledge, strategies, and skills underlying accomplished performance.

Observation

Teachers can acquire better understandings of the ways in which students are struggling just by becoming careful "kid watchers." Making careful notes in a log or journal about how students approach a task, the tasks they seem to enjoy or avoid doing, their attention during certain tasks, and what they seem to accomplish easily versus what they struggle with can help teachers draw conclusions about a student. For instance, in Angela's case, careful observation by the TESOL teacher during shared book reading might reveal some oral language issues when Angela was asked to describe what is happening in the book or talk about what she likes most. The TESOL teacher might notice that Angela does not use the type of vocabulary you might expect a second-grade student to use, nor does she respond with complex sentences. Instead, her oral language seems similar to a younger child's. By keeping observation notes, the TESOL teacher is collecting information that provides some insights into why Angela is having trouble reading: her oral language abilities need improving. When students do not have sufficient vocabulary or the ability to use complex syntax (e.g., grammar), their comprehension is often impaired and so is their ability to read text fluently. Because Angela's oral language abilities are depressed, even in Spanish, it is undoubtedly difficult for her to easily listen to or read text and comprehend it.

For observations to be useful, teachers need to have some key behaviors in mind that they hope to observe. For instance, when students are solving word problems in mathematics, they may take note of how the student approaches the problem. Does the student seem to read the problem first? Does he or she select the correct operation? Is the student able to set up the problem correctly? These are just some of the questions a general or special education teacher might ask when observing. Teachers will definitely want to develop questions or use checklists of the behaviors they hope to observe before collecting data.

Checklists of Academic and Social Behavior

Teachers can use checklists during observations to identify whether or not students have mastered skills or accomplished developmental expectations appropriate for their age and grade (Overton, 2004). These checklists might be teacher-constructed or found in commercial materials or curriculum guides. For instance, when a student is reading aloud, the teacher might want to note if the student (1) decodes phonetically regular words, or words that follow a pattern; (2) makes self-corrections; (3) stops for punctuation; and (4) reads phonetically regular and common sight words fluently. Recording notes about these different oral reading behaviors would enable the teacher to make judgments about students' decoding abilities, their comprehension of text, and their ability to decode fluently. If a student decoded most words and read fluently, but did not make self-corrections or stop for punctuation, then comprehension of text is likely the problem. See Figure 4.2 for a series of questions that teachers might ask themselves about a students' reading abilities.

Teachers can also use checklists to evaluate a student's behavior during instruction and other aspects of the school day, such as recess or lunch. Noting changes in academic behaviors when different instructional or social demands are present can help teachers hypothesize about a student's strengths and areas of need and develop behavioral interventions to support the student.

Interviews

By talking to students, teachers can secure a wealth of information about what their interests are, how they feel about school and certain subjects within school, how they approach tasks, and how they solve problems. As pointed out in Chapter 3, when students are motivated to learn a subject, they will remain more engaged in the learning process, and as a consequence are likely to achieve more. Special and general education teachers then are wise to improve their understanding about students' interests and experiences both inside and outside of school. Developing such an understanding is important for students with disabilities, particularly those coming from culturally and linguistically diverse backgrounds. Often these students feel disengaged from school as a result of repeated failure. When teachers can draw on these students' interests and experiences during instruction, they are more likely to foster their motivation to learn and improve their understanding of new concepts.

Teachers can also use interviews in combination with observations to better understand how students are approaching and solving tasks. For instance, teachers can ask students to talk about what they do prior to reading an expository text or ask them to describe what they were thinking about while reading a text. In mathematics, teachers can ask students to describe each step they will take while solving a problem. Cognitive interviews can provide insights into the strategies students employ to comprehend materials, organize their writing, and solve mathematics problems. Such insights will help teachers to decide on what strategies they should teach.

Error Analysis

The types of errors students make can provide insights into the struggles they are having. By examining patterns of errors, teachers can target specific areas for instruction in reading, writing, or mathematics. For instance, a teacher might

Decoding skills: Questions to Ask

Does the student attempt to decode both the initial and final consonant sounds in a word? ☐

Is the student able to recognize when a phonetically regular word contains a short-vowel sound or a long-vowel sound? ☐

Is the student able to discriminate easily between short-vowel sounds (e.g., /a/ and /e/ or /o/ and /u/)?☐

Is the student able to say each of the sounds represented in a blend? ☐

Is the student able to decode words using consonant diagraphs (e.g., *ch, sh, th, wh*)? ☐

Is the student able to decode words using vowel diagraphs (e.g., *oa, ee, ea, oo*)? ☐

Is the student able to decode words using vowel diphthongs (e.g., *oi, ow, oy*)? ☐

Is the student able to segment words into their individual sounds and represent those sounds with letters? ☐

Is the student able to blend sounds to decode words he or she does not know? ☐

Does the student have any approach/strategy for decoding multisyllabic words? ☐ What is it? _____

Does the student use context to decode unknown words? ☐

Vocabulary skills

Does the student understand the meaning of words appropriate for his or her grade level? ☐

Can the student state the meaning of appropriate vocabulary words using his or her own words? ☐

Can the student rephrase a sentence substituting a target vocabulary word with a word or phrase that is synonymous with the targeted word? ☐

Can the student use grade-level vocabulary words in class conversations? ☐

Can the student use grade-level vocabulary words when writing? ☐

Can the student use knowledge of vocabulary to support successful decoding of multisyllabic words? ☐

Fluency Skills

Does the student automatically recognize sight words appropriate for his or her grade level? ☐

Does the student automatically recognize commonly used decodable words appropriate for his or her grade level? ☐

Does the student read connected text using appropriate phrasing and pacing? ☐

Can the student read a certain number of words per minute with few errors, according to guidelines for his or her grade level? ☐

Comprehension Skills

Is the student able to make predictions about the text that are appropriate? ☐

Can the student set an appropriate purpose for reading (e.g., learn information for a test, understand the directions for an activity)? ☐

Can the student identify the main idea of a passage in expository text? ☐ In narrative text? ☐

Can the student summarize a passage in expository text? ☐ In narrative text? ☐

(cont.)

FIGURE 4.2. Reading checklist for upper elementary students.

Can the student recall key information about expository text (e.g., questions about key events in social studies text or important facts in science texts)? ☐

Can the student recall key information about narrative text (e.g., the main characters in a story, information about key events, setting, the main sequence of events in the plot, the problem the character has to solve)? ☐

Can the student respond to questions asking him or her to infer information from the text? ☐

Can the student respond to questions that ask him or her to evaluate certain ideas or aspects of the text (e.g., "Do you think the main character made a wise choice in supporting his son's plan to save the animals?")? ☐

Is the student able to make connections between his or her vexperiences and ideas in the text? ☐

FIGURE 4.2. *(cont.)*

analyze errors from a student's math homework to determine if the student is lacking conceptual understanding, failing to remember problem-solving formulas (e.g., the formula for determining the area of a figure), or is making simple calculation errors. Depending on the types of errors made, the teacher will develop a strategy for addressing the errors. For instance, Angela may consistently demonstrate mistakes while solving long addition problems. Upon closer analysis, Kristi and Desera notice that the mistakes always involve regrouping, so they decide to work on some regrouping with base 10 and 1's blocks to see if Angela understands that concept.

Work Samples

Students produce products in class such as essays or picture summaries of stories that can be analyzed to improve understanding of their academic strengths and needs. Work samples can provide a powerful portrait of student performance. For instance, writing samples can demonstrate students' ability to organize their ideas, use complex sentence structure, and spell correctly, and can also be used to evaluate students' vocabulary usage and understanding of concepts. Work samples in combination with scoring rubrics can be particularly useful for helping teachers focus on the key aspects of accomplished performance. For instance, when scoring Angela's picture summary of her story, the rubric could be used to determine if she was able to capture the gist of the story, use key details to support the gist, and present the picture summary in an organized way. Using rubrics to evaluate work samples can also help teachers communicate students' accomplishments as well as areas of need with parents, students, and other teachers. In addition to using rubrics, teachers can also employ error analysis to determine patterns of need across several work samples. For instance, in the case of Angela, writing samples can be analyzed to better understand how she is applying her emerging knowledge of phonics to spelling when generating texts.

Portfolios

Teachers interested in providing more comprehensive pictures of students' abilities can use portfolios. This assessment tool is usually developed collaboratively between teachers and students and is designed to provide a complete picture of a student's performance in a curriculum. Portfolios include multiple sources of information, such as curriculum-based measurement (CBM) data, checklists of academic or social behaviors, notes from observations of students, and work samples. Additionally, portfolios typically include products students have selected to represent their knowledge of a topic or their expertise in a particular subject area. Teachers can also help students design self-evaluations of their work. By encouraging students to participate in the assessment process, teachers can foster their ability to reflect on their strengths as learners and to set goals for improvement. Although portfolios have not been established as valid and reliable indicators of student progress, they can be helpful tools if designed carefully. In Angela's case, teachers could build a comprehensive picture of her reading abilities by first considering what it takes to be an accomplished reader (e.g., ability to work with the sound structure of language, ability to match sounds with letters, knowledge of vocabulary and grammar, ability to read text fluently, and ability to use comprehension strategies to make sense of text). They could then develop a portfolio that captures these fundamental abilities, including but not limited to, samples of her performance on various phonics measures, graphs of how many words she reads per minute, the TESOL teacher's observation notes from shared book reading, and picture summaries of texts Angela has read. With such information, the special education, general education, and TESOL teachers can begin to provide a comprehensive profile of Angela's reading abilities, share that information with Angela's mother, and target instruction accordingly.

Functional Behavioral Assessment

Teachers interested in understanding a student's problem behavior and gathering details about the events that predict a student's behavior would most likely administer a functional behavioral assessment (FBA). The purpose of the FBA is to provide information that will be used to design effective positive behavior support plans. To support a student who is engaging in problem behaviors in your classroom, it is important to consider the reasons why a student may be engaging in such behavior. Behaviors are not repeated unless they serve a function for the student. Thus, the FBA seeks to determine the antecedent to the behavior to better determine how to prevent and/or address the behavior when it occurs.

Students generally engage in a behavior for one of two reasons: to avoid or escape something unpleasant and to obtain something desirable. For instance, a student may try to escape from a difficult or boring task by becoming disruptive in class because he knows the teacher will send him to the office for misbehaving. In other situations, a student tells jokes and makes funny noises during independent seatwork because she is seeking attention from her teacher and peers. In this way, problem behavior can be seen as a form of communication. It is the student's way of telling others that he or she is tired, bored, needs a break, and/or wants attention.

An FBA is not completed in the same way every time. The type of information collected varies depending on the individual student's problem behavior, strengths, and needs. In some cases, specific tools are needed in an FBA to collect information about medications, sleeping patterns, or social and interactional skills and may require more time and energy to complete. Even though the FBA tools and level of complexity vary, the process remains the same. The FBA is considered complete when the following products have been documented:

- A clear and measurable definition of the problem behavior.
- Events that predict when problem behaviors will and will not occur.
- Consequences that maintain problem behaviors.
- One or more hypotheses about the function of ntaining problem behavior.
- Direct observations data supporting the hypotheses.

The process for conducting anFBA involves three different types of strategies: indirect assessment, direct observation, and functional analysis. These activities are completed by a team, including the teacher (or teachers), the student, parents, and other important individuals. A team approach ensures that the FBA gathers accurate information that reflects the perspectives of the student and the people within his or her social network.

Curriculum-Based Measurement

CBM is one of the most well-researched classroom-based assessment strategies, and therefore is viewed as an essential tool for determining the progress of students with or without disabilities as well as identifying them for special education services. CBM uses repeated measures from a student's curriculum to monitor his or her progress regularly. The purpose is to provide ongoing information on how a student's behavior changes on a "generic task" that is indicative of overall progress in that curricular area. Frequent progress monitoring helps teachers select more effective teaching methods when a student is not making adequate progress (Deno, 1985). CBM measures have been developed for reading, mathematics, and writing, although many teachers are probably most aware of those designed for reading.

For example, one of the most well-known CBM measures is oral reading fluency (ORF). ORF is the number of words read correctly in a minute. ORF helps teachers determine if students are acquiring important reading skills, as ORF is both an indicator of the ability to decode fluently and to comprehend. In writing, how many words a student produces in response to a writing prompt is an indicator of overall writing quality.

The ability of CBM to validly monitor students' progress in the curriculum has made it a useful tool for identifying students' specific needs, developing interventions targeting those needs, and calculating students' response to targeted interventions. Consequently, CBM is now recognized as integral to determining a student's RTI under the IDEA of 2004 (Public Law 108-446). The fundamental RTI concept is that students receive the high-quality instruction and intervention that enables them to be successful.

RTI AS IT RELATES TO CBM

RTI is a process that involves several important steps. Each of these steps is to be conducted within a collaborative problem-solving context that, at minimum, involves the general education teacher, special education teacher, and parents. Although each partner may not be involved in executing each step of the process, she or he should be engaged in collaborative conversations about how the process is unfolding as well as what information is being gathered about students.

1. Monitor students' progress in the curriculum with technically adequate assessments.
2. Choose and implement an evidence-based proven intervention to address students' deficits.
3. Follow explicit rules to decide which students are not making sufficient progress or responding to the intervention.
4. Monitor the student's outcomes in the intervention with at least weekly or biweekly assessments (e.g., CBM).
5. Ensure that the intervention is delivered in a manner in which it was developed and meant to be implemented.
6. Determine the intensity of the support that a student needs to be successful.

For assessment purposes, RTI's ongoing monitoring of a student's progress and his or her response to an intervention is referred to as progress monitoring (e.g., CBM). Progress monitoring under the RTI framework is seen as a flexible data collection process that can be implemented with individual students and/or across an entire class.

PROGRESS MONITORING AS IT RELATES TO CBM

Like CBM, the purpose of progress monitoring is to identify a student's current level of performance, establish educational goals for learning that will take place over time, and measure student's academic performance on a regular basis. Progress monitoring seeks to measure performance/progress by comparing expected to actual rates of learning. Teaching is adjusted as needed according to what is learned. The student's progression is thereby monitored and the instructional technique is adjusted on the basis of the data (e.g., individual student's learning needs). Thus, progress toward meeting the student's goals is measured by comparing expected and actual rates of learning and then analyzing and adjusting instruction as needed.

Progress monitoring requires educators to examine specific data of an academic event (e.g., reading fluency) and/or behavioral component (e.g., time on task). A way to look at overall direction of the observed learning/behavior can be demonstrated via a trend line. The trend line shows current performance with the said intervention. For struggling students, progress monitoring introduces an aimline that shows the rate of progress a student must make (e.g., words read correctly per minute) to reach his or her instructional goal within the allotted instructional time. Aimlines help show the expected rate of progress and offer a visual indicator to the teacher of what needs to be done over a period of time. For example, if three consecutive data points are below the student's aimline, the teacher should make an instructional change. However, if the data points are above the aimline, the student is making adequate progress, indicating that the teacher should consider setting a new instructional goal. Similarly, if the data are not above or below the aimline for three consecutive data points, no changes should be made. The idea here is that concrete data needs to be collected, organized for meaning, and used on a regular basis to determine the next steps of evidence-based instructional interventions for a specific student or group of students within a class.

By using progress monitoring, the expectation is that student learning will be accelerated because students are receiving more appropriate instruction. Similarly, regular documentation should lead to more informed instructional decisions and thus to higher expectations for the students by teachers. The efficiency of the process allows for targeted instructional techniques and goals, which together move all students to faster attainment of general education standards in the inclusive classroom.

When one looks at progress monitoring within the framework of RTI, one realizes that this gathering of data in a periodic manner serves two important purposes in schools. First, it is a powerful prevention process, designed to limit the amount of academic failure all students experience, not just those who have a specific disability. In other words, RTI helps to ensure that, at the first sign of academic problems or behavioral problems that can derail academic learning, a student receives the supports (e.g., evidence-based interventions) he or she needs to be successful. Thus, instead of waiting to fail and/or waiting for assessment data to identify a significant delay, RTI seeks to intervene as soon as possible with effective evidence-based instruction. The second goal of RTI is determining whether or not a student has a disability. If teachers can document that increasingly intense instruction was provided in the context of general education and students failed to respond, then students may be referred for special education services. Although the use of RTI for determining eligibility is not the focus of this chapter, general and special education teachers should understand that referral to special education is employed only as a last resort, that is, after all other interventions (e.g., tiered supports) have failed to be effective in any substantial way.

Organizing the Assessment Process

To better understand a child's behavior and/or academic progress, schools often engage a team that collects and shares information through a collaborative problem-solving process. These teams, sometimes referred to as student intervention teams (SITs), are school-based, problem-solving groups designed to assist school staffs and parents in the development of interventions and strategies to improve the learning or school adjustment of students. In Angela's case, the team involved the special and general education teachers, the TESOL teacher, Angela's mom, and the building principal. The purpose of the SITs is to provide schools with an efficient, effective, and clearly defined procedure for providing assistance to students, teachers, and parents. It is a collaboration model that provides a forum for routine and timely problem solving by building staff. School-based teams may have other names such as child study team, student review team, student assistance team, schoolwide assistance team, and so on. Regardless of the name, team membership generally involves three-to-five general and special education teachers, an administrator, a school counselor, and on a case-by-case basis related service personnel to inform team members about particular aspects of the child (e.g., reading coaches, speech pathologists, a school psychologist, behavior consultants).

For SITs to be useful, teachers need to collect specific data to better inform team members of the specific challenges the child is presenting, what evidence-based practices have been tried, and any relevant information particular to the student. For instance, Angela's teachers understood she struggled with reading but what specific components? What interventions were currently being used to address her reading challenges, specifically as part of whole-classroom instruction? How was Angela's general education addressing these needs? How did Angela respond to this intervention? How was the intervention selected? What type of data was collected to better illustrate the reading challenge (e.g., observation, interviews)? With this information, SITs are then able to assist teachers (Kristi and Desera) in offering possible solutions while also providing effective ways to collect data on ongoing progress. If the evidence-based solution works, wonderful. If it does not, the SIT and the teacher have more information (data) to better understand the challenge and to hopefully better identify a possible general education solution. We should note that this is often an ongoing process in which teachers and the SIT might interact over several months to ensure success for the teacher and the student.

Under the RTI framework, SITs increasingly view evidence-based interventions and the supports they suggest teachers employ with struggling students within a three-tiered model. RTI's three-tiered model seeks to address the needs of all learners in the general education setting with more intense interventions in the special education setting. Tier 1 represents evidence-based core instructional interventions that seek to be powerful differentiated instruction, providing instruction designed to meet the specific needs of students in the class. In respect to the SIT problem-solving process, SIT members are often engaged when a student struggles in the core instructional and/or behavioral intervention. As a result, the SIT is then tasked with suggesting additional evidence-based interventions applicable as Tier 1 or possibly Tier 2 types of interventions. The goal here is to address the student's unique needs while doing so within the general education inclusive setting. The data collected to monitor progress is also examined and SIT members may offer suggestions and actually participate in the data gathering.

For students that continue to struggle, SIT members may suggest more intensive services and interventions. Often seen as Tier 2 services, these interventions are provided in small-group settings with support from the general education teacher as well as other building specialists (e.g., reading specialist).

If continued monitoring of progress indicates the evidence-based interventions are not working, SITs may suggest that students receive Tier 3 individualized, intensive interventions that target the student's skill deficits. Students who do not respond to these targeted interventions are then considered for eligibility under special education. SITs can then use the data collected during Tiers 1, 2, and 3 to make the eligibility decision.

Family Involvement

Families are an essential part of the assessment process. They provide important information about students with disabilities that cannot be secured through any other source, and their participation in the educational process is essential to their children's success in school. Plus, families are designated under IDEA (2004) to be essential advocates and participants in students-with-disabilities educational programs. To obtain a comprehensive understanding of students-with-disabilities' strengths and needs, SITs must have productive relationships with families. Families can provide important insights about students' outside interests, what they value, their perceptions of school, their behavior outside school, and effective ways of communicating with and motivating them. All of these insights can be used to build rapport with students and their families, as well as to develop educational environments and strategies that support children's inclusion. To develop productive relationships, SITs build rapport with families. To build rapport, SIT members must first recognize misconceptions or stereotypes they hold about families because negative views of families will be the first barrier to any type of productive relationship. Many students in schools no longer come from families in which both a mother and father are present. Fifty percent of all children live with one parent at some point in their lives, and many children are living with grandparents or other family members, such as aunts or cousins. SITs must understand that a child's mother or father may not be the only person to call on for support and information about the child, and that family members, because of their circumstances, may not be able to be as actively engaged in their education.

Second, in order to gather information from family members, SITs will have to establish quality interactions with families. Such interactions will be far more consequential in establishing productive relationships than any technical information SIT members can provide (Bauer & Shea, 2003). To establish such relationships, SITs must be willing to listen to parents, understand any goals or concerns they may have for their child, communicate information about children in clear and respectful ways, and engage in effective problem solving. School professionals' interactions with parents can be consequential in establishing productive relationships, but they may have to sometimes readjust their expectations about what parent involvement means. Many children are growing up in homes where their primary caretaker works, sometimes at night or on the weekends, or cannot help children with homework because they do not have the skills to do so. If SITs believe that family involvement means active participation in overseeing homework and helping children learn key academic skills, they will be setting themselves and the families up for frustration and failure. As in the case of Angela's mother, Isabella, SIT members have to be aware of all the demands on Isabella's time as a single parent of two children as well as skill problems with the English language. The degree to which Isabella can participate in Angela's educational program will depend on the supports she has for shouldering family demands and her perceptions of the assistance she can provide Angela given limited proficiency with English. Understanding Isabella's daily challenges will enable SIT members to set realistic expectations for her involvement.

Building partnerships with families also requires excellent communication and skills for involving parents in the educational process. Rethinking stereotypes about families and being sensitive to their needs are first steps in facilitating communication. Such thinking helps SIT members to be less judgmental about what they expect from families and enables them to be honest about the level of assistance they can provide their children at home to improve school performance.

Integrating Technology into the Assessment Process

The data collected as part of the progress monitoring effort and similar information pertinent to the student is increasingly being supported via technology-based solutions. While most districts employ an online grade system and related management applications used by administration and select school personnel, general and special education teachers are now using technology to support traditional informal assessments.

Regardless of how often progress is measured, teachers' progress-monitoring documentation, which may include graphs or data charts, serves as useful information for modifying the instruction and/or intervention, or for referring students to the next tier of help, as necessary. With the use of technology-based applications, educators can better understand the data collected and how it applies to student interventions.

Today, it is difficult to find progress monitoring and/or RTI systems that do not employ technology-based components as a central part of their application. For example, AIMSweb (see *www.aimsweb.com*) consists of CBM testing materials and web-based software to provide schools with a three-tiered progress monitoring and RTI system. Similar to tools such as DIBELS (Dynamic Indicators of Basic

Early Literacy Skills) (and other assessment tools on the market), AIMSweb offers assessments from oral reading fluency to math computation. By integrating the web, educators have nearly immediate access to student-, class-, grade-, school-, and district-level reports. Flexible in use, these reports can be viewed in multiple formats to better understand the data, apply for specific schools, and address individual needs specific to classroom instruction. Of course, web-based information can be viewed, collected, and used with a variety of hardware devices including portable handheld applications. For instance, AIMSweb Palm Link (see *www.aimsweb.com/ products/palm-link-software*) offers educators access to data on the go where they can quickly, accurately, and efficiently access data, understand data specific to a student, and apply this data in a way relevant to the classroom need. We will examine this further when we discuss the use of handheld devices in overall data collection and management.

As an aside, the Internet houses a number of resources helpful to progress monitoring such as the National Center on Student Progress Monitoring's Review of Progress Monitoring Tools (see *www.studentprogress.org/chart/chart.asp*). The *Tools Chart* offers users access to a "guide" of sorts whereby one can access the reliability, validity, and overall progress monitoring standards of a respective instrument and compare it to similar products. While not a consumer reports guide, the review does offer a critical review process and includes detailed information for each standard. Thus, the center offers a standard to evaluate the scientific rigor of commercially available tools to monitor student's progress, making this available via an interactive web-based format.

Personal Digital Assistants

As mentioned earlier, handheld or personal digital assistants (PDAs) are increasingly being used to collect and analyze observation data (e.g., behavior) in classrooms, buildings, and across schools. For general and special education students, checklists and observation forms critical to progress monitoring can be loaded onto the device, allowing for quick access in the recording and review of the collected information. By using the PDA, the teacher has immediate access to information while also the ability to quickly tabulate it. For CBM purposes, PDAs capture data as assessments are given, HotSync uploads scores electronically, which allows for flexibility in the administration and scoring of assessments (e.g., reading fluency) and scores the assessment while automatically storing the information for future use.

When needed for direct observation, the PDA allows for flexibility in and outside of the classroom, automatically stores PDA data that can be uploaded to a computer for printing, storing, inclusion into a report, or exporting to a database. Likewise, frequency data and similar patterns are automatically tracked and tabulated by the application for teacher analysis. In addition to the hardware, software applications like *T-Observe* (see *www.soft32.com*) offer an interface to observe and collect information on classroom activities.

Spreadsheet Applications

Be it Microsoft's *Excel* or *Access* (see *office.microsoft.com*), the use of spreadsheets to manage, display, and tabulate data is a common practice. For the general and special education teacher to make data-based decisions, they require access to data in a manageable format. Excel and Access provide interface and interactive design capabilities that do not require deep database knowledge, allowing educators to track and report information pertinent to students. Prebuilt templates and formulas, a friendly user interface, and the ability to create tables and import/add data from various applications are all components educators are increasingly using within progress monitoring and CBM efforts.

For educators not equipped with knowledge or limited to an elementary understanding of spreadsheet application, the developers of the software (e.g., Microsoft's Help and How-To section—see *office.microsoft.com*) continue to develop tutorial and other helpful instructional experiences (generally web-based) that seek to enhance the understanding and subsequent use of the technology. Likewise, web-based products such as Atomic Learning (see *movies.atomiclearning.com/k12/home*) have developed (more than 35,000 tutorial movies for more than 110 technology-based classroom applications) easy-to-view-and-understand tutorials so that educators can quickly *see* what the software can do, how it works, and how others have used it for the classroom. For example, Atomic Learning has 66 video tutorials (averaging about 1 minute in length) that can be downloaded via the web on Microsoft's Excel application focused on teaching educators easy-to-create powerful spreadsheets and work with others to review and analyze them. For the advanced Excel user, Atomic Learning offers an additional 85 video-based learning modules (again averaging about 1 minute in length), with topics ranging from advanced charting to auditing and error correcting. While not the entire solution, web-based applications like Atomic Learning continue to provide general and special educators tools to enhance their understanding and subsequent use of technology-based applications in the inclusive setting.

Finally, for the educator and/or parent who requires a more visual illustration of data in order to understand and use it for instructional decisions, spreadsheet applications like Inspiration's *InspireData* (see *www.inspiration.com/InspireData*) are available. InspireData advertises itself as the visual way to explore and understand data and thus allows one to investigate, analyze, and represent data and information in dynamic graphs and charts. Its tools make it easy to change variables and plot types so users can explore data in multiple, meaningful ways. For educators and the parents who aspire to understand and apply increasing amounts of data, InspireData builds data literacy by basing it on visual representations. Beginning with data housed in any spreadsheet (e.g., Excel, Word, Access), InspireData allows users visual representation for their data using multiple plot types such as Venn, bar, stack, pie, axis, and time series. The interactive aspect of the application allows for a minimal learning curve and a visual representation of data involving color, object, movement, and various graphic-based illustrations. For the dataphobic or the individual who struggles to interpret data in meaningful ways and use it to make decisions, applications like InspireData offer a visual solution.

Software Progress Monitoring

An integral part of many reading, writing, and math technology-based solutions is an assessment management tool or progress-monitoring component. The tool facilitates data-driven, individualized instruction while also collecting data applicable to group and classroom-wide decisions. For example, Edmark's Destination Reading (see *hmlt.hmco.com/DR.php*) offers a flexible structure that allows one to work with the whole class, small groups, or individual students for specific tiered needs. Similarly, the assessment and reporting component correlates to the teacher's state standards and allows one to track student progress and individualize prescriptive content. Besides identifying the student, the software automatically tracks progress and provides data relevant to the success of the intervention, suggested improvement, and direction for subsequent instruction.

Reading programs like Scholastic's *Read 180* (see *www.scholastic.com*) or Houghton Mifflin Harcourt's *Earobics* (see *www.earobics.com*) provide similar progress-monitoring components. In these and other applications, data are automatically collected, managed, organized, and downloadable to other tools to assist educators in making instructional decisions. Writing software applications like Don Johnston's WriteOutloud (see *www.donjohnston.com*) provide specific word count, word use, number of words per sentence, number of sentences per paragraph, and similar data that assist educators to monitor the quantitative and qualitative progress of a student's learning. Completed independent of the teacher, these software applications continue to provide data and do so in a manner that is applicable to the needs associated with monitoring a student's progress.

Finally, instructional software applications can also create more effective intervention instruction by uploading assessment results (e.g., from DIBELS) and generate real-time reports of student performance with links to instruction specially tailored to each student's needs. For instance, Earobics is a PreK–3 reading program that includes interactive software that provides individualized instruction in critical areas of reading. A key component of this program is the Assessment Roadmap that organizes and uploads assessment data that are then linked directly to a comprehensive collection of innovative lessons. These lessons address specific skills and incorporate technology and multimedia for effective learning. Thus, without the need of another application, general and special education teachers can chart student progress and track performance via Earobics's graphical summary reports supporting planning and analysis.

Technology and Test Accommodations

While we have focused our discussion on technology-based solutions as they relate to progress monitoring, it is vital that we briefly mention how technology can be used as an accommodation and modification in the assessment of individuals with disabilities. Historically, permitted equipment/technology accommodations for assessment have included large-print test materials, Braille materials, calculators, and the use of electronic devices (mechanical speller, word processor, computer, augmented communication device, etc.).

With the continued advancements in technology-based solutions, assessment modifications for reading have begun to include digital books, audio books, text-to-speech applications, digital recorders, speech-to-text applications, headphones, and electronic dictionaries. Likewise, for written language some of the modifications used include speech-to-text, word prediction software, spell check, homonym check, audio spell checks, digital audio recorders, and headphones.

As learning and test-taking tools continue to integrate universal technology-based features, accommodations and modifications will be further blurred. For example, state assessments are increasingly becoming web-based whereby tests are administered on the computer via the Internet. A primary advantage is the immediate access to the test results as well as the flexibility on the part of the test administrator to ensure a reliable and valid test has been offered. By having the test online, the student then has immediate access to technology-based features that can accommodate learning challenges. That is, free text-to-speech applications are available on all computer platforms as well as on most Internet browsers. With the use of headphones, a student could easily have the entire test and related questions read to him or her. Of course, the question is whether having the test read to the student is an appropriate accommodation and what determines eligibility. While we do not have the answer, the point is that as technology solutions become integral to the computer and thus as instructional resources within our classrooms, the assessment process will be impacted and these and similar questions will need to be answered.

PART II

RESPONDING WITH EFFECTIVE INSTRUCTION AND TECHNOLOGY SUPPORTS

CHAPTER 5

Planning Effective Classroom Instruction

Study Guide Questions

- Why is effective, collaborative planning essential for students with high-incidence disabilities?
- What instructional and curriculum frameworks can teachers use for planning effective instruction?
- What are three ways that teachers can use technology to plan effective classroom instruction?

THE CASE OF MS. LONG

Ms. Long is a third-grade general education teacher at Sunflower Elementary School. Ms. Long is one of three third-grade teachers who have worked together for over 15 years after opening the building in the mid-1990s. Having worked together for so many years, Ms. Long and her peers have assumed different responsibilities in order to better facilitate third-grade activities across the three classrooms. For example, Ms. Long is in charge of the annual Dr. Seuss Extravaganza held every April in the school's gym, Mrs. Jones facilitates the fall family night, and Mrs. Carter always has the student teacher from the local university.

Recently, Ms. Long's class size has grown and her student population is shifting. She now has more students with learning challenges included in her classroom, especially those with disabilities. Accustomed to having students with IEPs, Ms. Long has regularly worked with the special education teacher and related service personnel. However, this influx of students has Ms. Long more perplexed about finding sufficient ways to structure and deliver her content in a manner that helps all her students. She wonders how she can plan for meaningful inclusion when she has students at such varying levels. To complicate matters, her special education co-teaching partner, Mrs. Loesel, is a new unlicensed special education teacher. While Mrs. Loesel has willingness and unlimited energy, her knowledge and expertise continues to increase while she completes university coursework and state-related requirements.

In order to provide the instruction needed, Ms. Long is realizing she needs to plan differently and alter current practice structuring her curriculum in a manner conducive to her changing student body. To assist, Mrs. Loesel mentions a framework she recently learned about that offers a structure to plan and deliver curriculum called universal design for learning (UDL). Ms. Long recognizes that the UDL planning framework could be very helpful to her students; she also knows that she can use the framework to co-plan with her third-grade team. Together, Ms. Long, Mrs. Loesel, and the other third-grade teachers set up a common meeting time every week to co-plan as well as to determine ways to use the principles of UDL to meet the varied needs of all their third-grade learners. Ms. Long is thrilled with the UDL approach and the chance to further co-plan for all her students; she sees it as a way to help her students and provide needed support to Mrs. Loesel.

WHAT SHOULD TEACHERS KNOW ABOUT PLANNING EFFECTIVE CLASSROOM INSTRUCTION

Students, like those in Ms. Long's class, present a wide mix of abilities and learning needs, for example, differing degrees of readiness and background knowledge, varied educational and cultural experiences, differing rates of skill acquisition, and broad diversity in their ability to learn through traditional educational methods and materials. In the past, schools made accommodations for student diversity and lowered curriculum expectations to address this diversity. In today's standards-based classroom, expectations prevent a "watering down" of the curriculum or limiting expectations for those students who are challenged. Instead, today's classroom finds educators striving to develop meaningful educational opportunities for all students, especially those with disabilities. This is achieved through well-organized planning with clearly defined objectives and goals that are based on student needs. Good instruction begins with meaningful planning that is structured and organized around principles that reflect the needs of all learners. When teachers know what they want their students to learn and can plan lessons accordingly, they demonstrate the qualities of accomplished teachers that we described in Chapter 3. They can clearly define the expected learning outcomes for each student, provide focused instruction, and offer equity of access to instruction appropriate to the age and grade level of students with diverse learning needs.

Planning, however, is not simple; it requires a model or framework to establish what is important, what is not, and how best to structure and convey this content. One of the major planning dilemmas you will face as a teacher is deciding what to teach. State and local standards, in addition to school system guidelines, curricula, textbooks, and related print materials, are all sources that are used. The troubling reality is that there are more standards than teachers can address in any deep and meaningful way, particularly when students who struggle to learn are considered. General and special education teachers need to think about how they can prioritize the standards, a task that is not so easy (Meo, 2008).

Research on teacher planning for inclusive classrooms tells us that teachers have limited planning time, considering the instructional challenges they face and the fast pace of their day (Carter, Prater, Jackson, & Marchant, 2009). Planning time in the schools is often taken up with administrative duties, appointments, and unexpected demands. Also, teachers can become sidetracked by classroom management issues (Stuart & Rinaldi, 2009). Teachers have much to lose in a classroom if students are not engaged. Thus, it is natural that teachers often focus their planning on creating activities for motivating and engaging students rather than focusing on the larger outcomes: what students need to know and understand.

It is important to remember, however, that teachers like Ms. Long and Mrs. Loesel play an instrumental role in constructing the curriculum that is taught in their classrooms. Standards shape only the broad outlines of what students should learn; it is teachers themselves who determine the specifics to be covered and how learning will be structured and guided. Planning to structure and guide learning that includes all students requires that teachers carefully think through what they want to teach and how they plan to teach it, and that they do this well before the class and/or school year begins (Carter et al., 2009; Meo, 2008). In the section that follows, we describe a framework to help teachers plan and structure curriculum and instruction for all learners, especially those with disabilities. Next, we offer strategies and solutions teachers can use to enhance the planning process. Finally, we feature technology-based solutions that support these planning activities.

A FRAMEWORK FOR PLANNING INSTRUCTION

Effective planning is at the foundation of good instruction and a well-structured and managed educational environment. While most teachers receive a daily planning time, planning goes beyond a designated time within one's schedule. Often, planning requires interaction with other colleagues within as well as outside the building. Finding a suitable time and place to meet can be quite a challenge. Teachers need tools to facilitate their interactions and to develop necessary frameworks for determining appropriate curriculum and subsequent instruction.

For struggling students and those with disabilities, an essential first step in the teacher planning process involves interaction with a colleague. In the best scenario, general and special education teachers collaborate to determine individual student needs and plan appropriate instruction. While collaborative planning appears practical, it is a complex process that requires the time, effort, and professional capacity of both the general and the special education teacher.

Collaboration for Inclusive Teacher Planning

Successful collaboration is predicated on fundamental principles of partnership and respect. Involved partners must view themselves and each other as equals. They voluntarily "come to the table" to address a challenge, and within this interaction they are recognized as equals bringing particular strengths and professional qualities (Conderman & Johnston-Rodriguez, 2009). For Ms. Long and Mrs. Loesel, this means they see each other as partners who respect and acknowledge each other's talents, skills, and field of expertise.

Teacher partners also have to realize they will need to redefine their roles in a collaborative effort. For example, the special educator's traditional responsibilities included providing instruction to students eligible for special education services in pull-out environments such as resource rooms, special classes, and special schools. In a collaborative relationship, a special education teacher might co-teach; serve as a collaborative consultant; work as part of a grade-level, content, or problem-solving team; and provide direct instruction to students with identified needs and those who are struggling in inclusive settings (Friend, 2007).

In contrast, traditional general education teachers taught children in their classrooms. Struggling students were pulled out or excluded completely from the general education setting in order to work with a special education instructor, reading specialist, or other professional beyond the confines and requirement of the general education classroom (Friend, 2000). When students were not meeting their needs in general education settings, the traditional approach called for students to be referred for diagnosis, remediation, and possible removal from the class or removal from certain activities (e.g., tests or statewide assessments). Within a collaborative experience, general education teachers teach all assigned students while seeking support from special educators and other school personnel for students experiencing difficulty in learning (Friend & Pope, 2005).

Effective collaborative teaching is predicated on professionals who are engaged in planning that is specific to the needs of a shared problem. To do this requires face-to-face interaction among educators to discuss, strategize, and plan for subsequent instruction. From a school perspective, collaborating means a shared time to co-plan, and thus requires encouraging leaders and teachers to work together to ensure common planning times (Conderman & Johnston-Rodriguez, 2009). Administrators in charge of scheduling teacher planning, as well as the teachers themselves, will need to adjust planning times to ensure that collaborators have the same time and day available to meet and plan.

Professional collaboration will not be easy. It often involves a change in perceptions about one's role in the classroom, thoughtful scheduling, and having a variety of professionals who previously may have had limited interaction; however, it is essential for successful planning for the inclusion of all students, especially those with disabilities in the general education classroom (Friend, 2007). In Chapter 10, we will further discuss the components of effective collaboration and its impact on instructional and behavioral practices for students with disabilities.

Planning for Inclusive Classroom Instruction

Effective planning also depends on tools or processes to help teachers determine what to teach, how partners will share the instruction, and how that instruction will be designed to address students' varied needs. With state curriculum standards and district guidelines, curricula, and textbooks, teachers face the dilemma of deciding what to teach. Current curriculum conceptualization often promotes content coverage rather than learning. Wiggins and McTighe (1998) described this approach as "teaching by mentioning it," or covering the topic and ideas by drawing attention to them without developing them for students. Tools to structure the planning process are essential because research suggests that effective teacher planning influences both content coverage and students' opportunity to learn (Clark & Yinger, 1987).

A first step in our approach to curriculum planning should involve a "backward design," whereby teachers decide what to teach on the basis of sorting information into three different levels: "enduring understanding," "important to know and do," and "worth being familiar with" (Wiggins & McTighe, 1998, pp. 9–10). This framework helps teachers think about curriculum with respect to state standards because it provides a way of sorting information according to its importance to the learner. For example, by using a structure collaboratively, teachers can decide what *all* students should be expected to know and be able to do and what *most* students should be expected to know and be able to do. Schumm, Vaughn, and Harris (1997) conceptualize this framework about what all, most, and some students should know and be able to do around a tool described as a planning pyramid.

The Planning Pyramid

The *planning pyramid* is a tool that assists in the design of inclusive curriculum. Schumm et al. (1997) describe the planning pyramid as a framework for general and special education teachers to plan instruction across content subject areas, critical concepts and vocabulary, state standards, or other curricular components that require a flexible tool.

The planning pyramid is structured around three layers, or the degrees of learning. As Figure 5.1 illustrates, the layers are meant to represent what all, most, or some students are expected to learn. For example, the layer at the base of the planning pyramid (the largest of the three sections) represents what "all" students are expected to learn. The middle layer (second largest layer) represents what "most" students will learn, but not all. The third, top, or smallest level is meant for what "some" students will learn. The framework recognizes that while all students can learn, not all students need to learn course content required by every state standard, benchmark, and indicator. The challenge for teachers is to determine what curriculum is critical and then develop an instructional solution to best engage the student and convey the content.

The planning pyramid is a tool that assists educators in prioritizing the critical elements of curriculum and then planning instructional interventions to best

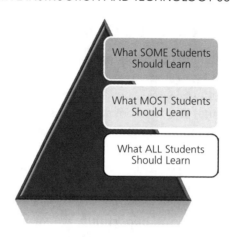

FIGURE 5.1. Planning pyramid.

address these components. With this said, the planning pyramid is not to be used to track a student or place a student within a certain layer, thereby limiting his or her options and/or structuring instruction in a manner that does not properly engage student learning. Likewise, tasks or activities should not be specific to a layer (e.g., worksheets for "all" students, enrichment problem-based activities for "some"), thus limiting engagement and subsequent learning (Vaughn & Linan-Thompson, 2003).

Now that we have established the basic premise for the planning pyramid, we next consider what is described as the "point of entry." The point of entry is used to determine where a teacher and student enter the pyramid and is guided by questions that help teachers plan lessons and courses. The point, or axis, is meant to represent one aspect of instruction (e.g., teacher, student, topic, content, instructional practice). Questions related to each point of entry include questions pertaining to the topic, student, teacher, context, and instructional strategies (Daniels & Vaughn, 1999). Special and general education teachers use these questions to determine entry into the planning pyramid and subsequent use of the tool.

As special and general education teachers collaboratively plan, their first meeting might utilize the questions from the points of entry as a guideline. Next, teachers can use the layers of degrees of learning to identify concepts, recording them within the traditional structure of a lesson plan. Textbook objectives, state standards, and teachers' understanding of the subject will determine and prioritize the content. In placing the concepts within a specific layer, teachers can identify potential challenges for struggling students or those with disabilities. Prerequisite skills and pre-teaching tools could be identified to ensure that the key concepts are mastered.

The planning pyramid's three layers and point of entry questions then offer collaborative partners a framework from which to begin planning curriculum and sorting through the various state standards to determine what all, most, and some of the students will learn specific to a course, unit, or individual lesson. The planning pyramid offers inclusive educators a visual framework with which to determine the essentials of the curriculum, and thus offers a foundation from which to develop and plan subsequent instruction.

Course Planning

Another tool developed to help teachers differentiate critical information from less critical information and build instruction around important ideas is the SMARTER Planner (Lenz & Deshler, 2004). The SMARTER Planning process provides a structure for reflective planning that assists teachers in shaping critical questions about their content, organizing content in a visual map, analyzing the content for learning difficulties it may pose, reaching decisions about how to enhance teaching to overcome learning difficulties students may have, teaching strategically to help students learn how to learn, and then evaluating student mastery of their content and revisit learning outcomes (Lenz, Bulgren, Schumaker, Deshler, & Boudah, 2003).

SMARTER Planning is an acronym to guide teachers through the major steps of the planning process (see Figure 5.2). First, teachers identify "big idea" questions that reflect what is critical about the content to be learned. Teachers shape these questions by considering what is really critical for all students to know in the course, unit, or lesson they are planning. They use "how" and "why" questions to identify the ways in which students should understand the information to be learned. Good critical questions help students to organize the information to be learned because they are tied to the supporting information students learn, helping them make the connections (Bulgren, Deshler, & Lenz, 2007). For general course planning, teachers should develop about 10 questions that every student in a class will be able to answer by the end of the year.

Second, collaborative teachers use critical questions to construct a graphic representation of how the content might be organized or sequenced. The graphic representation assists the collaborative teachers in structuring the plan while helping students visualize the content's organization. Thanks to this graphic map, students are provided a schema for organizing their newly learned content (Lenz, 2006).

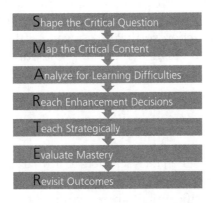

FIGURE 5.2. SMARTER Planner.

Third, collaborative teachers can use critical questions and graphic organizers to reflect on whether students will have difficulties learning the information and ideas set forth. The expertise teachers bring to this process in knowing their content and its complexities allows them to better identify potential challenges, especially when considering the strengths and weaknesses of the specific learner. For example, is memorizing required in order to have the knowledge foundation on which to build further learning? Are steps that might offer complexity for some learners involved? Is the information abstract, requiring generalizations and conclusions to be drawn based on previous knowledge?

Fourth, teachers need to select teaching strategies or techniques to guide student learning. Teaching strategies are methods taught to students so that they can complete tasks and approach learning independently. Planning for the explicit use of a teaching strategy is critical to ensure that students understand how to learn and what good learners use to ensure success. When these strategies are applied, teachers are actually developing a teaching routine. Teaching routines—ways for teachers to organize and teach content—are introduced to the entire inclusive classroom, ensuring that the strategy is used by the students in need. In Chapters 6, 7, and 8 teaching routines and strategies for helping students mediate their own learning are introduced and explained within the context of reading, mathematics, and other content-based areas (Bulgren et al., 2007).

In the final step, teachers need to revisit outcomes chosen during the planning stage. That is, they need to reflect on whether students have learned the critical information and, if not, identify the additional instruction that should be given (Bulgren et al., 2007). Therefore, a part of SMARTER Planning involves student outcomes as well as an evaluation of teaching planning and instruction. In the final step, teachers ask themselves whether devices and routines are effective. Do they need to do some reteaching with the routine or adapt it? Or, is it possible that the outcome selected for the student is not really critical? This final step allows the teacher an opportunity to further evaluate curricular decisions and student learning needs.

The SMARTER Planning process helps teachers to share plans with students so that they can see what and how learning will occur. Doing so will develop learning partnerships among the teachers (e.g., special and general education) and their students as the teacher assumes the role of the instructional leader while engaging students in shaping instruction so that it is meaningful and relevant. Finally, as one's strategic teaching evolves, it is important that students understand that they are expected to be engaged and to take advantage of the instruction and to utilize the strategies for learning.

Unit Planning

While the SMARTER Planner enables teachers to utilize a macrostructure for reflectively planning and evaluating courses, units, or lessons, the Unit Organizer structures planning for the specific unit. Both are part of the Content Enhancement routines developed by Deshler and his colleagues (Bulgren, Deshler, & Schumaker,

1993) at the Center for Research on Learning at the University of Kansas. The Unit Organizer routine is used by teachers to launch and maintain a content unit so that all students in an academically diverse class understand the "big ideas" of the unit, their relationships to each other, the unit questions to be answered (derived from standards and proficiencies), learning strategies to use when answering these questions, and their assignment responsibilities.

The routine structures how a teacher introduces, builds, and gains closure on "chunks of information," or the critical ideas and information in an instructional unit. Again, this planning tool is not simply for teachers but also is to be used by the student him- or herself to understand the intent of instruction and have a tool for organizing the content, so that it may be acquired more easily and applied in other instructional contexts.

Deshler and his colleagues conceptualize unit planning into three major phases:

1. What are the big ideas for the unit? Here the teacher decides what students should know at the conclusion of the unit.
2. What evidence should the teacher collect to evaluate student learning? Here the teacher must consider how he or she will develop assessments to determine if students have learned the big ideas.
3. What knowledge and skills do students need to have in place at the conclusion of the unit? Here the teacher designs the learning experiences and determines the strategies he or she will use to help students acquire the knowledge and skills supporting the big ideas.

The Unit Organizer, illustrated in Figure 5.3, is a visual routine that accompanies the planning process. This visual organizer helps teachers to articulate both the unit's big and supporting ideas. It is used to help teachers introduce and build a unit so that everyone has a visual representation demonstrating (1) how the unit is part of the broader course and (2) how information is organized according to main ideas and subideas. Teachers and students can then use this visual routine to determine those concepts that have been learned and those that still require additional study. Moreover, students can be taught to self-question themselves regarding concepts they still need to learn. The visual organizer helps all students, but particularly students with attention and learning issues, to know where they are going, how long it will take to get there, and what assignments will be done along the way.

The Unit Organizer has 10 sections designed to correspond with the three major phases of planning outlined above. While the sections have a specific purpose, they can be grouped around five general areas.

1. *Articulating the relationship between the unit of interest and other units in the course.* The first four sections (see Figure 5.3) help students understand the conceptual structure of the unit. Section 1 identifies the title of the current unit (classifying plants and animals), section 2 identifies the previous unit

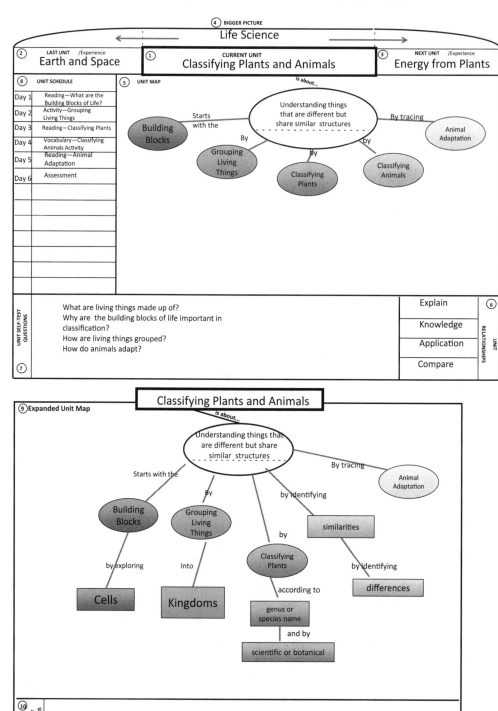

FIGURE 5.3. Unit Organizer. Reprinted from Lenz et al. (2006). Copyright 2006 by Edge Enterprises, Lawrence, Kansas. Reproduced by permission.

(earth and space), section 3 the next unit (energy from plants), and section 4 indicates a theme or idea that connects multiple units (life science).

2. *Providing the visual map of the unit content.* Section 5 contains the unit paraphrase that summarizes the key concepts of the unit in a brief sentence: "understanding things that are different but share similar structures." Below the paraphrase is the map linking supporting concepts (grouping living things, etc.) to the unit paraphrase using labeled lines that indicate the relationships between supporting concepts and the central concept of the unit.

3. *Providing unit relationships and self-test questions for the learner.* Section 6 helps students structure their thinking about the key unit concepts. The self-test questions in section 7 identify what the student needs to know to be successful in this unit and can be connected to the specific state standard or related substandard (e.g., benchmark, goal). Each question is tied to the type of thinking the students will be asked to do (e.g., classify, compare, contrast) and is written in section 6.

4. *Showing the unit schedule.* Section 8 lists the activities/assignments and due dates, providing a clear picture of what will take place, when, and how the sequence of activities build upon one another.

5. *Expanding the unit map and questions.* Section 9 provides an expanded map that adds details about unit concepts and offers a visual in which concepts and subtopics are tied together via specific geometric shapes (e.g., circles, squares). Section 10 provides additional questions that complement the original self-test questions, helping students extend and elaborate on their knowledge.

The Unit Organizer is most effective if it is developed in collaboration with professionals but can also be effective when developed with students (Lenz et al., 2006). Of course, as a planning tool, inclusive teachers identify the critical elements of the unit, the questions to be asked and answered, the structure of the daily activities, and similar components. At the same time, the student needs to be aware of the structure of the Unit Planner and how it is to be used. Thus, it is critical for teachers to engage students in an understanding of the Unit Planner and the development of its sections.

Lesson Organizer

Course and unit planning is often followed by specific lesson planning to ensure that the big ideas and general standards are addressed within specific daily or multiple day lessons. As many teachers know, the traditional lesson plan often reflects four basic elements including (1) objectives, (2) materials, (3) procedures, and (4) assessment. A good lesson plan also identifies state, national, or professional standards that are woven into instruction and learning outcomes. The traditional format is generally described as a "linear lesson plan" model in that the lesson is developed and presented in a logical and hierarchical sequence. We know and appreciate that there are several variations on the steps, or stages, that are included in a lesson plan. For the inclusive classroom, however, teachers need to develop lessons that scaffold or support learning. That is, at the lesson-plan level, the information a teacher collects about students is used to guide daily decisions and interactions with students. While a sequential model is useful, a strategic visual representation, similar to those used in the Course and Unit Organizers, is more practical and effective for struggling learners. Furthermore, the principles, components, and performance options can be integrated within the lesson plan organizer, just as they were in the Course and Unit Organizers.

The Lesson Organizer routine is another component of the Content Enhancement series (Bulgren, Deshler, & Lenz, 2007; Lenz et al., 2003) that allows teachers to frame a lesson. By offering structure, the inclusive teacher assists students to see the "big picture" of the lesson. For example, the Lesson Organizer routine introduces and crafts a lesson in which students understand the main idea of the lesson; relate the lesson to previous context/knowledge; understand how the lesson is structured and how the information is visually organized; distinguish the most important parts; and understand the lesson's tasks and associated expectations. In this way, the lesson plan is useful to teachers (e.g., identifying the structure for the day, materials needed) and provides a clear structure for students.

A critical component of the Lesson Organizer is that it is introduced to the entire class, so that students can understand how it will be used, and, more important, what their role will be and how their participation can markedly improve their learning. The Lesson Organizer expands on the Unit Organizer (Lenz, 2006). While it is a classwide intervention, the Lesson Organizer can also be adapted to meet students' unique needs. When using the Lesson Organizer, the teacher introduces the routine allowing for students to be engaged in expanding the organizer and/ or co-developing the organizer, enhancing student understanding and application. Thus, through the integration of the routine students become actively engaged as partners in the process with their teacher and peers (Deshler & Tollefson, 2006). The Lesson Organizer routine is structured around a series of linking steps that can best be remembered through the acronym CRADLE. The CRADLE steps are outlined and described in Table 5.1, and a completed Lesson Organizer routine is provided in Figure 5.4.

INSTRUCTIONAL PLANNING IN ORDER TO ACCESS LEARNING

For Ms. Jones and Mrs. Loesel, the Content Enhancement routines and the planning pyramid are essential to their planning process. In the use of the routines and the Pyramid, Ms. Jones and Mrs. Loesel are able to identify the most important content to be taught, how that content should be structured, and what they want students to ultimately learn. Likewise, these approaches to planning fit well within

TABLE 5.1. The CRADLE Strategy

Strategy step	Description of step
Consolidate goals.	The teacher helps students understand the goals of the lesson by (1) naming the topic of the lesson plan (food groups), (2) paraphrasing the topic in words the students understand (choosing a balanced dietary intake), (3) identifying the important relationships that students need to be looking for within the lesson content, and (4) naming the strategy or strategies students will be using to achieve learning outcomes.
Review knowledge.	The teacher helps students build background knowledge needed for the lesson by reviewing topics from previous lessons and student background knowledge or experiences.
Assemble anchors.	The teacher develops a visual anchor for connecting the new information to previously learned information. The purpose is to graphically depict the previous information, connect to the new, and illustrate how new information fits within the unit or students' background knowledge.
Describe and map content.	The teacher uses a visual graphic organizer to further detail how the lesson's information is connected to previous learning and the unit. The graphic organizer is developed by drawing arrows between information (e.g., balanced diet to combination of foods) with bulleted information below each subtopic to further describe them.
Link content to anchors.	The teacher further links visual anchors to students' lives by using visual resources that further connect the students' context to the content—for example, the use of additional stories, examples, and explanations of how the content relates to the students' lives.
Explore questions and tasks.	The teacher offers students a series of questions that communicate outcomes of the lesson and indicate what the student should be able to answer at the end of the lesson. These questions are listed in Section 7 of the organizer, describing the expectations students must meet. This way the student is aware of what he or she needs to learn to be successful, and teachers are directed in their teaching to ensure that the questions are answered as a result of their instruction.

two broader frameworks that allow curriculum and instruction to be designed in ways that enable day-to-day instruction to be more accessible.

The two frameworks are differentiated instruction (DI) and universal design for learning (UDL). While UDL is at the forefront of special education efforts to develop universal accommodations to assist a wide variety of users, including those with disabilities, DI is also part of the equation for many general education initiatives impacting classroom and schoolwide planning. We introduce both models with respect to planning to further illustrate ways teachers can plan and design curriculum and instruction for the needs of all students, especially those with disabilities. As we introduce both models, we should note that UDL embodies the key concepts of DI addressing curriculum and instructional considerations for *all* students. We introduce both frameworks below but emphasize UDL as the primary model for consideration and further exploration (Edyburn, 2010; Tomlinson, 2009).

The Lesson Organizer

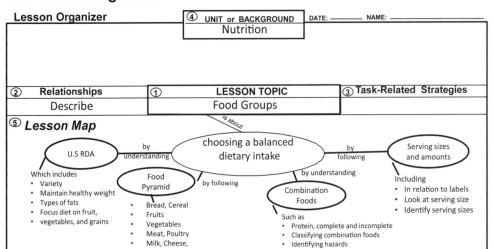

FIGURE 5.4. Lesson Organizer. Reprinted from Lenz et al. (1993). Copyright 1993 by Edge Enterprises, Lawrence, Kansas. Reproduced by permission.

Differentiated Instruction

DI comes from the literature on gifted education and is a model that requires teachers to be flexible in their approach, adjusting the curriculum and presentation of information to learners. Teachers are expected to organize the curriculum content and instruction to accommodate learners rather than expect students to meet a specific expectation. DI is based on the premise that instructional approaches should vary and be adapted in relation to diverse student needs (Scigliano & Hipsky, 2010). According to the model, differentiation can occur within one or more of the following four classroom elements: content, process, product, and learning environment (Tomlinson, 2009).

Content

In a differentiated classroom access to content is seen as key, and thus the manner in which students gain access is critical to learning. In planning, then, DI requires a teacher to align tasks and objectives to learning goals. Objectives are frequently written in incremental steps resulting in a continuum of skills-building tasks. An objectives-driven menu makes it easier to find the next instructional step for learners entering at varying levels. Examples of differentiating content at the elementary level include (1) using reading materials at varying readability levels; (2) putting text materials on tape; (3) using spelling or vocabulary lists at readiness levels of students; (4) presenting ideas through both auditory and visual means; and (5) meeting with small groups to reteach an idea or skill for struggling learners, or to extend the thinking or skills of advanced learners.

Process

The process element of DI centers on activities used to help students make sense of or master the content. Flexible grouping is used consistently to facilitate learning. Here, learners are expected to interact and work together as they develop knowledge of new content. Teachers may conduct whole-class introductory discussions of content "big ideas" followed by small-group or pair work. Next, the teacher may coach student groups based on need to work collaboratively to complete the task or independently. Examples of differentiating process or activities at the elementary level include (1) using varied activities ensuring all students work to develop understanding and skill; (2) offering manipulatives or other hands-on supports for students who need them; and (3) providing interest centers that encourage students to explore aspects of class topics they find interesting (Tomlinson, 2008).

Product

Culminating projects that ask students to rehearse, apply, and extend what they have learned in a unit are considered products. Products can be differentiated by (1) giving students options for expressing required learning (e.g., create a puppet show, write a letter, or develop a mural with labels); (2) using rubrics that match and extend students' varied skills level (see Figure 5.5); (3) allowing students to work alone or in small groups on products; and (4) encouraging students to create their own product assignments if they contain required elements.

Learning Environment

To make differentiation possible, the learning environment must be arranged to maximize student development. Examples of differentiating learning environments at the elementary level include (1) designing the class to ensure places for quiet, distraction-free work as well as "centers" that invite group interaction and/ or student collaboration (see Figure 5.6); (2) establishing structures that guide independent work and match individual needs; (3) developing routines that support students in a timely manner regardless of whether the teacher is available for one-on-one or small-group help; and (4) developing an environment whereby students understand and appreciate the varied way peers learn (e.g., moving around, sitting in seats, reading simpler texts) (Tomlinson, 2008, 2009).

    A DI framework complements the Content Enhancement routines not only by helping teachers focus their planning on the concepts, principles, and skills that

CATEGORY				
Point of View— Awareness of Audience	Strong awareness of audience in the design. Students can clearly explain why they felt the vocabulary, audio, and graphics chosen fit the target audience.	Some awareness of audience in the design. Students can partially explain why they felt the vocabulary, audio, and graphics chosen fit the target audience.	Some awareness of audience in the design. Students find it difficult to explain how the vocabulary, audio, and graphics chosen fit the target audience.	Limited awareness of the needs and interests of the target audience.
Voice— Consistency	Voice quality is clear and consistently audible throughout the presentation.	Voice quality is clear and consistently audible throughout the majority (85–90%) of the presentation.	Voice quality is clear and consistently audible throughout some (70–84%) of the presentation.	Voice quality needs more attention.
Voice— Pacing	The pace (rhythm and voice punctuation) fits the story line and helps the audience really "get into" the story.	Occasionally speaks too fast or too slowly for the story line. The pacing (rhythm and voice punctuation) is relatively engaging for the audience.	Tries to use pacing (rhythm and voice punctuation) but it is often noticeable that the pacing does not fit the story line. Audience is not consistently engaged.	No attempt to match the pace of the storytelling to the story line or the audience.
Images	Images create a distinct atmosphere or tone that matches some parts of the story. The images may communicate symbolism and/or metaphors.	Images create an atmosphere or tone that matches some parts of the story. The images may communicate symbolism and/or metaphors.	An attempt was made to use images and create an atmosphere/tone but it needed more work, image choice is logical.	Little or no attempt to use images to create an appropriate atmosphere/tone.
Duration of Presentation	Length of presentation was 4 minutes.	Length of presentation was 3 minutes.	Length of the presentation was 2 minutes.	Presentation was less than 2 minutes long OR more than 4 minutes.
Point of View— Purpose	Establishes a purpose early on and maintains a clear focus throughout.	Establishes a purpose early on and maintains focus for most of the presentation.	There are a few lapses in focus, but the purpose is fairly clear.	It is difficult to figure out the purpose of the presentation.

FIGURE 5.5. Digital storytelling: The planets.

Front of the Classroom

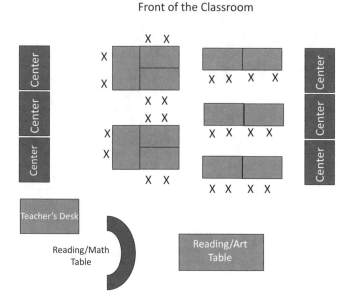

FIGURE 5.6. Seating options in classroom design.

students should learn, but also by helping them think about how they can organize concepts by their degree of complexity. Instruction can be further adjusted according to three student characteristics: readiness, interest, and learning profile. Thus, as teachers plan for the specific needs of the students they examine *readiness*, which is assessed by determining a student's current knowledge, understanding, and skill as it relates to what is being studied within the context of the entire class. *Interest* is made apparent by observing what a student enjoys learning about, thinking about, and doing. Finally, a *learning profile* can assist a teacher in identifying a student's preferred model of learning as influenced by factors such as intelligence, gender, and culture (Tomlinson & Edison, 2003).

UDL for Planning: The Framework

UDL also serves as a blueprint or framework for educators in designing flexible curriculum and instruction. For teachers working with students with disabilities, one should be aware that provisions for UDL implementation were key ingredients in the reauthorization of the IDEA (2004) as well as the 2008 Higher Education Opportunity Act. We note this connection to reinforce the emphasis UDL is receiving from an instructional as well as a legislative perspective.

UDL is an approach that seeks to address an inflexible one-size-fits-all traditional curriculum that often presents barriers to struggling learners by replacing it with universally designed curriculum or curriculum that is created with the intention of including all learners (see Figure 5.7). In planning, then, teachers can

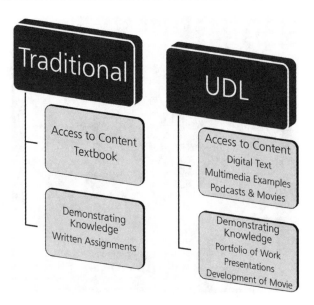

FIGURE 5.7. Traditional solutions versus UDL solutions.

utilize the UDL framework to embed features within curriculum and instruction that will help those with disabilities as well as benefit everyone in the process. In many instances, these features are technology-based, utilizing the power of ever-changing features of technology solutions to make the classroom more inclusive and effective for all. A universally designed curriculum is shaped from the outset to meet the needs of the greatest number of users, making costly, time-consuming, and after-the-fact changes/accommodations to the curriculum unnecessary (Edyburn, 2010; Flores, 2006).

UDL Principles

The UDL framework is structured around three core principles: (1) provide multiple means of representation, (2) provide multiple means of expression, and (3) provide multiple means of engagement. Multiple means of representation focuses on the "what" of learning, concentrating on how learners perceive and comprehend information presented to them (Spooner, Baker, Harris, Ahlgrim-Delzell, & Browder, 2009). For example, text or print is often a primary way we represent material for learning (e.g., textbooks) in schools. Yet students with learning disabilities and other struggling learners may require a different means to approach content. Some may simply grasp information better through visual or auditory means than through printed text. In reality, no one type of representation will be optimal for all students, so providing options in representation is essential.

Multiple means of expression refers to the "how" of learning, or how students will express or demonstrate what they know according to their individual abilities. For example, individuals with learning challenges often have language barriers that might make developing writing responses, a frequent response mode in schools, difficult. Thus, they require a different way to demonstrate their mastery of knowledge, perhaps by using speech-to-text software that allows them to record their oral response.

Multiple means of engagement focuses on the "why" of learning and considers that students differ markedly in the ways they can be engaged and motivated. Some students thrive on structure and preplanned transitions while others need constant change and activity to be engaged in learning. Providing multiple options for engagement is essential.

UDL in Use

The purpose of the UDL framework is to help teachers (and others such as parents, related service personnel, building leaders) plan and design flexible curricula that reduce barriers to learning and provide learning supports to meet all learners' needs from the onset rather than developing accommodations once initial curriculum and instruction has been planned and implemented (McGuire, Scott, & Shaw, 2006) . As a planning tool, UDL helps educators evaluate both new and existing curriculum— including instructional goals, materials, methods, and assessments. Guidelines for the UDL framework have multiple purposes and can be used in a variety of ways when planning instruction, deciding curricula supports, and determining the focus of instruction.

DEVELOPING ACCOMMODATIONS

After identifying curriculum goals and collaboratively planning around diverse student needs, accommodations are often integrated to further support meaningful learning in the inclusive classroom. As we discussed in Chapter 3, accommodations help students to become more proficient learners. That is, classroom accommodations make it possible for students to demonstrate their learning in inclusive classrooms.

In many schools, the use of accommodations is widespread. Typically, it is the general education teacher who is responsible for determining how to integrate them into the general education curriculum. Even though research shows that general education teachers are willing to make accommodations, evidence suggests that they tend to use the simplest accommodations, without regard for the specific or unique needs of the students (Nevin, Cramer, Voigt, & Salazar, 2008; Parker, 2006). For example, it is common to find accommodations offering preferential seating, extended time on assignments and tests, reduced workload, and a quiet place to take a test. Often, these easy-to-implement accommodations are not individualized for the student or monitored for their effectiveness. Similarly, classroom accommodations may be unrelated to test accommodations. Regardless, in respect to planning, general and special education teachers need to work together to plan for effective instructional accommodations to have a meaningful impact on the needs of those with disabilities.

Ideally, accommodations for assessment and instruction should be integrally intertwined; yet there are some accommodations that are appropriate for classroom use that would not be appropriate in testing situations. For instance, some states will not allow state assessments in reading to be read aloud to students, as decoding fluently is considered an important component of the reading process. No accommodation should be recommended for an assessment that a student has not had a thorough opportunity to learn to use comfortably and effectively during classroom activities. If an IEP team considers an accommodation appropriate to ensure accurate testing, then it is vital that this accommodation be used throughout the year to assist in a student's learning while also developing competency in use of the accommodation. The bottom line is that the use of accommodations takes planning and collaboration to further extend identified instructional goals.

Instructional accommodations are typically categorized according to whether they are different in presentation, response, setting, or timing/scheduling. Table 5.2 offers examples for each of these areas. A complete list of accommodations for instruction and assessment can be found at the National Center on Education Outcomes' website (see *data.nceo.info/pa-summaries.asp*).

Presentation Accommodations

Presentation accommodations allow students to access instructional materials in ways that do not require them to decode standard print. Students with print disabilities (e.g., dyslexia) may require alternate visual, tactile, or auditory formats. Some learners may simply require the use of large print or the use of a magnification system that will enlarge the print as the student accesses the test or instructional resource. Other students may require that the text be read to them by a teacher, aide, or paraprofessional. Readers should use strategies that do not improve students' ability to comprehend. For instance, they should use even inflection so as not to give any portions of the text extra emphasis. Readers must also read test items/questions exactly as written. Readers may not clarify, elaborate, or provide assistance to students. Similarly, readers should follow this pattern on information access across the learning environment, allowing the student access to the intervention and enabling him or her to get accustomed to the approach.

Text can also be read by a more fluent reader into audio files that students can listen to later. Advantages include ease of operation and low cost. Audio versions need to be supplemented with a print or Braille version of the text so that a student can have access to complicated graphic material. Increasingly, "Books on Tape" (e.g., Recordings for the Blind) are readily available to schools, and many textbook companies provide digital recordings of texts and supplementary materials. Easy-to-use digital recordings are an important tool for enhancing access to text-based materials. Additionally, text-to-speech applications, available free on the Windows

TABLE 5.2. Examples of Instructional Accommodations

Instructional accommodation	Examples

Presentation accommodations	• Visual
	  ○ Large print
	  ○ Magnification devices
	  ○ Visual clues
	  ○ Highlighters
	• Tactile
	  ○ Braille
	  ○ Nemeth code
	  ○ Tactile graphics
	• Auditory
	  ○ Human reader
	  ○ Audiotape or compact disk
	  ○ Audio amplification devices
	• Visual and auditory
	  ○ Text-to-speech
	  ○ Videotape and descriptive video
	  ○ Talking materials

Response accommodations	• Different ways to complete assignments, tests, and activities
	  ○ Express response to a scribe through speech, sign language, pointing, or by using an assistive communication device.
	  ○ Type on or speech-to-word processor.
	  ○ Type on Brailler.
	  ○ Speak into digital recorder.
	  ○ Write in test booklet instead of on answer sheet.
	  ○ Monitor placement of student responses on answer sheet.
	• Materials or devices used to solve or organize responses
	  ○ Calculation devices
	  ○ Spelling and grammar assistive devices
	  ○ Visual organizers
	  ○ Graphic organizers

Timing and scheduling accommodations	• Extended time • Multiple or frequent breaks • Change testing schedule or order of subtests • Divide long-term assignments
Setting accommodations	• Change location to reduce distractions • Change location so student does not distract others • Change location to increase physical access • Change location to access special equipment

and Apple OS platforms, are increasingly altering the way students can access text. In this instance, students can have the digital text read to them "on the fly" without the need of a prerecorded version and/or a live person. The text is highlighted either word by word or in complete sentences, allowing students to hear but also to see the text as it is being read. Finally, descriptive videos are increasingly part of a textbook series (CD or online appendices) that provides the reader anchors or visual connections to enhance understanding of the readings (see *streaming.discoveryeducation.com*). For example, as students become engaged in learning about Dr. Martin Luther King Jr., teachers and students have immediate access to the video and audio of Dr. King's 1963 "I Have a Dream" speech at the Lincoln Memorial in Washington, DC. The visual component contextualizes the speech for the student, aiding comprehension.

Response Accommodations

Response accommodations allow students to record their work in alternate ways or to correct or organize their work using some type of material or device. The most common is dictation to a scribe (e.g., paraprofessional, teacher, aide). A scribe is someone who writes down what a student dictates through speech, sign language, pointing, or an assistive communication device. The student is responsible for telling the scribe where to place punctuation marks, how to indicate sentences and paragraphs, and how to spell certain words. The skill involved in using a scribe requires extensive practice. Too often a scribe, assigned at the time of local or state assessment, may be untrained and easily complete work for the learner and/or not provide opportunities for the student to develop the right skills. In these cases, the individual is not appropriate and does not perform as an accommodation but instead misrepresents the student's knowledge and his or her actual abilities.

The use of a word processor or a speech-to-text application is an option that may increase a student's independence and reduce the need for a trained scribe. Of course, the student's ability to effectively use a word processor is based on his or her keyboarding skills as well as his or her ability to spell. Thus, keyboarding training and testing for skill level should be part of any word-processing use. Recent improvements in speech-to-text conversion or voice recognition software (e.g., *Dragon Naturally Speaking*) allow students to use their voice as an input device. Voice recognition may be used to dictate text into the computer or to give commands to the computer (such as opening application programs, pulling down menus, or saving work). Applications such as *Microsoft Word* offer a speech-to-text option, but it should be noted that these often require extensive training. As this technology improves, students will have a technology option that reduces their dependence upon an adult/scribe. Likewise, initial findings suggest that students prefer the independence of the technology-based solutions, reducing the need for human support and offering more flexibility and meaningful use in and out of the school setting (Fletcher et al., 2009).

Timing/Scheduling Accommodations

Timing and scheduling accommodations change the length of time allowed to complete assignments, tests, and activities, and may also change the way the time is organized. Timing accommodations give students the time and the breaks they need to complete assignments, tests, and activities. Other changes may include the particular time of day, day of the week, or number of days over which a particular activity takes place. If done well, time/scheduling accommodations can enhance students' learning as well as their ability to convey what they know (Parker, 2006).

Setting Accommodations

These accommodations involve changing the location or conditions in which instruction is provided. Students are allowed to sit in a different location than the majority of students to reduce distractions, receive accommodations that may be distracting, or increase physical access. For an elementary school student, this might mean placement in the group "pod" or commons area where sound and activity might be reduced to enhance attention and understanding.

Getting Accommodations into Practice

The continued growth and access to accommodations offers a variety of supports from which to consider and use for a student with a disability. The tendency may be to recommend a variety of accommodations, with the assumption that "the more accommodations, the better," or "at least something will help" a student access academic content. Unfortunately, this hit-or-miss approach does not necessarily enhance a student's access to learning. Every student with a disability does not need an accommodation, nor do all students with the same disability need the same accommodations. For example, a student with difficulty reading print may use any of the following depending on the severity of his or her reading problem: no accommodations, a human reader, a digital audio file, or a text-to-speech reader.

Ultimate decisions about whether to use accommodations should be made collaboratively with the IEP team, the parents, and the student and should rest on learning goals, each student's needs, and each student's preferences. Further, each student's accommodations should be understood and supported by the student and all school personnel involved with the student, including general and special education teachers, paraeducators, and related services staff such as speech clinicians, school psychologists, and therapists.

If technology-based solutions are considered, then including the building or district assistive technology (AT) and/or instructional technology expert would be helpful. The AT consultant can offer further information by conducting an assistive technology needs assessment to ensure the technology being considered is appropriate to accommodate the student's needs. This expert will also consider what training the student, educators, and parents require to ensure successful implementation.

Using Technology for Instructional Planning

Technology, in many facets of effective teaching, increasingly offers solutions that assist teachers in instructional planning by fostering meaningful time and providing venues in which to interact and collaborate. Teachers use technology in planning, both in terms of collaborative interaction with peers and in supporting students during direct instruction. As illustrated earlier in the chapter, technology is a key component in the application of the UDL framework as well as in the use of instructional accommodations. Likewise, Web 2.0 technologies (e.g., applications that facilitate interactive information sharing) offer ever-growing solutions that enhance teachers' abilities to share and plan. In this section, we provide information about how technologies can be used to support the planning process specific to teacher collaboration, Content Enhancements routines, and UDL principles.

Teacher Collaboration and Planning

When face-to-face planning and collaboration is hampered by daily activities (e.g., IEP meetings, school building obligations, parent meetings), Web 2.0 applications can help. There are multiple Web 2.0 applications accessible to teachers within their classroom, school, and home environments. Many are free and applicable not only to planning needs but also to the needs of students. For example, Wikis (e.g., *wikispaces.com, pbworks.com*) are being used by teachers to post information; share thoughts and resources; organize instructional courses and units; post videos of classroom practices and lessons; and correspondingly share information with students and parents. A Wiki is a website that allows a user to create, edit, and maintain a site on the Internet that is accessible to the entire web-based community or specific users designated by the developer of the Wiki. The Wiki provides an easy-to-use website that is edited with a simple text editor, which is similar to a basic word-processing tool and menu bar. Users can upload documents, images, video, audio, and other multimedia files to their selected Wiki space. The principle elements of a Wiki allow users to create collaborative websites where a teacher, for example, can create a Wiki and allow multiple users (e.g., teachers, students, parents) access to edit the site, upload materials, post information, comment on each other's ideas, and communicate in real time via a central website accessible to designated individuals. For example, Ms. Long and Mrs. Loesel recently posted materials essential to an upcoming unit on the settling of Lawrence, Kansas. Kidspiration (see *www.inspiration.com*) graphic organizers, study notes, plans for daily activities, a Lawrence History unit study guide, and similar information were posted, edited, and discussed all via the Wiki. By placing the information on the Wiki, Ms. Long and Mrs. Loesel reviewed and contributed to the information when their schedules allowed and engaged in specific planning when face-to-face meetings were not possible.

Course, Unit, and Lesson Planners

Planning tools, like the Course Enhancement Routines, also feature technology-based solutions for teachers and students. For the Content Enhancement routines, the GIST (Graphic Interactive System for Teaching) (see *www.gistplan.com*) software was developed and incorporates research-based templates of the routines with interactive tools making the planning templates easier to develop and richer in visual representation, expanding the original use of the paper-and-pen/pencil planner template. GIST software offers technology-based templates for the Course, Unit, and Lesson Organizer routines described earlier in this chapter. The application also provides users technology-based supports for over a dozen Content Enhancement routines developed by the Center for Research on Learning at the University of Kansas (see *www.ku-crl.org* for more detail).

Available on both the Windows and Mac platforms, GIST provides users with a complete template for each of the planning routines. Here, teachers and students can complete the planner as described earlier in the chapter. The beauty of GIST is that it extends the typical paper-and-pen/pencil routine, allowing teachers (and students) an interactive tool capable of altering the text size, font, color, and the background color of the planning routine. Whether developing from a template or scratch, users have the full functionality of a word processor combined with a graphic organizer and an intuitive tool bar allowing users to add graphics, text, arrows, and other visual objects specific to the Unit, Course, or Lesson Organizer. Links can also be provided to websites, multimedia, and other GIST files. If teachers need ideas for initial development, GIST links to a web-based library where teachers from across the country have added and continue to add free completed Content Enhancement routines to share with others. Organized by subject, grade, or routine, a searchable database makes the web-based resource user-friendly for the novice or veteran teacher. Once a routine is found, users can download the completed routine for free and then open, modify, and generally use it as needed for inclusive planning and student instruction.

For example, Figure 5.3 offers an example of a Unit Organizer developed with the GIST application. Like the paper-and-pencil template, GIST visually organizes the materials for the user with objects, sections, and arrow structure, which can be further differentiated with the use of color and/or patterns separating content for comprehension. Furthermore, the underlined text offers live links to web-based resources identified by the inclusive teachers for additional examples and further understanding. With GIST, teachers can also use text color and font (style/size) to further differentiate the various sections that can be easily modified specific to the entire class, small groups, or the unique individual. Graphics and related images could also be embedded to further illustrate the visual building context and understanding.

UDL Planning

UDL principles encourage teachers to use alternate materials and media, often technology-based, to maximize student's access to curriculum and instruction. By planning for a combination of flexible materials and media to be used as well as allowing students to choose the materials they work with, teachers can incorporate the UDL principles: representation, action and expression, and engagement.

For example, text-based materials (e.g., textbooks, handouts) require a level fluency and comprehension competency in order to access information and apply concepts to learning. If static print is an obstacle, teachers need to plan for alternative ways to represent this material. The most common type of flexible media is digital text, a format in which the content is separate from the manner in which it is presented. For example, the digital text on a computer screen can be manipulated in many different ways (e.g., by increasing the font size, switching on the text-to-speech feature, highlighting text as it is read) to make it more accessible to more students. Text-to-speech applications are available for free (e.g., *Readplease*) or nominal charge and are increasingly available on most Window and Mac platforms throughout our school buildings. Teachers need to plan for these applications and select textbooks that offer digital text resources and/or that are available in both print and digital format.

When designing lessons using the UDL principles, teachers need to be not only flexible in the way they present and teach information but also offer their students options in the learning environment. For example, Ms. Long assigns a final project for the unit on Lawrence history. She asks her students to present information on one aspect of the founding and settling of Lawrence. In a UDL-planned environment, Ms. Long allows her students to choose a medium that works best for them. In response, the students choose to create oral reports, short films, hand-written papers, or presentations constructed on the computer.

Teachers also need to be aware of the influence that the learning environment (e.g., classroom noise, structure of task) has on student learning. Because students prefer certain contexts, it is important for teachers to utilize a variety of learning environments. Digital media are often designed to help control many of these factors (e.g., options for turning off background music, help balloons). Likewise, computer games often integrate environments that sustain engagement, reinforce positive learning, and prompt appropriate responses and learning. Thus, using technology within UDL's third principle (engagement) can provide adjustable levels of challenges, allow students to choose from a variety of meaningful reinforcers, and have access to varied options for the learning environment.

CHAPTER 6

Fostering Concept Development

Study Guide Questions

- Why is instruction that fosters concept learning important?
- How do teachers select appropriate concepts and associated vocabulary to teach?
- What instructional principles and strategies are effective for teaching concepts?
- In what ways can teachers use technology to support students' acquisition of essential concepts?

THE CASE OF MATTHEW

Matthew is a third-grade student in Ms. Dienno's inclusive elementary class-room. Ms. Akers, his special education teacher, works closely with Ms. Dienno to provide instruction that allows Matt, as well as other students in the class, to learn both simple and complex concepts across content areas. Matt poses particular challenges for these teachers because he has difficulties organizing and integrating information within and across subject areas. His struggles also make it difficult for him to remember and recall information during class-room activities.

To ensure Matt's and his classmates' academic progress, Ms. Dienno and Ms. Akers know they must help their students understand and organize concepts across content areas to increase their learning efficiency. To address their students' needs, they provide explicit and systematic instruction. They use small-group instruction to work intensively with those students who are struggling to learn. In these small groups, they use concrete manipulatives, visual–spatial displays, multiple examples and nonexamples of concepts taught, and authentic, or actual, problems and events to enhance concept learning. To provide a motivating and engaging approach to continued practice, the teachers use a range of technology-based solutions for reviewing the concepts reinforced in small groups. After a few months, they notice that Matt's comprehension, retention, and integration of the information taught has improved, he is observed using the information learned in new ways, and has increased his learning of related information. By carefully monitoring Matt's progress, the teachers will be able to provide him, and others in his class who need additional instructional support, with the intensive and carefully designed instruction necessary for successful concept learning.

WHAT SHOULD TEACHERS KNOW ABOUT CONCEPT DEVELOPMENT?

To think and reason well, children must be able to form concepts, problem-solve, use rules, think logically and critically, create and brainstorm ideas, and represent ideas in their minds (Levine, 1998). Forming, or developing, concepts is particularly important for learning in school because it allows students to extend and refine knowledge they already possess and to generate new ideas about subject areas such as science, social studies, and mathematics. Concept learning also improves students' ability to extract meaning from texts and is associated with improved comprehension (Snow, 2002).

Concepts consist of organized information we hold in our minds about objects, events, actions, qualities, and relationships. Sternberg and Ben-Zeev (2001) suggest that there are five types of concepts: simple, complex, verbal, nonverbal, and process. Simple concepts can be seen, touched, or heard (e.g., lamp, pomegranate, thunder). Complex concepts are learned through communication without support from objects or observed actions. Verbal, nonverbal, and process concepts are complex concepts. Understanding verbal concepts, such as *friendship*, is acquired through language. Nonverbal concepts, such as *perimeter, volume*, and *mass*, are understood when students make mental pictures to represent important attributes of these concepts. Process concepts represent methods such as *photosynthesis* or an *atomic reaction*. Students who accurately and fluently construct concepts are able to retrieve well-integrated information from memory, allowing them to build new knowledge and, in general, to better understand the world they live in. Without this skill, students experience difficulties making sense of and remembering the massive amount of information they encounter over time.

It is important to understand how simple and complex concepts differ because these differences have implications for designing classroom instruction. Cognitive psychologists suggest that when we organize simple concepts mentally we place them into categories. For instance, all types of horses belong to the category "horse" because they have a mane, a long tail, four legs, a similar shaped head, and give birth to live young. Simple concepts are easier to teach because their meaning remains fairly constant across different contexts (i.e., if we see a horse while watching a cowboy movie or when mounted police trot down a city street, we understand each horse to be a horse). Alternatively, complex concepts are more difficult to teach because they are represented in our minds as links among associated, or related, concepts. Unlike simple concepts, complex concepts often have distinct meanings depending on the context in which they are used. Consider the complex concept of *love*; the love you have for your spouse or parents may mean something very different to you than the love you have for your country. In general, complex concepts tend to have more meanings than simple concepts do, underscoring how difficult they can be to learn (Crutch & Warrington, 2005). Yet simple and complex concepts are not necessarily mutually exclusive. Simple concepts can be used as anchors for learning more complex concepts or unknown simple concepts. Consider the complex concept *photosynthesis*. To understand photosynthesis, students must first understand simple concepts such as *gas, oxygen, carbon dioxide, light, water, food, sugar*, and so on.

In addition to understanding the nature of simple and complex concepts, it is also important to understand that people tend to group and sort information based on their interests, beliefs, values, and experiences. Think about the concept *snake*. To one child it may mean a dangerous, venomous reptile; to another it may be a valuable creature capable of eating disease-carrying rodents. How concepts are defined and classified by students have implications for teaching and later learning.

The teacher's task is to identify essential concepts students need to learn, and consider students' prior learning, or background information, when teaching new concepts. In Table 6.1, examples of simple and complex concepts are presented across four content areas. We explore distinctions between these concept types again when we discuss approaches to teaching.

TABLE 6.1. Examples of Simple and Complex Concepts across Content Areas

Content area	Simple concepts	Complex concepts
Science	• Nonliving things • Animal homes	• Hypertension • Gravity
Social studies	• Oceans of the world • Presidents of the United States	• Slavery • Politics
Mathematics	• More, less, same • Numbers 1 to 9	• Place value • Proportionality
Literacy	• Letter names • Letter sounds	• Literary devices in poetry • Themes within a classic novel from non-Western traditions

HOW IS VOCABULARY RELATED TO CONCEPT LEARNING?

The difference between simple and complex concepts is one important aspect of concept development. Understanding how concept learning and vocabulary words are related is another. Words (vocabulary) are used to label concepts. They represent the concept. Students learn new words in relation to concepts represented by familiar vocabulary. If a concept is understood well, students can come to understand unknown words associated with the concept by tapping into their prior understandings. For example, if students understand the concept of *addition*, they may better understand *multiplication* when it is introduced and taught as *repeated addition*. If the concept is not understood well, and a new word is taught, the new word will most likely be forgotten within a few days (Kame'enui, Dixon, & Carnine, 1987).

Vocabulary associated with complex concepts in science and mathematics, for example, cannot be learned well by simply looking up words in a dictionary or glossary and writing their definitions. This type of rote learning does not produce the usable knowledge students need for future learning (Nagy & Scott, 2000). Teachers can help students develop concepts and associated vocabulary words by improving their ability to recognize and understand common features of objects, events, actions, and qualities, and the relationships between them. Making explicit the patterns and connections between concepts helps students develop well-integrated knowledge and is important for facilitating acquisition of new knowledge.

WHAT DO TEACHERS NEED TO KNOW
ABOUT STUDENTS' LEARNING NEEDS?

As we consider simple and complex concepts and associated vocabulary words, it is important to think about problems students with mild disabilities may encounter when learning them. In Chapter 2, you read that students with mild disabilities often struggle to learn because of difficulties attending to, processing, storing, and/or retrieving information. Specifically, they may possess inadequate concept and vocabulary knowledge because of deficiencies in language production, such as problems retrieving words from memory. Although students with mild disabilities can organize concepts conceptually when given the categories, they may have difficulties generating categories on their own and may use ineffective strategies for grouping concepts into categories. They may also lack proficient reading skills, resulting in less time spent learning concepts and words through independent reading (Baker, Simmons, & Kame'enui, 1998; Stanovich, 1986). In general, students with mild disabilities experience problems with cognitive functioning that affect their ability to plan ahead and independently organize information. Though all students need help developing the well-formed and organized concepts required to progress as learners, students with disabilities often need more support. The challenge for teachers in inclusive classroom settings is to design and deliver high-quality, effective instruction that will allow heterogeneous groups of students to learn and retain important information.

WHAT INSTRUCTIONAL STRATEGIES ARE RECOMMENDED?

In this chapter and several chapters that follow, the instructional practices recommended and described are based on features of effective instruction, including the use of researched instructional supports and routines that have been shown to improve the learning of students with mild disabilities as well as how technology can be used as both a support and a teaching tool. To design optimal instruction, teachers begin by deciding which critical concepts to teach. They then determine if these concepts are simple or complex and what instructional approaches are appropriate to use. Research-based instructional principles for teaching simple concepts involve (1) defining and discussing attributes of a concept, (2) creating and discussing examples and nonexamples of the concept, and (3) helping students use the conceptual knowledge they have developed. Teachers use graphic learning devices and activities-oriented instruction for teaching complex concepts. Instruction is explicit and intensive, includes demonstration and discussion, and emphasizes the relationships, or connections, within and across concepts.

What Concepts and Vocabulary Should Teachers Select?

In Chapter 5, we discussed planning strategies that enable teachers to determine key concepts all students should learn in a content area. Effective teachers begin by identifying *big ideas* that thread throughout a student's academic course of study and then provide instruction targeting these concepts (Kame'enui, Carnine, Dixon, Simmons, & Coyne, 2002). Planning what to teach occurs at different levels (e.g., grade-level concepts, unit-level concepts, daily lesson plan concepts) and in response to students' needs. For concept teaching in particular, it is important to assess students' misconceptions, or concepts that have been learned incorrectly or inadequately, before deciding what to teach. Students' misconceptions are resistant to change; instead of using new information they have been taught, students tend to continue to apply the original concepts as they have acquired them. Identifying students' misconceptions, selecting these for instruction, and reteaching them directly can improve students' conceptual understanding (Muller, Sharma, & Reimann, 2008).

Researchers have developed many classroom-based techniques for teaching vocabulary words (Beck, McKeown, & Kucan, 2002). In deciding what to teach, teachers must consider the utility of concepts and associated vocabulary words. Categorizing words into three tiers can be helpful for deciding what to teach. Tier One words are basic words, such as *shoe* and *jump*, and require little instructional attention. Tier Two words are words that appear frequently in grade-level material and have potential for enhancing students' reading comprehension, oral language, and written expression. Depending on the content to be taught and the age and grade levels of students, words such as *hermit, altered*, and *ridiculous* might be Tier Two words. Beck et al. (2002) recommend teaching these words explicitly because of the role they play in improving reading and writing. Tier Three words include words children encounter infrequently, such as *lateral* and *silo*, and are best taught when related topics arise during content instruction.

Effective Strategies for Teaching Concepts

Once concepts and associated vocabulary words have been selected for instruction based on utility, students' needs, and important curricular content to be learned, teachers then select research-based instructional strategies. As discussed earlier, concepts can be simple or complex, and because people tend to store these concepts differently in their minds (i.e., simple concepts into categories, and complex concepts as linkages to other concepts), we describe instructional strategies effective for teaching that are aligned with these notions of learning. We also classify instructional strategies as either generic or content-specific. Generic instructional strategies can be used across content areas. Content-specific strategies are designed specifically for teaching in a content area (e.g., mathematics, science, social studies). When using any strategy, teachers need to ensure that the features of the concept being taught are supported by the strategy.

Generic Instructional Strategies for Teaching Concepts

We begin our discussion of instructional approaches by focusing on generic instructional strategies for teaching simple and complex concepts. These strategies are appropriate for teaching a variety of topics across content areas. Table 6.2 presents selected generic instructional strategies for learning simple and complex concepts.

SIMPLE CONCEPTS

Concept Attainment (e.g., Joyce, Weil, & Calhoun, 2004) is a generic instructional model for teaching simple concepts supported by learning theorists (e.g., Bruner, 1966). Concept Attainment involves teachers in (1) creating and discussing examples and nonexamples of the concept, (2) defining and discussing the attributes of

TABLE 6.2. Generic Instructional Strategies for Teaching Concepts

Types of concepts	Generic instructional strategies
Simple concepts	Concept attainment
Complex concepts	Concept enhancement routines Semantic feature analysis Semantic mapping

a concept, and (3) helping students use newly developed conceptual knowledge. In Concept Attainment, simple concepts have four elements: (1) an associated vocabulary *word* (e.g., *dog*), (2) *examples* (e.g., chihuahua, great dane) and *nonexamples* (e.g., Siamese cat), (3) *attributes* (e.g., four legs, barks), and (4) *attribute values* (e.g., bark is essential, tail is not). Table 6.3 shows how the concept of *mammal* might be taught using this instructional approach.

COMPLEX CONCEPTS

Teachers must keep in mind that complex concepts are difficult to learn for several reasons. First, they are understood by using language rather than physical evidence. They also have multiple, distinct meanings depending on the context in which they are used. And they are represented in our minds as links to other related concepts

TABLE 6.3. Concept Attainment Procedures

What the teacher does	What students do
1. Begins by using pictures, words, and/or actual objects to present the concept using an example. Then the teacher presents subsequent examples, followed by a nonexample, and then additional examples presented in random order (use three examples for every one nonexample). The teacher presents the examples and asks if the example represents the concept (e.g., "Is this a mammal?"). Possible examples of a mammal include (tiger, goat, human, meerkat), possible nonexamples (fish, flamingo, ladybug).	Respond to teacher's examples by saying "yes" or "no."
2. Asks for additional examples from the students.	Provide their own examples of the concept of mammals (e.g., leopard, whale, squirrel).
3. Presents an example that might stump students causing them to deliberate (e.g., duck-billed platypus).	May talk among each other to come up with a response.
4. Asks students to identify the critical attributes apparent in the examples (e.g., has hair, produces milk to feed young) and nonessential attributes (e.g., lives on land) and lists these on the board, chart paper, or overhead projector.	Contribute to the list of critical and nonessential attributes and help develop a definition of the concept.
5. With students, derives a definition of the concept.	Provide a possible definition ("All mammals have hair and produce milk to feed their young").
6. Evaluates student learning of the concept.	May, for example, recite the definition from memory, create a concept map, or illustrate the concept.

rather than within categories as simple concepts are. In this chapter, we high-light three generic instructional strategies for teaching complex concepts: Content Enhancement routines (CERs; Bulgren, Deshler, Schumaker, & Lenz, 2000; Bulgren et al., 2007), semantic mapping (SM), and semantic feature analysis (SFA; e.g., Bos & Anders, 1990). All three strategies have been researched with students with mild disabilities using both science and social studies content.

Content Enhancement Routines. CERs were designed to assist secondary stu-dents, including those with mild disabilities, to succeed in inclusive science and social studies classrooms. CERs and the accompanying graphic devices ensure that students have (1) adequate background knowledge for learning new content; (2) opportunities to manipulate information through activities such as categoriz-ing, comparing and contrasting, and inquiring into critical questions; and (3) ways to generalize what they have learned by predicting, inferring, problem solving, and synthesizing information. We focus on one CER, the *Concept Anchoring Rou-tine* (CAR) and its associated graphic device, because it creates opportunities for students to organize information about concepts, and make connections between known and new concepts, enabling retrieval of information from memory.

The CAR and its associated graphic device, the Anchoring Table, emphasize an important principle in concept teaching (i.e., using a familiar concept to teach a new, similar concept); the authors refer to this approach as *teaching by analogy.* Teach-ing by analogy is particularly useful for complex concept development because the approach allows the teacher and students to make explicit linkages or associations between concepts through classroom discussions. The CAR consists of three com-ponents: (1) the Anchoring Table; (2) the *Cue–Do–Review* sequence, and (3) seven linking steps within the *Do* phase. During the *Cue* phase, the teacher explains the importance of the concept to be learned and tells students they will complete, as a group, a graphic display to learn the concept. In the *Do* phase, seven linking steps for completing the graphic are followed. In the *Review* phase, the content in the graphic display is reviewed to ensure students' understanding and retention of the concept. Additional instructional details for the CAR are presented in Table 6.4.

When compared to traditional classroom instruction, the CAR has been found to enhance the subject-matter content learning of high school students identified as high, average, and low achievers, including students with learning disabilities. Fur-thermore, teachers have been shown to quickly learn how to create the Anchoring Table and use the routine. An example of a completed Anchoring Table is provided in Figure 6.1.

Earlier in this chapter we referred to vocabulary words as labels for concepts. Recall also that when selecting vocabulary to teach, Beck and colleagues (2002) make a distinction between Tier Two and Tier Three words. Tier Two words are high-frequency words found in a variety of texts (e.g., *required, fortunate, maintain*). Alternatively, Tier Three words have lower frequency and are associated with uncommon concepts found across content areas (e.g., *photosynthesis, mitochondria, radioactive* in science). For Tier Three words, the focus of instruction is on teaching

TABLE 6.4. Concept Anchoring Routine

Phase	What the teacher does	What students do
Cue	1. Tells students they will be learning a new concept and completing an Anchoring Table. 2. Emphasizes the importance of learning the new concept and linking new information to what is known. 3. Distributes Concept Anchoring Table to students.	
Do	1. Names the new concept and provides a rationale for learning it. 2. Names the known concept and expresses confidence in students' understanding of the concept. 3. Collects information about the known concept by leading a brainstorming discussion with students; lists information generated during discussion on the far left side of the Anchoring Table under "Known Information." 4. Underlines most important characteristics of known concept that will facilitate learning of the new concept and places these under "Characteristics of Known Concept" in the table. 5. Examines characteristics of the new concept as they relate to the known concept and encourages student participation; lists characteristics generated on the right side of the table under "Characteristics of the New Concept." 6. Reveals shared characteristics between the known and new concepts and encourages student participation; the shared characteristics are listed in the table under "Characteristics Shared." 7. Directs students to write a definition of the new concept that includes its name and characteristics in the box labeled "Understanding the New Concept."	3. Provide important information and characteristics of the known concept during class discussion. 5. Provide characteristics about the known concept during class discussion that may relate to the new concept. 6. Identify shared characteristics between the known and new concepts during class discussion. 7. Demonstrate understanding of the new concept by writing a definition.
Review	1. Reviews briefly the key content covered in the lesson. 2. Asks students something about the Anchoring Routine (e.g., "How has the routine helped you learn about the new concept?" "How might you use the routine in other classes?").	2. Respond to questions posed by the teacher.

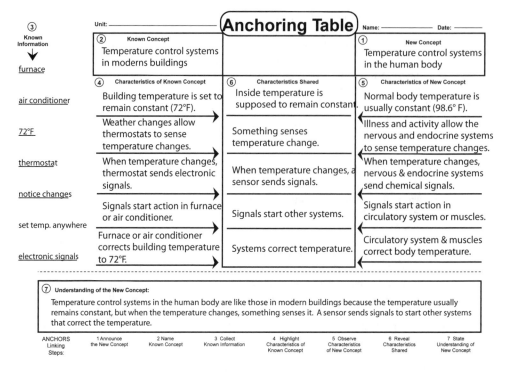

FIGURE 6.1. Completed Anchoring Table for the concept "temperature control systems in warm-blooded animals." From "Making Learning Easier: Connecting New Knowledge to Things Students Already Know" by D. Deshler et al. (2001, p. 84). Copyright 2001 by the Council for Exceptional Children. Reprinted with permission.

new concepts by integrating them with existing knowledge and helping students represent this information as sets of relationships. A number of instructional strategies are recommended for helping students relate new concepts to what they already know and to structure this information in organized ways that facilitate recall and understanding. These strategies are referred to as "graphic organizers," or visual–spatial displays that depict relationships among concepts (e.g., DiCecco & Gleason, 2002; Kim, Vaughn, Wanzek, & Wei, 2004). Two graphic organizers highlighted in this chapter are SFA and SM (Bos & Anders, 1990).

Semantic Mapping. SM is designed to help students categorize vocabulary words by identifying similarities and differences among related concepts. Teachers help students structure concepts as sets of relationships, not as lists of isolated information. SM can be used for initial instruction to illustrate relationships among concepts and as an assessment for measuring students' understanding of concepts. If used as an assessment, teachers might create a semantic map as in Figure 6.2, but leave some or most of the cells empty to allow students to fill in the words. Like other instructional strategies discussed in this chapter, SM involves teachers in helping students to activate and expand on background knowledge as well as to ask questions about and discuss the connections between the new concept and familiar concepts. SM also involves the use of a diagram that groups related concepts to visually depict relationships between and among concepts, as in Figure 6.2.

   Semantic Feature Analysis. SFA is also a generic instructional strategy that can be used across content areas. SFA helps students identify characteristics of a concept by comparing its features to those of other concepts falling in the same category. Bos and Anders (1990), for example, have studied SFA with students with disabilities using social studies and science content and have found this approach to be more effective for learning content than instruction using definitions only. The semantic features are the attributes that define a concept and cause them to be different from, or overlap with, other related concepts. Students place a "+" sign in the matrix when a concept aligns with a particular attribute. If the concept attributes do not align, students put a "–" in the grid. If there are instances when the attributes may or may not align with the concept, students use a "±". An example of a completed SFA grid is presented in Figure 6.3.

Content-Specific Instructional Strategies for Teaching Complex Concepts

Many research-based, content-specific strategies for teaching science, social studies, mathematics, and reading also exist. These domain-specific, or content-specific, instructional strategies help improve students' understanding of important concepts,

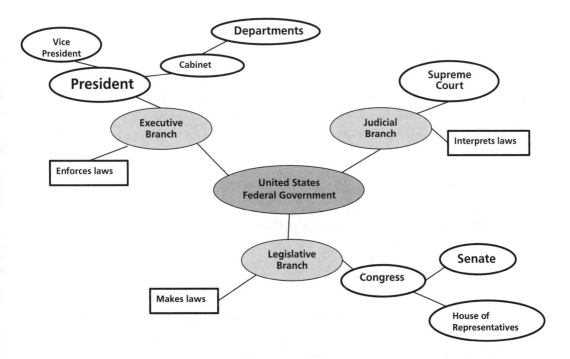

FIGURE 6.2. Semantic map.

		Queen	King	Tsar	Dictator	President
Attributes of World Leaders	Elected	−	−	−	−	+
	Complete power	+	+	+	+	−
	Limited authority	+/−	+/−	+/−	−	+
	Tyrant	+/−	+/−	+/−	+	+/−
	Appointed	+	+	+	−	−
	Chief executive	+	+	+	+	+
	Monarch	+	+	+	−	−
	Unlimited authority	+/−	+/−	+/−	+	−
	Commander in chief	+	+	+	+	+
	Royalty	+	+	+	−	−

FIGURE 6.3. Example of a semantic feature analysis matrix.

particularly in the case of students with disabilities (De La Paz & MacArthur, 2003). The example content-specific strategies to be discussed in this chapter include Supported Inquiry Science (Dalton, Morocco, Tivnan, & Rawson-Mead, 1997; Palinscar, Magnusson, Collins, & Cutter, 2001), Strategy-Supported Project-Based Learning (SSPBL; Ferretti, MacArthur, & Okolo, 2001, 2007; De La Paz, 2005), the concrete–representational–abstract (CRA) teaching sequence (Miller & Hudson, 2007), and robust vocabulary instruction (Beck & McKeown, 2007). Table 6.5 provides an overview of the content-specific instructional strategies for teaching complex concepts.

SCIENCE INSTRUCTION

Hands-on approaches to science instruction that include concrete experiences have been used effectively to enhance science-concept learning of students with mild disabilities (e.g., Mastropieri & Scruggs, 1999; Scruggs & Mastropieri, 2004b). Students with behavior disorders also seem to benefit from hands-on science instruction by

TABLE 6.5. Content-Specific Instructional Strategies for Teaching Complex Concepts

Content areas	Content-specific instructional strategies
Science	Supported Inquiry Science (SIS) Guided Inquiry Science Instruction (GISI)
Social studies	Strategy-Supported Project-Based Learning (SSPBL)
Mathematics	Concrete–Representational–Abstract (CRA) teaching sequence
Literacy	Robust vocabulary instruction

performing better on science assessments than students who receive traditional textbook instruction (McCarthy, 2005). Although the hands-on science approach can be effective for helping students demonstrate their understanding of the science concepts, it can also require a fair amount of "behavioral support" (p. 259). Thus, teachers need to carefully consider effective classroom management routines (see Chapter 9) when implementing hands-on science instruction.

Supported Inquiry Science (SIS; Dalton et al., 1997) and *Guided Inquiry Science Instruction* (GISI; Palinscar, et al., 2001) are examples of hands-on science approaches that directly address the needs of students with mild disabilities. Specifically, these approaches are designed to help students who experience difficulties (1) drawing inferences across science experiences, (2) making sense of new information that conflicts with what they already know, (3) using materials to enhance their conceptual knowledge, and (4) participating in peer-supported learning experiences. In particular, the instructional approaches focus on building deeper understandings of science concepts by addressing students' misconceptions, involving them in problem-solving activities, and offering them multiple ways to communicate what they know and have learned. A listing of the key features of SIS instruction along with an explanation for how each component addresses the needs of students with mild disabilities is included in Table 6.6.

The GISI approach to science instruction incorporates teaching principles that emphasize student understanding of the content, and also involves pairs and small groups of students in inquiry-based activities. GISI includes four phases: Engage, Investigate, Explain, and Report. Instruction typically begins with a question (Engage). Then students are provided multiple opportunities to learn science concepts through cycles of investigation related to a single topic (Investigate and Explain). In the end, students share claims and evidence (Report). A GISI program of study occurs over 2–6 weeks depending on the grade level and the science topic, 5 days a week, for about 45 minutes to 2 hours each day. Table 6.7 provides a more detailed description of the practices that may occur during a GISI lesson.

GISI and SIS require both general and special educators to understand the content and the specific ways of thinking and reasoning about the subject matter to be learned. Although inquiry-based approaches can be effective for enhancing concept learning in students with and without mild disabilities, teachers must invest considerable preparation time if they are to implement the approaches properly. Low-performing students' participation during peer-mediated learning situations can be minimized if teachers do not plan carefully how to involve them and monitor their participation. Teachers are referred to Chapters 5 and 9 for planning instruction and ensuring effective learning among peers during lessons.

SOCIAL STUDIES INSTRUCTION

Students with and without mild disabilities have been found to make significant gains in their understanding of history content and use of historical inquiry when

TABLE 6.6. Supported Inquiry Science

SIS components	Needs addressed
1. Creating a classroom environment in which students are comfortable expressing their ideas about science	Students' lack of participation and need to provide only correct answers
2. Designing instruction around a unifying concept (e.g., the environment and energy)	Students' lack of integrated information
3. Discussing students' misconceptions, providing opportunities for them to examine conflicting evidence, and allowing time for students to reconstruct their thinking	Students' misconceptions are typically resistant to change, even when presented with conflicting information
4. Facilitating conversations about students' hands-on learning experiences	Teacher assumes the role of knowledgeable facilitator to support students' understanding as they are engaging in hands-on experiences
5. Using whole-class, small-group, and individual learning arrangements	Flexible groupings and individual work give students opportunities to work with others and have adequate time to work on problems on their own
6. Offering students multiple ways to explore science concepts and processes such as manipulating materials and using visual representations	Students have opportunities to manipulate materials and to talk, draw, or write about what they are doing
7. Embedding assessment within instruction including hands-on performance tasks	Assessments are embedded at important points to help teachers modify their instruction to fit students' learning needs
8. Teaching students how to work together collaboratively and providing them with opportunities to discuss what is and is not working during the collaborative process	Students learn how to work with each other and assume productive roles on the team

involved in *Strategy-Supported Project-Based Learning* (SSPBL; Okolo & Feretti, 1996; Ferretti et al., 2001). SSPBL lessons are designed to enhance students' (1) understanding of historical concepts, (2) awareness of the ways historians analyze and interpret historical evidence, and (3) productivity during group work. To achieve these goals, SSPBL includes the instructional features depicted in Table 6.8.

Studies suggest that students with and without disabilities progressed in their understanding of history concepts and use of inquiry techniques when teachers engaged them in SSPBL. In particular, teacher scaffolding during collaborative small-group and large-group discussions was found to be important for developing student understanding.

TABLE 6.7. Guided Inquiry Science Instruction

Phases of GISI instruction	What the teacher may do during each phase	What students may do during each phase
1. Engage	• Pose broad-based questions that cover the topic area of interest—for example, "How do plants and animals live in the desert with very little water?"	• Respond to teacher questions.
2. Investigate	• Involve students in authentic tasks through structured, experiential learning in and outside the classroom. • Provide students with opportunities to build cognitive strategies (from basic skills such as organizing materials to more difficult skills such as synthesizing information). • Monitor and mediate students' ideas and claims.	• Participate in two types of investigations related to the question(s) posed: 1. *Firsthand investigations.* These are direct experiences (such as taking a field trip to observe animals and plants in their natural environment); 2. *Secondhand investigations.* Students use the science text or other sources to find out what they want to know. • Gather data, decide if the data provide evidence for the claims they are forming, share and evaluate claims with their peers.
3. Explain	• Help students interact productively by modeling and encouraging an appreciation for diverse ideas, good listening skills, and shared ownership of the learning activity. • Help students needing support to think through their ideas or rehearse how they will share their ideas with the class.	• Work in small groups or pairs to create an explanation for the question(s) they are investigating. • Conduct further investigations to test (support or refute) their claims.
4. Report	• Encourage students to engage in constructive criticism by focusing on the question(s) at hand. • Assess students' progress in developing conceptual understanding.	• Share (in small groups or pairs) their data and findings by reporting to the class and asking for feedback. • Compare and contrast data collected and findings that emerged related to the question(s) posed during whole-class discussions.

TABLE 6.8. Instructional Features of Strategy-Supported Project-Based Learning

Pretest and small groups

Students are pretested to assess their knowledge of the historical concepts to be taught and placed in small groups that include students with adequate to above-average knowledge and those with limited knowledge of the topic.

Conceptual framework

The teacher uses a framework for organizing the essential concepts within a unit of instruction. For example, in a unit focused on the migration of people, students may study the reasons for migration, conflicts between migrants and prior residents, and long-term outcomes.

Background knowledge

Units of instruction include stories (e.g., a movie or documentary) designed to pique students' interest in the topic and supply necessary background information. Students work together gathering information that extends this story using elements of a narrative as a guide (e.g., the people, the problems they faced, reasons for their decisions, and outcomes that occurred).

Historical inquiry and reasoning

Students are involved in a number of activities, including:

1. The teacher provides student groups with authentic sources from the period (e.g., news clippings, diaries, letters, political cartoons from the U.S. westward expansion in the 1800s) and uses a three-step historical reasoning strategy to examine the historical evidence:
   a. First, students consider the author, or source of the text, by responding to three questions:
      i. What was the author's purpose?
      ii. Do the reasons make sense?
      iii. Do you find evidence of bias?
      The teacher then guides students to examine the author's word choice and point of view to detect bias.
   b. Students then use five questions to search the documents for conflicting points of view:
      i. Is an author's view inconsistent?
      ii. Is a person described differently?
      iii. Is an event described differently?
      iv. What is missing from the author's argument?
      v. What can you infer from reading across sources?
   c. Finally, students are prompted by the teacher to make notes on what appears to be credible information within each source.
2. Students are taught a compare–contrast writing strategy to compare, for example, the ways of life of migrants and prior residents.
3. The teacher scaffolds students' collaborative discussions between peers in both small and large groups focusing on rectifying misunderstandings and clarifying information.

Project-based inquiry

Student groups create and present multimedia projects to their teacher and peers that include both text and images.

MATHEMATICS INSTRUCTION

Despite significant changes in the standards for learning and teaching of mathematics (National Council of Teachers of Mathematics (2000), Gersten and his colleagues (2009) reaffirm the widespread support for systematic and explicit mathematics instruction for students with disabilities (e.g., Kroesbergen & Van Luit, 2003). Fuchs et al. (2008) further expand the definition of effective practice in mathematics for students with disabilities to include (1) precise explanations to reduce misunderstandings; (2) the use of manipulatives, number lines, and other concrete materials to enhance conceptual understanding; (3) drill and practice; (4) cumulative review; (5) strategies for helping students maintain attention and persistence, and regulate their behavior; and (6) ongoing progress monitoring. In particular, the *concrete–representation–abstract* (CRA) *sequence* incorporates many essential instructional design features for ensuring conceptual understanding in mathematics for students with disabilities (Miller & Hudson, 2007).

At the concrete level of the CRA sequence, manipulatives are used to represent the concept to be taught. A variety of manipulative devices can be used to show, for example, the relationship between repeated addition and multiplication. To begin, the teacher demonstrates by separating counters into equal subsets (e.g., five subsets with three counters in each set) and writing a number sentence that reads: $5 \times 3 = 3 + 3 + 3 + 3 + 3$. After several similar demonstrations, students then have opportunities to practice creating their own subsets and number sentences with teacher guidance. When students perform independent practice activities at the concrete level with 80% accuracy, instruction progresses to the representational level of the CRA sequence. At this level, instruction is the same as the concrete level, except that it involves the use of pictures or tallies to represent the concept taught, instead of manipulatives. Research suggests that students with disabilities should participate in three concrete and three representational lessons using about 20 problems during each lesson to develop understanding (e.g., Butler, Miller, Crehan, Babbitt, & Pierce, 2003). Again, when mastery is achieved at 80% accuracy on independent practice tasks at the representational level, instruction proceeds to the abstract level. The abstract level involves the use of numbers and symbols only (e.g., $5 \times 3 = ?$). Finally, the CRA sequence has been implemented effectively using concrete and representational levels only, skipping the abstract level, a variation in the approach that may be more appropriate for teaching young children, or students with more significant learning problems.

Research also supports an instructional approach associated with the Content Enhancement series (Bulgren, Lenz, Deshler, & Schumaker, 1995) that involves embedding various structures into the CRA instructional sequence aligned with the teaching of mathematics concepts (Hudson & Miller, 2006). For example, the *compare/contrast structure* can be used to illustrate similarities and differences between fractions, such as comparing equivalent and nonequivalent fractions. In addition, the *example/nonexample structure* may help students distinguish between various geometric shapes that are only minimally different, such as a parallelogram and a rhombus. Effective concept teaching in mathematics also entails linking two previously learned concepts (e.g., addition to subtraction) or relating a previously learned concept to a new one (e.g., understanding simple *more*, *less*, and *same* concepts for later learning of equivalent representations for the same number). In sum, the CRA instructional approach has been effective for learning algebra, basic operations, money, and place value with students with learning disabilities.

LITERACY INSTRUCTION

Research suggests that effective vocabulary instruction for students with learning disabilities must emphasize instructional methods that teach words directly (Jitendra, Edwards, Sacks, & Jacobson, 2004). However, it is not enough to directly teach words. If the instructional goals are to enhance text comprehension and what students might talk and write about, words must also be encountered frequently over time and students must be actively engaged in thinking about and using the meanings to develop sufficient word knowledge that is maintained (Beck, McKeown, & Omanson, 1987).

Teaching Tier Two words focuses on explaining the meaning of the word rather than providing a dictionary definition and provides students with opportunities to interact with word meanings. Beck et al. (2002) provide an example of how the word *dazzling* is best explained to emphasize its meaning:

> If something is *dazzling*, that means that it's so bright that you can hardly look at it. After lots of long, gloomy winter days, sunshine on a sunny day might seem dazzling. (p. 55)

In Table 6.9, we present four brief activities researched by Beck and her colleagues (pp. 44–45) that require students to use and interact with words by thinking about word meanings.

Integrating Technology Into Concept Development

Technology can be a powerful tool for concept development. Teachers can use technology to assist students in organizing the different types of concepts (e.g., simple, complex), both in terms of learning and identifying objects as well as observed actions. Technology tools can further represent concepts by offering a visual support; allowing the student to recognize and understand the common features of events, actions, or objects; and basically break down complex concepts or unknown simple concepts. In the use of pictorial representations, multimedia anchors (e.g., audio, video), and interactive visual organizers, technology tools can enhance concept development by combining supports into one tool. In this section, we provide information about how available technologies can be used to support concept development for the struggling learner.

TABLE 6.9. Robust Vocabulary Instruction

Activity	What the teacher does	What students do
Word associations	Presents explanations for words (e.g., *apprentice, bookworm, tutor*). Asks, "What word goes with *chef*?"	Explain: "An *apprentice* helps the head chef."
Have you ever. . . ?	Asks a student to explain "a time when. . . ."	Describe a time when they were an *apprentice*.
Applause, applause!	Asks, for example, "Have any of you been a *tutor*?"	Clap to indicate how much they would like to be described by the target word and explain why they feel that way.
Idea completions	Presents a sentence stem: "A *bookworm* went to the library to. . . ."	Think about the target word and complete the sentence.

TEACHING COMPLEX CONCEPTS: MULTIMEDIA TOOLS

Teachers and students can use ever-growing multimedia applications (e.g., Internet-based, applettes, software) to provide visual anchors, a graphic display to learn the concept, or an interactive sequence to order events. Many of these tools are free and available via the web where they have often been developed to enhance Web 2.0 resources or provide interactive visual tools for user engagement. For example, Animoto (see *animoto.com*), Domo animate (see *domo.goanimate.com*), Voice Thread (see *voicethread.com*), and Kerpoof (see *www.kerpoof.com*) are often categorized as digital storytelling tools. While varying in specific features, they all allow teachers and students to visually represent concepts, events, vocabulary, and more through images, documents, and video. Teachers or students can add their own voice (directly through the computer microphone), input text (including doodles), upload audio files (e.g., music from their iTunes), or add video (e.g., via a webcam). The interactive nature of these tools allow for other users (e.g., students, parents) to view, post comments, embed other websites, or be exported for portable learning via an MP3 player or even burned as a DVD. For example, Kerpoof is a free web-based tool that allows students to develop animated movies, visual and interactive stories, postcards, and more. The tool has numerous embedded features enabling the student in his or her own resource development. The beauty of many of these free web-based tools is that they are developed with features seeking to engage as many learners as possible in their own meaningful development. As a result, the universal components provide enhanced access, engage the learner at his or her own level, and offer an outlet to develop meaningful representation of a variety of concepts, especially concept development related to content.

Teachers and students can also use software programs to detail the importance of a concept through a graphic organizer, visual representation, or meaningful anchor. Microsoft's *Photostory* is a free Windows-based (Mac users look to *iPhoto*) digital storytelling application (students produce short movies). Like its web-based counterparts, Photostory allows users to upload images (e.g., photos, graphics), music (e.g., MP3 files, from your CD), and text (e.g., titles, captions). Thus, students and teachers can quickly develop a digital story—featuring visual representation, graphics to organize concepts, mental images to visual events or a process—to break down difficult concepts or introduce them in a meaningful way for comprehension and application. Likewise, Photostory features a five-step process whereby the user is directed to complete a task before he or she is able to continue. Each step is simple in nature and consistent in design and tools in order to complete the task. As a result, students of all ages and abilities are able to control their own learning in that they are developing the tool to enhance concept development.

Not everything is free. The software marketplace is increasingly developing for-pay solutions that seek to offer visual cues building on meaningful anchors and allowing teachers to visualize concepts for student understanding and application. An increasingly popular reading comprehension application is Scholastic's *Read 180* (see *teacher.scholastic.com/products/read180*). Read 180 is an intensive reading intervention program (often used as a Tier Two intervention to support reading development) focused on students in grades 3 and up. While technology-based, the program also includes print, graphic organizers, and direct instruction in small teacher-to-student reading groups. Essentially, Read 180 offers a multimodal approach whereby students gain access to the concepts through visual anchors (e.g., images, videos), direct vocabulary instruction featuring visual and audio representation of the term (e.g., drill and practice via computer-assisted instruction), audio supports (e.g., audio books), and small-group direct instruction. While a reading intervention, the program directly addresses individual needs through adaptive and instructional software, high-interest literature, and direct instruction in reading and vocabulary skills.

VIRTUAL MANIPULATIVES

Another example of a tool that can be used to help students during problem solving is the virtual manipulative, available through the National Library on Virtual Manipulatives (NLVM; see *nlvm.usu.edu/en/nav/vLibrary.html*). Developed through funding by the National Science Foundation, the NLVM offers free downloadable manipulatives housed in five distinct areas (numbers and operations, algebra, geometry, measurement, and data analysis and probability). Besides offering free access to varied manipulatives, the universal aspect to this tool is that those performing at a third-grade level, but in a sixth-grade class, can easily locate and use a manipulative targeted for sixth-grade material but developed with a third-grade cognitive and learning level in mind. Similarly, for those learners challenged with fine motor issues, limiting their effective use of traditional manipulatives, the web-based tool offers an array of manipulatives requiring only the ability to manage a computer mouse or keyboard. Specific instructions for using manipulatives, connections to national standards, and parent/teacher tips for using manipulatives are also available online. Although manipulatives can be used to help students learn concepts, students can also be taught to use virtual manipulatives to represent problems they must solve. Doing so can provide them with a strategy to rely on in order to check their understanding and determine if their solution is accurate. For instance, in solving simple linear equations (algebra, grades 6–8) students can use NLVM's Algebra Balance Scales, which allow students to solve simple linear equations using a balance beam representation. Unit blocks (representing 1's) and X-boxes (for the unknown, X) are placed on the pans of a balance beam where the object of the activity is to keep the beam balanced. The goal, of course, is to get a single X-box on one side, with however many unit blocks needed for balance, thus giving the value of X. At any time, the user can Clear the beam (to begin again), Create a Problem, or access a New Problem to further understand simple linear equations. The goal with these and other technology-based tools is to support the struggling learner with strategic solutions infused with interactive applications to enhance student learning. Furthermore, by using these applications, students gain further practice with an effective strategy, application of the strategy with additional interactive features, and engagement with a tool that can be used in subsequent learning situations, in and out of school.

CHAPTER 7

Creating Strategic Learners

Study Guide Questions

- Why is strategy instruction essential for students with high-incidence disabilities?
- What framework can teachers use for selecting appropriate strategies to teach?
- How should teachers teach students the underlying processes of effective strategies?
- What are ways teachers can use technology to support students' strategy acquisition?

THE CASE OF JAMAL

Jamal is a sixth-grade student in Mr. Black's social studies class. Both Mr. Black and the special education teacher, Ms. Hernandez, have been working together to help Jamal acquire comprehension strategies so that he can improve his understanding of the texts and novels he reads in social studies. To more effectively address all his students' needs, Mr. Black has selected a few key comprehension strategies and has been teaching them in class. He notices, however, that Jamal and a few of his classmates need more assistance than he can provide in class, so he seeks advice from Ms. Hernandez about how to help these students.

To provide Jamal and his peers with the more intensive instruction they need to access social studies materials, Ms. Hernandez groups the students for more intensive instruction during her learning strategies class. In her class, she reteaches the strategies Mr. Black has taught, ensuring that each student receives explicit instruction in how to use the strategies and has multiple opportunities to apply using them in different types of history texts, including the class text, historical novels, and trade books. Ms. Hernandez also uses available technology to scan text and insert prompts that will help students remember to use the strategies. To determine if students are mastering the strategies, she asks them to think aloud while using the strategies. The coordinated efforts of Mr. Black and Ms. Hernandez pay off; by the end of the year they notice that Jamal and other struggling students are beginning to more easily paraphrase the main points of the text, and their ability to respond to different types of comprehension questions has improved. Additionally, Jamal has started to write more organized paragraphs.

WHAT SHOULD TEACHERS KNOW ABOUT CREATING STRATEGIC LEARNERS?

For students like Jamal to become effective and efficient learners, they must approach tasks in ways that allow them to complete them well and in a timely manner. Students who learn effectively and efficiently are often described as "strategic" because they employ helpful approaches to solving problems, comprehending text, or generating written compositions. As mentioned in Chapter 2, students with disabilities, particularly those with learning disabilities, do not always approach academic tasks in strategic ways (Deshler, Ellis, & Lenz, 1996). Often they are unaware of the effective strategies that more accomplished learners acquire over time. For instance, they do not paraphrase what they are reading to ensure understanding. Or they do not develop a plan for organizing ideas before writing. Further, they see successful academic performance as the result of ability or luck and do not realize that by employing effective strategies they can become more successful learners (Tabassam & Grainger, 2002).

The good news is that students with disabilities can learn to use cognitive and metacognitive strategies if they are taught the processes underlying them. *Cognitive strategies* are specific approaches to tasks, such as summarizing or organizing the main ideas of a chapter into a semantic web. *Metacognitive strategies* involve approaches to planning and monitoring how well one is learning information, solving problems, or completing a task. Research on cognitive and metacognitive strategy instruction shows that when teachers select powerful strategies and provide students with explicit instruction in using them, they can help students become more efficient and effective learners. In the sections that follow, we describe a framework to help teachers provide strategy instruction.

A FRAMEWORK FOR TEACHING STRATEGIES

To provide high-quality strategy instruction, teachers need to be able to identify (1) those strategies that hold the greatest promise for improving student performance, (2) use instructional routines effective for teaching strategies, and (3) use technology to support strategy instruction and scaffold students' basic comprehension and skills problems.

What Strategies Should Teachers Select?

Curricular materials often present teachers with a vast array of strategies to teach students. For instance, open any basal reader and you will quickly see that teachers are faced with a multitude of strategies, including compare and contrast, inferencing, prediction, summarization, cause and effect, KWLs, and so on. Presenting teachers with a multitude of strategies to use can be counterproductive. First, such an approach does not allow teachers to focus their instruction on those strategies with the most potential for improving comprehension; and second, teaching multiple strategies simultaneously to students with learning problems overwhelms them. Fortunately, researchers have identified strategies that offer strong support for improving student performance in reading, writing, and mathematics. These strategies are listed in Table 7.1 and described briefly in the text that follows. These strategies have been researched in both general and special education classrooms. Though a complete accounting of available strategies are beyond the scope of this book, you can refer to other books in this series and references included in the following section to learn more about the strategies teachers can use to assist students with disabilities and those who struggle.

Reading Strategies

Research on comprehension instruction suggests that students with reading difficulties can learn to comprehend text more effectively if they acquire strategies for

TABLE 7.1. Research-Based Strategies in Reading, Writing, and Mathematics

Reading strategies
Prediction and activating prior knowledge
Think-alouds employing self-questioning
Mental imagery
Summarization
Strategies for learning text structures
Word identification strategies

Writing strategies
Planning strategies
Organizing strategies
Sentence-writing strategies
Revision strategies

Mathematics strategies
Using graphic and visual organizers
Schema activation strategies for solving word problems
Using think-alouds during problem solving

activating prior knowledge, monitoring their comprehension of text, summarizing text, understanding text structure, and reading unknown words.

Prediction

Prediction refers to a family of strategies that assists students with making educated guesses about the content of text, activating background knowledge about what they will read, and previewing text to determine its main contents (Duke & Pearson, 2002). Prediction strategies attempt to help students draw on existing knowledge to improve their understanding of texts. For instance, a teacher may ask the student to preview a chapter on mammals and predict some of the information they might acquire about mammals in the text. In this case, a teacher would direct students to look at the title and pictures and ask students to predict what type of information they will learn about mammals; or perhaps, in activating prior knowledge, a teacher might ask students to notice what the animals have in common. Prediction strategies are effective only if students' predictions or prior knowledge are explicitly compared with information in the text. In the example just mentioned, teachers would want to determine if students' predictions about mammals were verified by information presented in the text.

Monitoring Comprehension through Think-Alouds and Self-Questioning

To comprehend effectively, students also need to monitor how well they understand the text while reading. They need to be able to identify when their comprehension is breaking down while reading and rereading, or be able to describe for themselves what a passage was mainly about (Gersten, Fuchs, Williams, & Baker, 2001). To assist with comprehension monitoring, students can be taught to think aloud and ask themselves questions while reading (Kucan & Beck, 1997). Think-alouds that are effective involve several specific strategies including restating what was read in simpler language, backtracking or returning to the point in the text where comprehension begins to break down, and examining demanding relationships. As an example, during instruction in an earth science text, students can be taught to consider the following questions:

- *Restating what was read*: "What are the main concepts that I need to understand about the weather?"
- *Backtracking or returning to the point*: "I am not really sure what cirrus clouds are. I think I will go back and look at the pictures and reread the definition to see if I can understand better."
- *Examining demanding relationships*: "What does the appearance of cirrus clouds tell us about the weather?"

During think-alouds, students might also be taught to create mental images of the text. For instance, when reading about clouds, students might be prompted to think about days when they saw cirrus or cumulus clouds in the sky and to consider what type of day it was.

Summarization

Students also must be able to summarize what they have read and learn how to respond to questions about the text, particularly questions that require them to make inferences or evaluate what they have read (Duke & Pearson, 2002). Summarization is a difficult strategy to teach most students and can be a very challenging strategy for students who struggle to learn. Summarization requires "readers to sift through large units of text, differentiate important from unimportant ideas, and then synthesize those ideas and create a new coherent text that stands for, by substantive criteria, the original" (Duke & Pearson, 2002, p. 220). Time spent helping students learn to summarize, though difficult to teach, is worthwhile. Teaching summarization improves their ability to comprehend what the text is mainly about, and to recall important information. Several groups of researchers have attempted to teach summarization strategies to students with disabilities and have met with a degree of success. In these summarization strategies, teachers help students learn to employ questions or follow steps that enable them to summarize information. In the "Paraphrasing Strategy" (Schumaker, Deshler, & Denton, 1984), students are taught to use the RAP mnemonic to summarize text:

- Read the paragraph.
- Ask yourself, "What were the main ideas and details?"
- Put the main idea and details in your own words.

Teachers providing instruction in the Paraphrasing Strategy or any summarization strategy must realize that many students with high-incidence disabilities and those who struggle to learn will have difficulty identifying the main idea. Teachers will have to show students how ideas are repeated in a paragraph or that many of the details are about one main topic. Sometimes starting with expository text might make this task easier, as headings, subheadings, and pictures can be used to help students identify the main idea and subsequently make a summarizing statement or statements about it.

Understanding Text Structure

Learning strategies for understanding text structure are also important for improving reading comprehension. In school, students encounter both narrative and expository texts. When students understand the basic structure of these texts, they can use this understanding to improve their comprehension. One strategy for helping students understand the major components of expository text is POSSE (Englert & Mariage, 1991). The POSSE strategy employs a mnemonic and a graphic organizer that reminds students to engage in a sequence of steps when reading expository

TABLE 7.2. The POSSE Strategy

Strategy steps	What students do
Predict what ideas are in the story.	Make predictions about ideas contained in the text based on their background knowledge.
Organize your thoughts.	Organize predicted ideas and background knowledge based on the structure of the text. Use a concept map to help them focus on the main ideas.
Search for the structure.	Identify the main ideas of the text and organize them into a concept map, preparing them for the next step.
Summarize the main idea.	Summarize the main ideas, ask their teacher a question about the main ideas to make sure they are on the right track, and check for details.
Evaluate by comparing, clarifying, and predicting.	1. *Compare* the semantic map they generated in the Organize step to the one generated in the Search and Summarize steps in order to confirm or disconfirm predictions. 2. *Clarify* ideas and vocabulary that are unfamiliar or unclear. 3. *Predict* what the next section of the text will be about based on information provided in the text and/or the semantic map developed in the Organize step.
Summarize the entire passage or section of text.	Are directed to summarize an entire section of text by examining main ideas and details in their concept map and the summaries they have written thus far.

text. The steps of the POSSE strategy and purpose of each step are described in Table 7.2.

Decoding Words

In addition to comprehension strategies, students need to learn strategies for decoding unknown words, as their inability to recognize key words in the text can derail comprehension. As students progress through the grades, they encounter increasingly complex texts. These texts contain many multisyllabic words that carry substantial meaning. As an example, it would be difficult for students to understand the following passage if they could not decode the italicized words.

> Animals of *Australia* have *developed* many *unique characteristics* as a way of *adapting* to the harsh, *arid climate* of the *Outback*. For *instance*, the *kangaroo* can go for months without water.

Many students with reading difficulties, however, cannot decode these multisyllabic words. For one, they have not automatized the smaller letter-sound patterns that comprise such words (e.g., *dapt* and *ing* in *adapting* or *de, vel, op, ed* in *developed*).

As a result, researchers have developed several strategies for teaching students to decode unknown words (O'Connor, 2007). These strategies include analogizing and other strategies, such as recognizing syllable types, for decoding multiple-syllabic words. The point of these strategies is to assist students in learning about syllables, word patterns, and context to identify unknown words. One of the most well-known strategies, analogizing, is incorporated in the *Benchmark School Word Detectives* program (Gaskins, 2005), a program developed specifically for students with learning disabilities. In this program, students are taught to use what they know about phonograms and morphemes (e.g., *ail, oat, un, re*) to solve unknown words. For instance, in analyzing the word *slapdash*, students would be taught to look for patterns they have learned previously such as *sl-*, *-ap*, and *-ash*. They would then use these patterns to decode the word; students are using what they know about words as an analogy for decoding unknown words.

Researchers have also developed routines for decoding multisyllabic words that can be effective for students with disabilities and other struggling learners. One of these strategies, called the BEST strategy, has been shown to be effective with second- through third-grade students and is detailed in Table 7.3 (O'Connor, 2007).

Teachers should keep in mind that in order to teach the BEST strategy or any strategy well, they must provide instruction in important subskills involved in the strategy. For instance, students cannot isolate the suffix if they have not learned common suffixes. Additionally, students cannot decode multisyllabic base words if they have not been taught some strategy for decoding individual syllables. As mentioned in Table 7.3, one strategy for helping students recognize syllables involves underlining vowels. All syllables have at least one vowel or vowel team. Thus, in the word *regard*, students would be taught to underline the *e* and *ar* (since *a* is an *r*-controlled vowel), as a way of identifying and decoding the *re* and the *gard*.

TABLE 7.3. The BEST Strategy

Strategy steps	What students do
Break the word apart.	Read a word and look for prefixes, suffixes, root words, and recognizable word chunks (e.g., *ort*). If they see prefixes or suffixes, they are to underline them.
Examine the stem.	Look at the base word and try to decode it. If students do not know the base word, they can be encouraged to underline the vowels. Underlining vowels helps students identify the syllables in words.
Say the parts.	Say each part of the word they have analyzed.
Try the whole thing.	Attempt to blend each word part. When blending the word, students are asked to think about whether or not the word makes sense. Is this a word they have heard before? And does the word make sense in the sentence?

Writing Strategies

In order to write well, students must be able to generate ideas about a topic for writing a story or some other type of text, organize those ideas, generate text that communicates those ideas, and then revise their writing. Additionally, they must be able to write text that conforms to specific expectations for different writing genres, such as narrative or expository text. To assist students with the writing process, researchers have developed multiple strategies that classroom teachers can use to help struggling writers. Some of these strategies can be applied broadly and others are specific to a genre (e.g., narrative or persuasive text).

Planning

Planning and organizing are essential to writing well. Since students with high-incidence disabilities often struggle to generate ideas and organize them prior to writing, teaching them routines for the planning process can be helpful. The STOP and LIST strategy assists students with the preplanning process by helping them set goals for their writing as well as to brainstorm and organize their ideas (Graham & Harris, 2005). This strategy has three steps that students use to guide the preplanning process, which are detailed in Table 7.4.

TABLE 7.4. The STOP and LIST Strategy

Strategy steps	What students do	Example
Step 1: STOP, or Stop and Think of Purposes	STOP is a mnemonic device that is intended to remind students to stop and set goals for their writing before they begin.	If the student is writing about bats, the teacher will encourage her to think about what she would like to communicate about bats, such as this paper is about different types of bats, where they live, and what they eat.
Step 2: LIST, or List Ideas and Sequence Them	LIST is a mnemonic device that reminds students to generate as many ideas as they can and then organize them.	In the example above, the teacher would encourage the student to first list the different types of bats, describe where they live, and what they eat. After listing this information, the teacher would encourage the student to figure out a way to group the ideas. For instance, the student could be encouraged to group the bats by geographic location, such as bats that live in North America versus South America. At this point, the student will number the ideas according to the sequence for presenting them.
Step 3	Students are encouraged to use this plan when writing and to think about how they might add to the plan or revise it.	The student may realize through her reading that all bats, except for the fruit bat, eat insects so the teacher figures out how to help her regroup the ideas so that information about these unique bats stands out when describing bats in South America.

Note. Adapted from *Writing Better: Effective Strategies for Teaching Students with Learning Difficulties* by S. Graham and K. Harris (2005, pp. 55–56). Copyright 2005. Baltimore: Paul H. Brookes Publishing Co., Inc. Adapted by permission.

Generating Text

Generating cohesive, understandable text is the next step in the writing process. Several different research-based strategies can be employed by teachers to help students with this process. One of these strategies is the PLEASE strategy (Welch, 1992). In this strategy, students are taught the PLEASE mnemonic to remember to employ the steps listed in Table 7.5 when using the strategy.

In addition to generating cohesive organized paragraphs, students will also have to write sentences that are complete and coherent. This step can be a major hurdle for many students with writing disabilities, and traditional grammar instruction does little to help. Teaching students grammar does not help them to create more sophisticated sentences (Deshler et al., 1996); in fact, it has even been shown to have a negative impact on their writing (Graham & Perin, 2007). What does help, however, is instruction in writing complete sentences and instruction that helps students combine independent and dependent clauses into more complex sentences. Struggling writers can be taught that sentences are independent thoughts involving a subject and a verb (Shumaker & Sheldon, 1985). To identify the subjects, students can be taught to identify the "who" or "what" in the sentence. To identify verbs, students can be taught to recognize the "action." Students can then be taught to recognize whether or not the sentences they have written are independent thoughts

TABLE 7.5. The PLEASE Strategy

Strategy steps	What students do
Pick the topic	Pick a topic for their paragraph and decide on the type of paragraph they want to write.
List ideas about the topic	Write either enumerative, compare–contrast, or cause–effect paragraphs.
Evaluate	Look over their list to ensure that it contains all facts or ideas relevant to the topic and add or delete information if necessary.
Activate	Activate their paragraph by writing a topic sentence.
Supply	Supply or construct sentences to support the topic sentence using the list of relevant facts and ideas.
End	Write a concluding sentence and edit individual sentences in their paragraph using the COPS strategy. The COPS strategy teaches students to ask themselves four questions while editing sentences (Schumaker, Deshler, Alley, Warner, Clark, & Nolan, 1982): • Have I Captalized the first word and proper nouns? • How is the Overall appearance? • Have I used Punctuation, commas, and semicolons correctly? • Do the words look like they are Spelled right? Can I sound them out, or should I use a dictionary?

Note. Adapted from *Writing Better: Effective Strategies for Teaching Students with Learning Difficulties* by S. Graham and K. Harris (2005, pp. 41–42). Copyright 2005. Baltimore: Paul H. Brookes Publishing Co., Inc. Adapted by permission.

by identifying the subject and verb. Once students are capable of writing complete simple sentences, they can be taught to write more complex sentences through sentence-combining instruction (Saddler & Graham, 2005). Sentence-combining instruction teaches students four skills (see Table 7.6).

Each instructional skill in the sentence-combining strategy is taught through direct instruction. First, the teacher models how to combine sentences. Initially, the teacher uses sentences that provide students with two types of cues for combining sentences. For instance, students would be provided with the following two sentences and cue.

Jermall worked up an appetite.

Jermall <u>was playing soccer for two hours</u>.

because

Students would then use coordinating conjunction and underlined words to combine the two sentences. Once students are able to use these explicit cues, the teacher provides modified cues. She may present the two sentences above, but only underline *was playing* and put *because* in parentheses. As students become more

TABLE 7.6. Sentence-Combining Instruction

Instructional skills	What students do
Combine smaller, simple sentences into complex sentences using a conjunction.	First combine simple sentences by using three common conjunctions (*and, but*, and *because*). For instance, they would be taught to combine "The boy ate the cake" and "The cake was delicious" to "The boy ate the cake because it was delicious."
Insert adjectives or adverbs from one sentence into another sentence.	They are provided with two sentences that are related, but one contains an adverb or adjective. Students are then taught to combine the two sentences into one—for example, "The boy ate the cake" and "The cake was delicious" to "The boy ate the delicious cake."
Insert adverbial or adjectival clauses from one sentence to another.	They are provided with two sentences that are related and then taught to combine the two sentences to make a complex sentence with an adverbial or adjective clause—for example, "The boy stopped eating the cake" and "The boy was stuffed" to "The boy stopped eating the cake when he was stuffed." Or "Terrance listened to his new CD" and "Terrance bought the CD at the Fireside Mall" to "Terrance listened to his new CD that he bought at the Fireside Mall."
Combine sentences, adjectives, and adverbs, and adverbial and adjectival clauses into complex sentences.	Develop complex sentences by using skills learned in previous units. For instance, they might be presented with the following sentences initially. "The boy ate the cake." "The boy was stuffed." "The boy ate a huge dinner." They are then taught to combine these sentences into one complex sentence. "The boy, who had just eaten a huge dinner, ate the cake but stopped when he was stuffed."

competent, the teacher fades cues. Finally, students are encouraged to apply the new skill in their own writing.

Revising and Editing Text

Revising one's work is the last phase of the writing process. In this phase, good writers understand that their writing has to make sense to the reader. Thus, the text must present ideas in some logical format, support ideas with sufficient details so that the reader can understand what is going on, and be easy to follow. Good writers understand that creating this type of cohesive and clear text is a difficult job, and that they must spend time writing and rewriting. One strategy for revising text, researched in elementary and middle school inclusive classrooms, is the *Peer Revising Strategy*. In this strategy, students were taught the steps listed in Table 7.7 for two major parts of the revision process (Graham & Harris, 2005).

Text Structure

Many struggling writers need explicit instruction in text structure in order to generate text within a particular genre. Researchers have documented that when

TABLE 7.7. The Peer Revising Strategy

Part I: The revisor's job as a listener

- Step 1. Listen and read along as the writer reads the paper.
- Step 2. Tell the writer what the paper is about and what you liked best.
- Step 3. Read the writer's paper, making notes about the following two questions: Is everything clear? Write a question mark next to anything that is unclear. Can any details be added? Provide the writer with three suggestions for improving the paper.
- Step 4. Share your suggestions with the writer and give him or her a chance to ask questions.

Part II: The listener's job as an editor

- Step 1. Check the writer's paper for errors in:
    Sentences: Is each sentence complete?
    Capitals: Is the beginning of each sentence capitalized? Are proper nouns capitalized?
    Punctuation: Does the ending of each sentence have a punctuation mark?
    Spelling: Circle any words that do not look right and check with spell-check or the dictionary.
- Step 2. Share your suggestions with the writer.

Note. Between Parts I and II, the writer is directed to make the changes he or she deems necessary and then return the paper to the listener. Adapted from *Writing Better: Effective Strategies for Teaching Students with Learning Difficulties* by S. Graham and K. Harris (2005, pp. 64–65). Copyright 2005. Baltimore: Paul H. Brookes Publishing Co., Inc. Adapted by permission.

students are taught strategies for generating narrative, persuasive, and expository texts, their writing improves. One example of a strategy for writing persuasive text is the TREE strategy. This strategy has been researched effectively with second-, third-, fifth-, and sixth-grade students and involves a three-part process, along with the mnemonic TREE, to guide the writing process. The TREE mnemonic, explained in Table 7.8, is intended to help students generate ideas for their paper, develop a position that they will take in the paper as well as reasons for supporting that position, and then formulate a conclusion for the paper (Graham & Harris, 2005).

Many other strategies exist for teaching students to write within a particular genre. Teachers can find concrete descriptions of strategies for developing text structure in other sources published in this series and elsewhere (e.g., Graham & Harris, 2005).

Routines Involving Multiple Strategies for Reading and Writing

Researchers have also developed routines for helping students integrate the use of several strategies to improve reading and writing. The POSSE strategy described earlier was one of these strategies. In reading, one well-known strategy that has been researched in middle school inclusive classrooms is Collaborative Strategic Reading (CSR; Klingner & Vaughn, 1999). In CSR, students learn the strategies listed in Table 7.9.

TABLE 7.8. The TREE Strategy

Strategy steps	What students do
Step 1	Identify their goal for writing the paper and their audience, by addressing two questions: 1. Who will read my paper? 2. Why am I writing this paper?
Step 2	Develop a plan to guide the writing process using the mnemonic TREE: • Note Topic sentence. (Students are prompted to write their topic sentence, which states their position or what they believe.) • Note Reasons. (Students are prompted to jot down reasons that support their position.) • Note Examples. (Students are asked to generate examples for their reasons. When doing so, they are asked to reflect on the validity of their claims.) • Note Ending. (Students are prompted to write a concluding sentence that summarizes their ideas.)
Step 3	Use their plan to guide the writing process and determine where additional planning is needed.

Note. Adapted from *Writing Better: Effective Strategies for Teaching Students with Learning Difficulties* by S. Graham and K. Harris (2005, pp. 96–97). Copyright 2005. Baltimore: Paul H. Brookes Publishing Co., Inc. Adapted by permission.

TABLE 7.9. The Collaborative Strategic Reading Strategy

Strategy steps	What students do
Preview	Examine a passage prior to reading in order to recall what they know about the topic and predict what they might learn about it.
Click and clunk	Monitor their comprehension during reading by looking for words and concepts that they do not fully understand. Additionally, they are directed to use fix-up strategies when the text does not make sense. For instance, they are directed to reread the sentence or sentences to look for key ideas that will help them understand a word or concept that does not make sense. They are also directed to break words apart, looking for suffixes and prefixes or recognizable chunks.
Get the gist	First focus on identifying what the most important person, place, or thing is in the passage. Then they are asked to think about the most important idea about that person, place, or thing.
Wrap up	Summarize what has been learned and then think about questions that a teacher might ask on a test.

Teaching Reading and Writing as an Integrated Process

By now, you have probably noticed some similarities between reading and writing strategies. In both processes, the effective learner has to summarize information and understand various text structures. By combining reading and writing instruction, teachers can emphasize for students how certain strategies are helpful to both reading and writing, and they can provide extra practice in essential strategies. Research shows that doing so strengthens reading comprehension and writing (Haager & Klingner, 2005).

Mathematics Strategies

The What Works Clearinghouse of the U.S. Department of Education (see *ies.ed.gov/ncee/wwc*) has provided a review of research on teaching mathematics to students with disabilities (Gersten et al., 2009) to improve their classroom instruction. This review states that three cognitive strategies can be particularly helpful in improving struggling students' abilities to solve math problems. These strategies include teaching students to employ concrete manipulatives and graphic depictions, recognize schemas, and engage in think-alouds while problem solving.

Using Visual and Graphic Organizers

In Chapter 6, we described how concrete manipulatives and graphic organizers could be used to help students develop a conceptual foundation for understanding mathematics. Research examining these instructional techniques has demonstrated that they can be incorporated successfully into cognitive strategies for solving word problems. Students with disabilities can be taught to use manipulatives and graphic depictions to assist them in solving word problems involving whole number operations, fractions, and algebra (Butler, Miller, Crehan, Babbitt, & Pierce, 2003; Miller & Mercer, 1993; Witzel, Mercer, & Miller, 2003). As an example, when presented with the following problem, "Jose had 12 baseball cards. Sam asked him for a third of the cards. How many cards did Sam want?," students would be taught to use manipulatives or a graphic depiction to represent the problem. Schema-based problem solving, described in the next section, demonstrates another way that visual depictions can be incorporated in cognitive strategies for solving word problems.

Using Schema-Based Problem Solving

Word problems involving whole-number operations require students to recognize problem types (Reed, 1999) to select the correct operation. For instance, addition and subtraction problems can be grouped into four types: change, equalize, combine, and compare (see Table 7.10). These problems vary in difficulty depending on

TABLE 7.10. Problem Types Involved in Addition and Subtraction

Problem type	Definition	Example
Change problems	In change problems, an initial quantity is either increased or decreased and the unknown, which students must solve for, is the starting amount, the amount of change, or the ending amount.	Change problem so that the start is unknown: "Terrance had a bag of candy bars. Then Sam gave him 7 candy bars. Now Terrance has 34 candy bars. How many were in Terrance's bag to start with?"
Combine problems	In combine problems, students combine two or more amounts, and they are asked to identify the total amount or a subset of the amount.	Combine problem so that the subset is unknown: "Freddie and Sally have 15 tickets to the basketball game. Freddie has 7 tickets. How many does Sally have?"
Compare problems	In comparison problems, students compare two quantities to determine if one quantity is more or less than the other. These problems can involve a difference that is unknown, or involve a comparison where one of the quantities is unknown, or involve a referent that is unknown.	Compare problems in which the referent is unknown: "Rocky has 15 boxing tickets. He has 9 more boxing tickets than Ralph. How many tickets does Ralph have?"
Equalize problems	In equalizing problems, students must determine the quantity that one subset must gain in order to be equal to the other subset.	"Isabella has 16 bottles of soda. Taisha has 10 bottles of soda. How many more bottles does Taisha need to have as many as Taisha?"

problem type, and what is unknown in the problem. Change problems are often easier than compare problems; students also find it easier to solve change problems involving an unknown ending amount as opposed to an unknown starting amount. Multiplication and division problems also can be categorized according to problem types (see Reid & Lienemann, 2006).

In schema-based strategy instruction, students are taught the various problem types or schemas to mastery, how to differentiate between schemas, and how to use visual representations to represent schemas before solving word problems (see Figure 7.1). Jitendra and her colleagues (as cited in Reid & Lienemann, 2006) have taught students to employ the steps listed in Table 7.11 when solving word problems.

Using Think-Alouds during Problem Solving

Teaching students to engage in think-alouds while solving word problems can improve their mathematical problem-solving skill. When teachers provide think-aloud instruction, they explicitly teach students (using the teaching routines articulated in the following section) to employ a problem-solving process while solving math problems. First, teachers model the steps of a problem-solving strategy (e.g., schema strategy described earlier) while thinking aloud. Second, they encourage students to think aloud, using the steps of the strategy. During the think-aloud, students direct themselves through the mental processes necessary for solving problems by verbalizing the steps of the problem-solving strategy. Research has shown that when teachers spend considerable time modeling aloud how to solve problems, and then have students practice verbalizing solutions for similar problem types, they are able to have a strong influence on the mathematics performance of students in elementary, middle, and high school grades (Reid & Lienemann, 2006; Xin & Jitendra, 1999).

How to Teach Strategies

Effective instructional routines for teaching cognitive strategies show students when and how to use the steps of the strategy when performing a task or solving

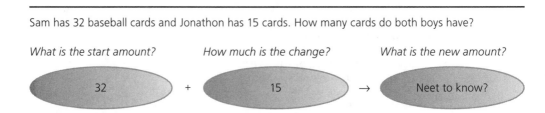

Sam has 32 baseball cards and Jonathon has 15 cards. How many cards do both boys have?

What is the start amount?   *How much is the change?*   *What is the new amount?*

32   +   15   →   Neet to know?

FIGURE 7.1. Sample graphic representation students can use for a change problem. For more examples of graphic representations, see Reid and Lienemann (2006).

TABLE 7.11. Schema-Based Strategy Instruction Steps for Solving Word Problems

Strategy steps	What students do
Identify problem schemas.	Learn how to identify a particular schema type and how to differentiate between schemas.
Create an appropriate diagram.	Learn how to diagram the different schemas. Students use these diagrams as graphic organizers to organize information from the problem and identify what is missing. (see Figure 7.1 for an example).
Flag the missing element with a question mark.	Put a question mark for the missing element in the diagram as a reminder that they must use a mathematical operation to figure out the number that goes in that box.
Apply the appropriate operation to solve the problem.	Learn what operation matches a particular schema or diagram and how to apply the operation for solving the problems.
Ask if the answer made sense.	After solving the problem, ask students to determine if the answer made sense. For instance, students can be prompted to consider if they should end up with more or less than what the largest number in the problem is.
Check the work.	Use the reverse operation to determine if their answer is correct.

a problem. Such instruction routines incorporate both principles of effective direct instruction and cognitive instruction. The routines teach students explicitly how to use the strategy while helping them to understand the cognitive processes that effective learners typically engage in as they execute the steps of the strategy. The purpose of well-designed strategy instruction is to enable students to take control over the strategy so that they can mediate their own learning. In Table 7.12, we outline major steps teachers can follow in providing strategy instruction. These steps comprise the most common approach used to teach cognitive strategies in numerous research studies.

To promote students' ability to regulate their own learning when using strategies, teachers should help students set goals for learning a strategy and then assist them in monitoring how their performance improves as a result of using the strategy (Reid & Lienemann, 2006). Once a strategy is introduced and the teacher provides a rational for its use, teachers should help students develop goals for learning and using the strategy. Goals should be achievable in a short period of time. For instance, a student could commit to using the summarization strategy every day for 1 month in order to increase his or her comprehension scores on weekly reading quizzes. Students could then create a chart that helps them keep track of how much they used the strategy and grades on weekly quizzes.

TABLE 7.12. Steps of Effective Strategy Instruction

Strategy steps	What the teacher and students do during each step
Selecting an appropriate strategy for instruction	The teacher identifies an area of student need, such as generating an organized essay, and then selects a research-based strategy to address that need.
Providing a rationale for using the strategy	The teacher must help students understand why a selected strategy is useful. During this step, the teacher helps students understand how a particular strategy can help them and the conditions under which it can be used.
Modeling the strategy while thinking aloud	The teacher describes steps of the strategy and shows students how to use it while thinking aloud, demonstrating the cognitive processes involved in completing each step of the strategy. The teacher is describing how he or she is thinking while using the strategy. For example, a teacher might say, "Let's see, in order to summarize this passage, I first have to look for ideas that are repeating themselves. Hmm . . . the title is about seals. In the first paragraph, it talks about where seals live. In the second paragraph, it talks about what seals eat."
Guided practice using the strategy	The teacher guides students to think aloud while performing the steps of the strategy. The teacher also provides students with multiple opportunities to apply the strategy under his or her guidance or the guidance of peers. While practicing, the teacher provides students with high-quality feedback, helping them understand both what they did correctly and what they will need to do specifically to improve their performance. The teacher should be aware that if he or she is providing too much corrective feedback to remediate student mistakes or misunderstandings, he or she should consider remodeling the strategy. The teacher must keep in mind that the purpose of guided practice is to move students toward independent and fluent strategy use.
Independent practice using the strategy	Students practice with materials and tasks that are similar to those used during guided practice. Students should be able to demonstrate facile use of the strategy. If students need too much support at any point during independent practice, the teacher should consider remodeling and/or providing more guided practice.
Maintenance and generalization practice	Once students have mastered the strategy with more controlled materials, the teacher then needs to ensure that students will continue to maintain strategy use and apply their learning to different types of texts. For instance, students should be able to use a summarization strategy when describing passages from a novel or sections of social studies and science texts. To facilitate strategy maintenance and generalization, the teacher will have to help students identify those situations in which they can use strategies and reinforce them for doing so.

Integrating Technology into Strategy Instruction

Technology can be a powerful tool for teaching strategies. Teachers can use technology to provide instruction in strategies, both in terms of modeling strategies and supporting students during guided and independent practice. Additionally, technology can be used to scaffold students struggling to apply the strategy independently. Likewise, technology (e.g., video, audio, interactive features) can enhance strategy implementation by combining multiple components of varied strategies into one tool. In this section, we provide information about how various available technologies can be used to accomplish these three broad instructional goals in reading, writing, and mathematics.

Reading Strategies

Teachers can use technology to model strategic processes in reading, as well as to support students during guided and independent practice. There are multiple technologies available to support students with disabilities when learning or using reading comprehension strategies that increasingly incorporate text-to-speech and tools for strategic instruction. As an example, with the software program entitled *Read and Write 3 Gold* (see *www.texthelp.com*), teachers can use several tools to teach summarization or note taking. Teachers can scan text to be projected. Once the text is projected, teachers can highlight text to show students how ideas are repeated and model for students how repeated ideas can be used to form the main idea. Additionally, they can help students use main ideas from various portions of a text to summarize sections of the text. After teaching students how to find the main idea, teachers can show students how to highlight and extract text to form an outline of main ideas and key supporting details. Students can use these outlines to study or develop research papers.

Teachers can also use software programs to provide extra instruction in reading comprehension strategies. *Thinking Reader,* developed through a collaborative effort involving the Center for Applied Special Education Technology (*www.cast.org*) and Tom Synder Productions (see *www.tomsnyder.com*), uses digitized text to provide students with instruction in seven reading comprehension strategies (e.g., summarization, prediction, clarification, and visualizing). After providing initial instruction in these strategies, teachers can tailor the program to work on specific strategies for students continuing to struggle. Additionally, the program provides students with both vocabulary and decoding supports that enable students to devote their attention to learning the comprehension strategies. For instance, students can click on a word they do not know and view its definition or have the text read to them.

A feature of both Read and Write 3 Gold and Thinking Reader that also improves comprehension is the text-to-speech function. Research shows that hearing the text read by a fluent, mature reader helps students with disabilities access and better understand the reading material. While these computerized read-alouds should not replace comprehension instruction, they can provide a scaffold during comprehension instruction. Increasingly text-to-speech software functions are available to students with disabilities at no cost. The National Instructional Materials Accessibility Standard (NIMAS; *nimas.cast.org*) guides production and electronic distribution of digital versions of textbooks and other instructional materials so they can be more easily converted into accessible formats. Access to digital materials has increased text-to-speech options, making audio output for reading an almost universal feature in classrooms today. Thus, struggling readers can see and hear the text, have each word/sentence/paragraph highlighted as the text is read aloud, and often have components of the strategies (e.g., prompts to preview or summarize text) infused as a central part of the tool.

The beauty of these software programs is that students can use them when working with peers or independently. For instance, after teachers have provided initial instruction in modeling how to summarize text, students can work with peers to highlight repeated patterns in text, so that the teacher can see how they determine ideas that are similar and draw on those ideas to develop a summary statement. Moreover, with Thinking Reader, teachers can set the program to provide more limited support as students acquire facility with the strategies.

Writing Strategies

In writing, software programs are available for teaching students how to organize their ideas prior to generating text. *Inspiration* (see *www.inspiration.com*) is an excellent example of one such tool. As discussed in Chapter 6, these programs can be used to create semantic maps of key concepts or ideas. However, unlike paper-pen/pencil maps, Inspiration (grades 6–12) or *Kidspiration* (PreK–5) generates semantic maps that revolve around images, shapes, colors, and patterns, allowing the user (both teacher and student) to quickly replace a picture with a shape and so on. If context can be enhanced through a digital image, these can be easily imported. Any text can be recorded and videos can be downloaded into maps (video limited to Inspiration). The use of images, audiotext, and videos can support students challenged by the mechanics of generating written text to organize and develop their ideas prior to generating text.

Teachers can also use these tools to model how semantic maps can be generated to assist the planning process for writing. Further, once the semantic web is developed, teachers can show their students how to develop their ideas by switching to the outlining tool. When students are ready, outlines and semantic maps created in Inspiration or Kidspiration can be exported to *Microsoft Word*, providing them with a structure to use when generating text. At this point, the teacher can model how notes collected during the research process, perhaps using Read and Write 3 Gold software, can be used to develop a detailed outline prior to generating text. Additionally, once detailed outlines are imported into a word-processing program, speech-to-text software can be used to generate the text. Speech-to-text software enables students to generate ideas by speaking into the computer (e.g., *WordQ, Dragon Naturally Speaking*), freeing them from struggles with handwriting and spelling (see *www.wordq.*

com). This example demonstrates how various technologies can be integrated successfully to support the writing needs of students with high-incidence disabilities.

Once students generate a written draft, word-processing programs, such as *Microsoft Word*, have editing features, such as grammar and spell check, that teachers can use to help students learn how to revise their text. As with reading, teachers can encourage students to use these technology applications during the guided and independent practice phases of strategy instruction. In fact, doing so would enable students with disabilities to make technology an important tool for their future literacy needs.

Comprehensive technology packages are also available to support students in using writing strategies and accommodate difficulties they experience with writing mechanics. An example of a comprehensive technology package for writing is Don Johnston's *SOLO* (see *www.donjohnston.com*). The *SOLO Literacy Suite* combines word prediction, a text reader, a graphic organizer, and a talking word processor into one interactive application. For example, *SOLO's Draft Builder* helps the struggling writer by providing a talking graphic organizer tool that enables the student to generate ideas. Specifically, the student can grab digital ideas (e.g., main ideas and details from digital text) or any information produced digitally and then organize these ideas into an outline. Then, when the student moves on to constructing and/or expanding complete sentences, *SOLO's Co-Writer* offers a word-prediction program that enables him or her to enhance vocabulary while improving grammar and spelling. Finally, *SOLO's Write Outloud* offers a talking word processor that enables students to hear what they wrote and revise their paper accordingly. Tools also include talking spell and homonym check, teacher features to direct strategic writing, and a graphic tool and menu bar for enhanced use. For example, to enhance the quantity and/or detail of the student's writing, a teacher could offer specific questions, directions, or steps of a proven strategy within the text of the document. Write Outloud also contains a locking tool that prevents the student from modifying the directions/questions/steps; thus, the teacher is guaranteed that students will have strategic supports immediately available within their unique document. The tool and menu bars also feature icons developed for easy comprehension and application. If the student wishes to center an image or text, he or she selects the align tool that moves him or her sequentially through left, center, and right alignment. Although similar to other word-processing applications (e.g., *Microsoft Word*), the icon image and its intuitiveness lends itself to easy student use.

Mathematics Strategies

Technology programs in mathematics can also be used to help teachers in inclusive classrooms work with students to develop problem-solving strategies. Software applications like Inspiration/Kidspiration or *Go Solve Word Problems* (see *www.tomsnyder.com*) can assist students in learning schema-based problem-solving approaches. With Inspiration/Kidspiration teachers and students can use the graphic organizer and visual learning application to develop schemas (e.g., color-based, shapes, object-oriented) that students are taught to use in translating a word problem into a mathematical equation. Of course, audio prompts, video illustration, graphics to build context, and similar components can easily be added to maximize learning. For example, a blue rectangle could represent the sum of an equation enhanced with an audio prompt that when selected describes/defines the sum and offers strategies to identify the sum within a word problem. Similarly, in Go Solve Word Problems, students are taught to recognize various problem schemas (as discussed earlier in this chapter) and select graphic organizers to represent various word problems. Worked examples are also presented to show students how they would develop a graphic organizer for solving the problem. An added benefit of this software program is that students can personalize word problems by adding their name to the problem or changing other aspects of the problem to represent objects or activities they enjoy. Such an approach has been demonstrated in a few research studies to improve student motivation for solving word problems.

CHAPTER 8

Building Fluent Skills Use

Study Guide Questions

- Why is instruction that fosters fluency important for students with high-incidence disabilities?
- What instructional practices are effective for building fluency across content areas?
- In what ways can teachers use technology to enhance students' fluency of essential skills across content areas?

THE CASE OF SHANNON

Shannon is a bright child in Ms. Hornet's fourth-grade classroom. In kindergarten and first grade, Shannon experienced considerable difficulties learning to read. Although she had strong oral language skills and seemed to comprehend information easily, she struggled to learn sounds and decoding patterns. Though Shannon is now reading and comprehending text on grade level, she still seems to have difficulty decoding novel words and her spelling skills are quite depressed. Currently, Shannon is receiving accommodations through a 504 plan. One of these services is a scribe so that she can write successfully on the state assessment. Ms. Hornet has noticed that when Shannon uses a scribe that she produces very interesting narrative text that is fairly well organized and rich in detail. Thus, Ms. Hornet thought it might be a good idea for

Shannon to use a computer when writing so that she could benefit from the spell-check capabilities of the software.

Shannon enjoyed using the computer to develop her written assignments, but that did not seem sufficient. Ms. Hornet noticed that Shannon's essays were not as elaborate as they were when she scribed for Shannon. She also noticed that Shannon misspelled many words, often failed to use capitalization and punctuation appropriately, and developed sentences that were grammatically incorrect. Ms. Hornet would tell Shannon to check her work, but Shannon often would just give up and refuse to try. Ms. Hornet went to her special education colleague, Mr. Futura, and asked if he could help her motivate Shannon. Mr. Futura explained that Shannon was not motivated because her spelling problems were creating enormous difficulties when generating text, even though she was using a word processor. Mr. Futura and Ms. Hornet worked together to help Shannon receive more intensive instruction in decoding and spelling. They also researched whether technology could be used to help Shannon; they found that speech-to-text software might enable Shannon to generate text more easily. Once the text was generated, Shannon could use grammar and spell check to edit her work. After 3 months, Shannon was showing some improvement in her ability to generate text, plus she was less resistant when asked to edit her writing.

WHAT SHOULD TEACHERS KNOW ABOUT FLUENCY BUILDING?

Fluent use of certain skills and concepts is essential to becoming a competent learner. If students develop fluent use of basic literacy and numeracy skills, they are better able to engage in higher order cognitive skills, as their cognitive capacity for learning new material is not diminished by weak facility with basic skills. In particular, fluent reading of connected text is essential to comprehension. When students are able to read words effortlessly, they have more cognitive capacity left to process the text's meaning. Similarly, the ability to write words easily and quickly and to retrieve vocabulary enables students to generate written text more readily, leaving more cognitive capacity for monitoring and revising text. Likewise, facility in recalling basic math facts and retrieving algorithms from memory for solving math problems affords students greater capacity to learn more challenging mathematics. In this chapter, we focus on fluency development and what teachers should know to foster fluency in reading, writing, and mathematics.

Reading Fluency

The National Assessment of Educational Progress (NAEP) defines *reading fluency* as the ability to read text "with speed, accuracy, and with proper expression" (2000, p. 11). The ability to read fluently depends on efficient processing at the word, sentence, and text level. Students who are able to read fluently demonstrate decoding efficiency. They are able to retrieve both orthographic (letters and spelling) and complimentary phonological information (speech sounds) rapidly and effortlessly when reading words. For example, students with decoding efficiency quickly recognize that the vowel combination *oa* is pronounced with a long *o* sound. For most students, repeated exposure to sound–letter relationships allows them to quickly retrieve common patterns or phonograms in words (e.g., *-oat, -an, -at, -eat*), aiding their ability to rapidly recognize words.

In addition to processing orthographic and phonological information quickly, fluent readers simultaneously and quickly process semantic, morphological, and syntactic knowledge about words. Students with semantic knowledge easily retrieve the meaning of a word, and such automatic retrieval supports decoding. Students with morphological knowledge quickly recognize both the orthographic representation and the meaning of morphemes (e.g., *please* in *pleasant* and *sincere* in *sincerely*). Students also have syntactic knowledge of words or an understanding of how words function in sentences (e.g., adjectives typically come before nouns in English). Strong readers retrieve all of this information effortlessly to process individual words while they are reading and to make sense of text simultaneously (Wolf et al., 2000; Wolf et al., 2009). Teachers should understand that the relationship between reading fluency and reading comprehension is strong and that fluent reading is acquired over years of substantial practice in these various subskills as well as through practice reading connected text (NAEP, 1995, 2000, 2001).

Students with mild disabilities are typically less fluent readers. Their oral reading is slow, they hesitate while decoding individual words, they may group words together in ways that do not mirror spoken language, and they experience serious comprehension deficits. Consequently, dysfluent readers lack motivation to read and spend little time reading. Reading fluency is difficult to remediate in struggling readers because they may experience difficulties in all or some of the subcomponents of fluency mentioned earlier (Hudson, Pullen, Lane, & Torgesen, 2009; Torgesen, Rashotte, & Alexander, 2001; Torgesen, Rashotte, Alexander, Alexander, & MacPhee, 2003; Wolf et al., 2009). Therefore, fluency instruction that focuses on multiple aspects of reading is important for students with reading difficulties.

Writing Fluency

Like fluent reading, fluent writing involves integrating many skills and processes, and developing "multiple aspects of competence" (Graham & Harris, 2005, p. 20). When students write, they simultaneously rely on thinking, memory, sustained attention, spelling, and handwriting (or typing). Despite the complexities of written expression, U.S. elementary school teachers report teaching writing for only about 15 minutes each day (Gilbert & Graham, 2010); other studies reveal that students may actually write for fewer than 30 minutes each week (Graham & Harris, 2003). These findings may explain why many students, particularly students with disabilities and those from minority groups, repeatedly fail to attain acceptable levels of writing proficiency on achievement measures (e.g., Salahu-Din, Persky, & Miller, 2008). Disregarding this lack of writing progress is counterproductive given that students are regularly required to use written expression to demonstrate what they know in elementary, secondary, and postsecondary education, underscoring the need for strong writing skills and knowledge.

Researchers have found that spelling and handwriting fluency influence students' ability to produce written text, accounting for differences in quality and length of papers produced by developing writers (Graham, Berninger, Abbott, Abbott, & Whitaker, 1997; Graham, Harris, & Chorzempa, 2002). Facility with vocabulary and syntax (i.e., the structure or grammar of language) also influences the ease with which students can write. Effective writing instruction addresses all of these multiple aspects of writing fluency.

Mathematics Fluency

The National Research Council (NRC; 2001) published a comprehensive view of mathematical proficiency as involving five intertwined strands: (1) adaptive reasoning, (2) strategic competence, (3) conceptual understanding, (4) productive disposition, and (5) procedural fluency. In this chapter, we focus on mathematics *procedural fluency*, or the "knowledge of procedures, knowledge of when and how to use them appropriately, and skill in performing them flexibly, accurately, and efficiently" (NRC, 2001, p. 121). Even though we are turning our attention to procedural fluency, we want to emphasize its close relationship with the other four strands. Students must comprehend basic addition, subtraction, multiplication, and division in order to use computational procedures accurately and efficiently. Procedural fluency then facilitates students' mathematical problem solving, and allows them to focus on justifying and explaining their answers, and working diligently and confidently to understand and use more complex mathematics over time. The five strands are "interwoven and interdependent" (NRC, 2001, p. 5) and important for teachers to consider collectively when designing optimal mathematics instruction.

Fluency with mathematics procedures is a common learning problem for students with mild disabilities, attributable, in part, to memory problems (Geary, 2004). Computational speed has been found to be a significant predictor of word-problem-solving performance (Zentall & Ferkis, 1993), explaining why these students may also experience delays and difficulties with mathematics problem solving (Pellegrino & Goldman, 1987). Lack of procedural fluency also affects students' involvement in math class discussions (Woodward & Baxter, 1997) and their mathematics use in daily living (Royer, Tronsky, Chan, Jackson, & Marchant, 1999). Instruction designed to enhance mathematics procedural fluency, and also foster conceptual understanding, is essential for all students, but particularly important for those students who struggle to learn. We now turn to a series of discussions of research-based instructional strategies for building fluency in reading, writing, and mathematics.

EFFECTIVE INSTRUCTIONAL STRATEGIES FOR BUILDING FLUENCY

Reading

Although some students develop fluent reading by simply reading, many students require specially designed, teacher-guided instruction in order to become fluent readers. Specifically, students with reading difficulties require targeted instruction in the subcomponents of reading as well as multiple, supported opportunities to read connected text to become more fluent readers. Chard, Pikulski, and McDonagh (2006) advocate a "deep construct" (p. 48) of reading fluency that incorporates multiple aspects of reading and teaching practices into a single instructional approach for struggling readers. A discussion of these aspects of reading and how to improve reading fluency in these areas follows.

Developing Decoding Efficiency

To develop decoding efficiency, teachers need to use powerful decoding strategies combined with fast-paced practice in phonograms. Two powerful strategies for teaching decoding incorporate blending and segmenting with letters. Teachers help students consciously blend each letter–sound correspondence in a word (e.g., /s/, /a/, /t/ in the word *sat*) by using strategies such as stretched blending. In particular, the teacher helps students learn to hold out a sound, without stopping between sounds, as they point to its corresponding letter, thereby helping students attend to each letter–sound in the word, and at the same time, realize that the sounds combine to make a word (e.g., /mmmmaaaat/ is blended together to then produce the word *mat*). Alternatively, they can also break the word *mat* into its individual sounds using letter tiles (i.e., segmenting). Once students learn single letter–sound correspondences, they learn to identify letter combinations in words (e.g., /ea/ in *peach*). Again, stretched blending and segmenting will be used. For instance, while students learn the *oa* letter combination, the teacher uses small tiles with printed letters to segment the word *float* into four continuous sounds (i.e., /f/, /l/, /oa/, and /t/). The long *o* sound represents the vowel combination *oa*. After spelling the word, the teacher then points to each letter–sound correspondence and asks students to slowly blend them together. This combination of stretched blending and segmenting with letter–sounds helps students consolidate their orthographic and phonological knowledge.

Another strategy that assists teachers in developing decoding efficiency is *analogizing*. In this strategy, students are taught to use both new and known words to decode novel words. As an illustration, teachers help students understand that the word *each* can be used to decode the word *impeach*. Analogizing is most powerful when combined with stretched blending and rapid practice (Lovett, Lacerenza, & Borden, 2000). In a rapid practice routine, the teacher works with students on several key words they have been learning (e.g., *oat, each,* and *eat*). First, the teacher quickly reviews the words students have been learning, and then encourages them to rapidly decode new words using these words (e.g., *goat, float, beach, teach, feat,* and *treat*).

Developing Sight-Word Efficiency

Sight words, or high-frequency words, are words that students encounter in most anything they read and should therefore recognize instantly. A sample of sight words found in early elementary school texts include *from, people, little, said,* and *something.* Readily available lists of sight words include the *Dolch Sight Word List* and *Fry's 300 Instant Sight Words;* similar lists are found in teacher's manuals of basal reading series.

Although good readers may learn sight words simply by reading a wide range of print materials (e.g., books, magazines, newspapers) and genres (e.g., narrative, expository, poetry), students with disabilities and other struggling readers do not read widely and require regular opportunities to practice reading in school. O'Connor (2007) discusses principles for effective sight-word teaching in another book in this series, *Teaching Word Recognition: Effective Strategies for Students with Learning Difficulties.* She suggests that teachers (1) practice new, or unknown, sight words in isolation before practicing them with other known words; (2) review sight words daily until students can read them on multiple occasions across different types of text (stories and information text); (3) avoid teaching sight words that students may confuse (e.g., *pen* and *pin*) in the same lesson; and (4) teach sight words as a part of a comprehensive approach to reading instruction that also addresses decoding, reading of connected text, comprehension, spelling, and writing. O'Connor also describes a number of evidence-based strategies for increasing students' sight-word fluency. Constant time delay and speeded word recognition are teaching techniques that provide opportunities for fast-paced practice. Constant time delay is used to teach a small number of new words, while speeded word recognition could be used to review a longer list of words. *Word walls* and *word banks* also allow students to review previously taught sight words. An overview of these practices is provided in Table 8.1.

Reading Connected Text

Repeated readings is supported by research on effective instructional practices for building reading fluency, and has been found to improve reading fluency in elementary students with learning disabilities (Chard, Vaughn, & Tyler, 2002). Having multiple opportunities to practice reading connected text with corrective feedback can improve reading rate, accuracy, and comprehension (Chard et al., 2002), and students will make greater gains in reading fluency when they read text matched to their reading level (O'Connor et al., 2002). In particular, comprehension is enhanced when students hear a teacher read a text passage first, or listen to a recording of the passage, before reading the passage on their own. Teaching assistants and adult

TABLE 8.1. Effective Practices for Developing Sight-Word Efficiency

Teaching strategy	Teaching procedures
Constant time delay	1. The teacher presents five new word cards, one at a time, by first saying the word, waiting 3 seconds, then asking students to say the word (this can be done as a group or individually). 2. After the first trial, the teacher mixes up the words, shows students the word, waits 3 seconds, then asks students to identify each word. 3. If students identify the words correctly, the teacher praises them. 4. If students incorrectly identify a word, the teacher supplies the word and points out a noteworthy feature (e.g., "Remember that *something* has two words in it, *some* and *thing*."). 5. The teacher repeats procedures 1 through 4 until students correctly identify each word twice.
Speeded word recognition	1. The teacher provides students with a list of 25 recently taught and learned sight words. 2. Students read the words as quickly as possible (a rate of one word per second is ideal). 3. On subsequent days, the teacher presents the list again but reordered.
Word wall and word bank	1. *Word wall*—The teacher arranges previously taught and learned sight words alphabetically or by letter patterns (e.g., *-ike* words such as *like, hike, Mike, bike*) on a bulletin board or wall in the classroom. 2. Students practice word wall lists with peers or in small- and large-group instruction with the teacher. 3. *Word bank*—Using a data-processing program such as *Excel*, teachers store sight words in electronic files that are updated as students learn new words. Files can be used to create *speeded word recognition* lists.

tutors can also serve as reading models if they are well trained. Even peers with proficient reading skills can be effective models if they are carefully chosen, prepared, and monitored by the teacher. Although fluent and independent silent reading is a fundamental goal of fluency instruction, in-class silent reading with insufficient teacher guidance and feedback has little support from the research literature. In short, allocated time for reading instruction is better spent providing direct instruction in fluency and its subskills. Table 8.2 provides several instructional approaches to repeated readings that are appropriate for improving the reading fluency of students in inclusive classrooms.

Two well-researched approaches to building text fluency are *classwide peer tutoring* and *peer-assisted learning strategies* (Haager & Klingner, 2005; Maheady, Harper, & Malette, 2003). Classwide peer tutoring (CWPT) refers to a set of instructional strategies in which peers teach each other skills and strategies in reading, spelling, and math. These peers are trained and monitored by classroom teachers. The oldest approach to improving oral reading fluency, CWPT has been researched for nearly

TABLE 8.2. Repeated Readings

Instructional approaches	Procedures
Reading with an adult	• The adult reads the text first, modeling appropriate speed and prosody. • The student reads the same passage to the adult as the adult provides corrective feedback and encouragement. • The student rereads the passage until the desired level of performance is attained (this may require three to four rereadings).
Reading with a peer	• More fluent readers are paired with less fluent readers. • The more fluent reader reads the passage first, modeling appropriate speed and prosody. • The less fluent reader reads the passage again while the stronger reader provides corrective feedback and encouragement. • The less fluent reader rereads the passage until he or she is able to read it independently. • *Note*: Peers with similar fluency levels may read together after the teacher has read the passage with them.
Reading with an audio recording	• The student follows along, pointing to each word, as he or she listens to an audio recording of the passage. • The recording is played again while the student tries to read along with the tape. • The student should continue to read along with the recording until he or she is able to read the passage independently. • *Note*: Record the passage reading at 80–100 words per minute.
Choral reading	• The teacher reads a big book, poem, or passage aloud. • The teacher and students then reread the text in unison. • The teacher and students reread the text several times, over a few days, until students are able to read the text independently. • *Note*: Students must be able to see the big book or have individual copies of the text to participate in choral reading.

30 years in general education classrooms. In a CWPT approach teachers use oral reading fluency scores to rank students from fastest to slowest. The teacher then splits the group in half, so that there is a more-fluent and a less-fluent group. The teacher then pairs the fastest reader in each group, the second fastest readers, and so on, until all the students have been paired. The point of this pairing arrangement is to avoid the frustration that might occur when a very fluent reader is paired with a very dysfluent reader. Also, even the least fluent readers will end up being paired with readers that are more typical in their skills. Once the readers have been paired, the teacher provides students with reading materials geared to the level of the less fluent reader in the pair and teaches them to engage in the following routine:

- The stronger reader reads aloud for 5 minutes, while the weaker reader makes note of errors. After 5 minutes, they switch roles.
- When the peer reading makes a mistake, the peer playing the tutor role asks the reader to stop. The peer tutor tells the reader: "You missed that word. Can you figure it out?" If the peer reading cannot figure out the word in 4 seconds, the peer tutor says: "That word is _____. What word?" The peer tutor then asks the peer reader to read the sentence again.
- After 5 minutes, the peer tutor records the number of words read correctly with the peer reader prior to switching roles.

Peer-assisted learning strategies expand the CWPT routine to include two key comprehension skills: summarization and prediction. To teach summarization, students engage in an activity called *paragraph shrinking*.

- After students have finished the repeated reading routine, the stronger reader continues reading the new text and stops to summarize a paragraph after reading for 5 minutes.
- The weaker reader then asks the stronger reader to "Name the who or what. Tell the most important thing about the who or what. Say the main idea in 10 words or less."
- The two peers switch roles and repeat the routine with the next portion of the passage.

To teach students to make predictions, students are taught *prediction relay*. They can do this simultaneously with paragraph shrinking.

- The stronger reader, prior to reading the new text, makes a prediction about what will happen next.
- The stronger reader reads a half page, then checks to see if the prediction came true and then uses the paragraph shrinking strategy.
- The stronger reader repeats this process for 5 minutes. After 5 minutes, the stronger reader switches with the weaker reader and they repeat the process.

To be successful with paragraph shrinking and prediction relay, either the general or special education teacher will need to provide direct instruction to the class in using the strategies. They must help students understand what characterizes a strong summary statement and prediction.

In Chapter 4 on assessment practices, we briefly discussed oral reading fluency (ORF). Fluency-based measures, such as ORF, have been found to be reliable and valid measures that accurately identify individual differences among students, and as such can be used as part of the screening, diagnostic, progress monitoring process. ORF measures, collected at least once a week, can also serve to help students monitor their own progress and therefore be powerful instructional tools.

In this chapter, we present additional information related to ORF from the work of Hasbrouck and Tindal (2006). These authors provide ORF national norms for grades 1 through 8 to allow teachers to make important placement and instructional decisions about their own students. According to the authors, scores collected in either the fall, winter, or spring that are within 10 words above or below the 50th percentile should be considered within the average range for grade-level performance at that time of year. In Table 8.3, we provide norms for grades 1 through 5. For a full list of norms for grades 1 through 8, see Hasbrouck and Tindal (2006).

Hudson, Lane, and Pullen (2005) provide specific procedures for measuring ORF that include the following:

1. Identify a passage of text written at the student's grade level.
2. Ask the student to read the passage aloud for 1 minute.

TABLE 8.3. Oral Reading Fluency Rate Norms

Grade level	Percentile	Fall (WCPM)	Winter (WCPM)	Spring (WCPM)
1	90		81	111
	75		47	82
	50		23	53
	25		12	28
	10		6	15
2	90	106	125	142
	75	79	100	117
	50	51	72	89
	25	25	42	61
	10	11	18	31
3	90	128	146	162
	75	99	120	137
	50	71	92	107
	25	44	62	78
	10	21	36	48
4	90	145	166	180
	75	119	139	152
	50	94	112	123
	25	68	87	98
	10	45	61	72
5	90	166	182	94
	75	139	56	168
	50	110	27	139
	25	85	99	109
	10	61	74	83

Note. WCPM, words read correctly per minute.

3. Mark any uncorrected word-reading errors (e.g., substitutions, omissions, reversals) made by the student.

4. Determine ORF by dividing the number of words read correctly per minute (WCPM) by the total number of words read (WCPM + any uncorrected errors).

Finally, compare student's performance to grade-level norms presented in Table 8.3. If students are below grade level, the teacher will want to choose measuring progress passages for that are less frustrating for the student to read. For instance, if a fourth-grade student is reading at a level commensurate with other fourth-grade students in the bottom 25%, then the teacher might want to drop back to third-grade passages and do an ORF timing until the students can comfortably read these passages at about 120 words per minute. At this point, the teacher can move the students back to fourth-grade passages.

Weekly ORF measures can be used to monitor student progress and help students learn to monitor their own progress in fluency. After a timed reading, students can graph the number of words they read correctly. In addition, students can make goals for improvement, such as reading two more words correctly per week. Research in reading has demonstrated fluency's importance in the development of proficient readers. Fortunately, a number of effective assessment and instructional practices are available for use in inclusive classrooms. As teachers use these practices, and remain mindful of struggling students' need for intensive and explicit fluency instruction that addresses multiple aspects of reading (i.e., decoding, sight words, connected text), better reading outcomes for all students are possible.

A Comprehensive Approach

Table 8.4 presents one of the most comprehensive, well-researched approaches for fluency building. This approach can be used in tiered instruction, as it is more appropriate for teaching small groups of elementary school students who need intensive instruction. Maryanne Wolf and her colleagues (Wolf et al., 2000, 2009) have developed the RAVE-O (Retrieval, Automaticity, Vocabulary Elaboration, Orthography) reading program, a comprehensive instructional approach designed for students who experience great difficulty with reading fluency. RAVE-O integrates three primary aspects of reading development (i.e., phonology, orthography, and semantics) during small-group instruction with second- or third-grade students. Wolf and her colleagues argue that students will retrieve words more efficiently in passages if the connections between the phonology, orthography, and semantic information about words are strengthened.

A brief overview of the RAVE-O program components is presented in Table 8.4. This approach can be used by general education teachers, special education teachers, and even paraprofessionals, making it a preferred option for tiered instruction. For a more thorough discussion of the program, consult the articles listed above, or

TABLE 8.4. Summary of RAVE-O Program Components

Activities and manipulatives	Description	What the teacher and students do	Skill(s) addressed
Spelling or orthographic pattern cards	Color-coded cards with high-frequency rime patterns, onsets, and suffixes. For example: For the word *cat*, *c* is the onset and *at* is the rime; *-ed* is a suffix.	The teacher helps students manipulate the cards to build and deconstruct words.	Letter–sound correspondences, decoding, common orthographic patterns
Core word cards	Word cards that include common rime patterns and have multiple meanings	The teacher discusses students' prior knowledge of the word meanings.	Decoding, word identification, word knowledge
Image cards	Cards with pictures and definitions of each core word	The teacher introduces the meaning of each core word. Students are involved in matching and memory games using both image and orthographic pattern cards.	Word meaning, word identification
Word wall "bricks"	Core words on larger cards that are added to a word wall display at the end of each week	The display is arranged by vowel and rime patterns, and by word meaning.	Word meaning, decoding
Spelling pattern dice	Dice printed with consonants, vowels, onsets, blends, or rime patterns	Students are guided by teachers to roll the dice to make words and to use words they constructed to form phrases and sentences.	Word recognition, common orthographic patterns, decoding, writing
Sound sliders	"Sliders" are made using file folders and lists of rime patterns on one side and onsets on the other.	With teacher guidance, students slide the folders up and down to form words.	Common orthographic patterns, decoding
Speed Wizard computer game	Five, five-level computer games (one for each vowel)	Students play the computer games independently, the teacher accesses student data and assigns levels based on student performance.	Fluency building of orthographic pattern recognition
Minute stories	Short stories written to include RAVE-O core words, rime families, and sight words and to be read completely in about 1 minute	The teacher introduces stories to students and involves them in repeated reading practice and writing activities.	All aspects of reading

access further information from the Center for Reading and Language Research at Tufts University (*ase.tufts.edu/crlr/RAVE-O/About_RAVE-O.html*).

Writing

Research demonstrates that individual differences in handwriting and spelling predict how well students write, and that mastering basic writing skills is difficult for students with learning disabilities and other low performers (e.g., Graham & Harris, 2009). To help these learners, researchers have developed supplemental strategies for spelling and handwriting instruction. These strategies have a positive impact on students' writing fluency (i.e., how much they write) and their sentence construction, as well as their handwriting and spelling skills (Graham et al., 2002). In this section, we discuss in greater detail the supplemental spelling and handwriting instruction developed by Graham and his colleagues.

Supplemental Spelling Instruction

The supplemental spelling instruction includes eight units with six 20-minute lessons per unit and seven types of lesson activities. Each unit focuses on at least two spelling patterns, as listed in Table 8.5.

Table 8.6 provides a sequence and description of spelling lesson activities included in each unit of the program. Teachers will note that this approach to spelling is powerful in that it will also help to improve students' decoding skills, a primary objective of any research-based approach to spelling instruction.

TABLE 8.5. Spelling Patterns Taught in Each Instructional Unit

- **Unit 1:** Short-vowel sounds for /a/, /e/, and /i/ in CVC, CCVC, and CVCC words.
- **Unit 2:** Short-vowel sounds for /o/ and /u/ in CVC, CCVC, and CVCC wordzs.
- **Unit 3:** Short-vowel sound for /a/ in CVC, CCVC, and CVCC words and long-vowel sound for /a/ in CVCe words.
- **Unit 4:** Short-vowel sound for /o/ in CVC, CCVC, and CVCC words and long-vowel sound for /o/ in CVCe and CCVCe words.
- **Unit 5:** Short-vowel sound for /i/ in CVC, CCVC, and CVCC words and long-vowel sound for /i/ in CVCe and CCVCe words.
- **Unit 6:** Short-vowel sounds and /ck/ at the end of monosyllabic words and long-vowel sounds and /ke/ at the end of monosyllabic words.
- **Unit 7:** Adding the suffix *-ed* to monosyllabic words with a short-vowel or long-vowel sound (i.e., the doubling rule).
- **Unit 8:** Adding the suffix *-ing* to monosyllabic words with a short-vowel or long-vowel sound (i.e., the doubling rule).

Note. CVC, consonant–vowel–consonant; CCVC, consonant–consonant–vowel–consonant; CVCC, consonant–vowel–consonant–consonant; CVCe, consonant–vowel–consonant–final *e*; CCVCe, consonant–consonant–vowel–consonant–final *e*

TABLE 8.6. Spelling Lesson Activities

Lesson 1

- *Word sorting*: The teacher helps students sort word cards (11–12 cards) into the spelling patterns emphasized in the unit (see Table 8.5). For example, students are presented with words such as *cat, bed,* and *pin*. The teacher pronounces each word once, and then again by emphasizing target sounds. The teacher then models aloud how the letters and sounds in the words are the same and different, and then discusses why each word card is sorted as such. Then students are given opportunities to sort the cards on their own with teacher monitoring and feedback.

- *Word hunt*: Teacher involves students in a hunt, or search, for words in their regular reading and writing material that fit the spelling patterns presented in the word sort.

Lesson 2

- *Word hunt check*: Students present words they found at school or at home that fit the spelling unit patterns.

- *Phonics warm-up*: Students practice identifying common letter–sound correspondences for short vowels, consonants, blends, digraphs (two letters with one sound, such as *ch* and *ea*), and rimes (e.g., *at* in the word *cat*) in words.

- *Introduction of spelling words*: The teacher helps students learn eight previously misspelled high-frequency words that correspond to the spelling-unit patterns, or words selected from lists of words that commonly appear in children's written products (e.g., Harris, Graham, & Loynachan, 1993).

- *Word study*: Students study new words using the following five steps: (1) say the word and study the letters, (2) close your eyes and say the letters, (3) study the letters again, (4) write the word three times without looking at it, and (5) check the spellings and correct any misspellings. The teacher then helps students graph the number of words spelled correctly.

- *Word building*: Using a card containing a rime introduced previously that fits one of the spelling unit patterns (e.g., *ip*), the teacher says the rime and then adds a consonant or blend at the beginning to make a word. For example, the teacher uses *n* or *fl* and models how the words *nip* and *flip* are formed. Students then work together to build real words. If they build a nonsense word, the teacher tells them it is not a real word.

- *Word hunt* (see Lesson 1).

Lesson 3 (changes from Lesson 2)

- *Word study*: Same procedures as Lesson 2, but students try to increase the number of words spelled correctly and then assess this goal by graphing the results.

- *Word building*: Teachers help students build words using a second rime that fits one of the spelling unit patterns.

(cont.)

TABLE 8.6. *(cont.)*

Lesson 4 (changes from Lesson 3)

- *Word study*: Students study the words assigned in Lesson 2 but students study using a game format taken from the Spell-it Write spelling series (Harris, Graham, Zutell, & Gentry, 1998).

- *Word building:* Teachers help students build words using a third rime that fits one of the spelling unit patterns.

Lesson 5 (changes from Lesson 4)

- *Word study*: Students use either the five-step study procedure or a spelling game to study words.

- *Word building*: Students build words using the rimes introduced in the three previous lessons.

Lesson 6

- *Unit spelling test*: Students are tested on their mastery of the eight spelling words introduced in Lesson 2.

- *Correction of test*: Students correct any misspelled words, graph the number correct, and set a goal to spell all new words correctly on the next unit test.

- *Word-building test*: Students are tested on their ability to spell words that contain the three rimes used in the word-building activity.

- *Review*: Starting with Unit 2, students review spelling patterns and skills introduced in earlier units.

Supplemental Handwriting Instruction

Despite widespread use of technology in written expression, research also suggests that a lack of basic transcription skills can negatively impact students' writing (Graham & Harris, 2005). For example, children who must focus on producing manuscript or script letters may not be able to attend to other writing processes, such as the planning and content development involved in writing. In addition to the spelling instruction discussed above, providing supplementary handwriting instruction has been found to improve students' sentence construction and overall writing output immediately after instruction up to 6 months later (Graham, Harris, & Fink, 2000). This approach to handwriting instruction includes nine units with three 15-minute lessons per unit and four types of lesson activities. Instruction in lower-case letters begins with letters that occur more frequently in English words and those deemed easier for young children to shape. The sets of letters taught within units are as follows: Unit 1 (*l, i, t*), Unit 2 (*o, e, a*), Unit 3 (*n, s, r*), Unit 4 (*p, h, f*), Unit 5 (*c, d, g*), Unit 6 (*b, u, m*), Unit 7 (*v, w, y*), Unit 8 (*x, k, z*), and Unit 9 (*j* and *q*). Zaner-Bloser (Columbus, Ohio) continuous script is used during the instructional sessions conducted with individual students. Table 8.7 provides a detailed description of the activities included in Lesson 1 of the first unit. All other units follow a similar instructional format.

Graham and Harris (2009) note that because supplemental spelling and handwriting instruction improves not only students' handwriting and spelling skills, but also their overall writing performance, this instruction should be provided during the primary grades to possibly prevent writing difficulties. Furthermore, although poor spelling and handwriting skills can constrain children's writing development, even young children are capable of learning how to use more sophisticated writing tools, such as planning strategies (e.g., Graham & Harris, 2005). This finding suggests that teachers should not use the supplemental spelling and handwriting

TABLE 8.7. Activities for Handwriting

	Lesson 1 (Letters *l*, *i*, and *t*)
Alphabet warm-up (2 minutes): Students practice naming, matching, and sequencing letters in the alphabet.	1. Students sing the alphabet song while pointing to the corresponding letters on an alphabet chart. 2. The teacher names letters on the alphabet chart while students point to each letter. 3. The teacher points to letters on the chart while students name letters. 4. The teacher says a letter and asks students what letter comes before or after it in the alphabet (the teacher uses the alphabet chart to reinforce or correct student responses).
Alphabet practice (6 minutes): Students practice writing letters in isolation.	1. The teacher traces and describes aloud how to form each of the target letters (i.e., *l*, *i*, and *t*) using cards with numbered arrows that show the direction of the strokes for each letter. 2. Students imitate the teacher, tracing each letter and describing how to form it. 3. The teacher and students discuss how the three letters are the same and different. 4. Using lined paper, students trace the target letters written with numbered arrows once and letters without the arrows, three times, using a pencil.
Alphabet rockets (5 minutes): Students copy a sentence (26–34 letters long) that contains the target letters.	1. Students write the sentence for 3 minutes. 2. Students and the teacher graph student performance and assess whether or not each student met his or her goal.
Alphabet Fun (2 minutes)	1. Students write one of the target letters in an uncommon way (e.g., very large or small) or use it as part of a picture (an insect drawn around the letter *i*). Or 2. Students practice writing the letter.

instruction without simultaneously teaching students more sophisticated writing strategies and processes such as planning, revising, and text organization.

Mathematics

Experts in mathematics education acknowledge that we need a stronger research base if we are going to teach learners that struggle. The National Council of Teachers of Mathematics (NCTM) recently acknowledged a need for "research on the various types of interventions teachers use to support struggling students develop mathematics proficiency" (Arbaugh et al., 2010, p. 26). Even though we lack a solid research base in mathematics, a few instructional approaches have been found to be effective for teaching students who experience difficulties learning mathematics concepts and skills. These strategies are outlined in Gersten et al. (2009) and include solving word problems based on common underlying structures, depicting problems visually and graphically, building fluent retrieval of basic mathematics facts, and teaching mathematics concepts and principles using explicit and systematic strategy instruction. Traditional instructional goals of mathematics learning (such as fluent retrieval of math facts) remain important, but are no longer sufficient as end goals of mathematics education. Instead, students must develop well-connected conceptual knowledge as a foundation underlying mathematical procedures. That is, students must understand "both the patterns or relationships as well as their linkages to operations" (Marshall, 1995, p. 67) to reason well mathematically.

To become proficient in basic mathematics, students must understand counting and decomposition strategies, and develop fluency in math facts (Fuchs et al., 2010). We provide modified descriptions of two researched approaches for building math fact fluency. The first approach described is designed for younger students (third graders) and involves both counting and decomposition strategies as well as practice opportunities (Fuchs et al., 2010). Teachers begin by assessing students' understanding of basic number concepts, and if necessary, teaching these concepts before intensive instruction in counting strategies, decomposition strategies, and addition and subtraction facts begins. These basic concepts and whole-number properties include:

1. The number that comes after (e.g., 5 comes after 4).
2. The commutative property of addition (e.g., $3 + 2 = 2 + 3$).
3. The additive identity property of zero (e.g., $5 + 0 = 5$).
4. The idea that a whole number can be broken down into parts in different ways (e.g., 8 can become 4 and 4 or 5 and 3).
5. The inverse relationship between addition and subtraction ($5 + 3 = 8$ and $8 - 3 = 5$).

Once students demonstrate understanding of these concepts and properties, instruction proceeds in the following order: first, teach counting strategies; second, teach decomposition strategies; and third, use practice activities to facilitate fact retrieval. When teaching counting strategies, teachers must remember that children typically use the *max strategy* (i.e., counting from the first addend, such as the 2 in 2 + 4) before they discover the more efficient *min strategy* (i.e., counting *not* from the number that occurs first but from the largest number, such as the 4 in 2 + 4). Moreover, children with mathematics difficulties do not naturally derive efficient counting and decomposition strategies and need explicit instruction to do so. Counting strategy instruction researched by Fuchs and her colleagues involves teaching the *counting up* strategy for addition and the *minus number* strategy for subtraction. When teaching decomposition strategies, children learn that whole-number sentences can be decomposed, or broken down, into parts in different ways. Students can partition and combine small numbers to find larger sums, and using the number 10 and doubles facts (i.e., facts such as 4 + 4) tend to be easier to manipulate and remember. Finally, teachers use practice activities, such as *flash card practice*, and encourage students to use counting and decomposition strategies if needed, to facilitate fact retrieval. Table 8.8 provides additional details related to these three teaching strategies.

Other researched teaching sequences and instructional strategies are also available for helping students learn multiplication facts. For example, Woodward (2006) suggests teaching the easiest multiplication facts first (i.e., 0's, 1's, doubles, perfect squares, and then 5's, 9's, and 10's). Once students are fluent with these facts, more difficult facts are taught using a doubling strategy and a number line (e.g., $6 \times 7 = 6 \times 6 + 6$ more). Facts such as 6×4 can be taught using the doubling strategy and doubling again (i.e., $6 \times 2 = 12$ and then $12 \times 2 = 24$). Number lines and arrays of blocks projected visually can be used to help students create mental pictures of the fact strategies. Furthermore, Woodward recommends helping students understand and express the connections between basic facts, extended facts, the partial product algorithm, and methods of approximating answers to multiplication problems. He also suggests using daily, 2-minute practice worksheets containing 40 facts (50% are review, 50% are new facts) to increase fluency. Table 8.9 provides a more detailed description of the components of effective multiplication fact instruction.

Developing procedural fluency, or automaticity, in math facts and algorithms remains important for improving students' mathematical competence. However, procedural fluency in the absence of conceptual understanding is not sufficient. Approaches such as those described in Tables 8.8 and 8.9, which link practice opportunities with strategy instruction, are recommended.

Integrating Technology into Strategy Instruction

With ever-expanding instructional technology, teachers now have access to some wonderful tools for practicing fluency. These tools can help students with disabilities and those who struggle secure the extra practice they definitely will need in general education classrooms. In this section, we highlight some of the tools available in reading, writing, and mathematics.

TABLE 8.8. Instructional Strategies for Remediating Math Facts

Counting strategies instruction

- If necessary, the teacher preteaches the basic number concepts as described above using number lines and manipulatives.
- Then, the teacher helps students learn two strategies. For addition, the teacher uses the following language to teach the *counting up* strategy: "Say the bigger number, then using your fingers count up with the smaller number; the answer is the last number spoken."
- For subtraction, the teacher teaches the *minus number* strategy in this way: "Say the minus number, then using your fingers, count up to the number you started with; the answer is the number of fingers used to count up."
- If students "just know" the fact, then the teacher tells them to "pull it out of their heads."

Decomposition strategies instruction

- The teacher helps students learn two types of decomposition strategies: one emphasizing facts in relation to a set of 10, the other using doubles (such as 3 + 3).
- For teaching facts in relation to the 10 set, the teacher uses a number line made up of squares with a heavy outline designating a set of 10 (as shown below) and blue (B) and yellow (Y) blocks. The blocks are used to represent the two numbers in the addition or subtraction facts.
- Start with facts that fall exactly within the heavy outline of the 10 set (e.g., 8 + 2 = 10). Note that 8 is represented by the blue blocks (B) and 2 is represented by the yellow blocks (Y) below

B	B	B	B	B	B	B	B	Y	Y										

- Once students are familiar with facts that equal 10, teach facts other than 10 (e.g., 8, 9, 11, 12) in relation to 10, in the way 9 + 5 = 14 is represented below.

B	B	B	B	B	B	B	B	B	Y	Y	Y	Y	Y						

- For a subtraction fact, such as 14 − 5 = 9, the 14 is represented by the blue blocks (B) and 5 is represented by the shaded blocks as those subtracted.

B	B	B	B	B	B	B	B	B	B	B	B	B	B						

- After the facts are represented in this way, the teacher shows students how the facts can be decomposed on the number line. For example, 14 − 5 = 9 becomes (10 + 4) − 5 = 9 or (10 - 5) + 4 = 9. The teacher adds and subtracts blocks as appropriate while talking through the changes made to the number sentence and relating the number sentence to the 10 set and relevant properties (e.g., commutative property of addition).
- Using steps similar to those described above, the teacher demonstrates how facts can be decomposed using doubles (e.g., 2 + 2, 3 + 3, 4 + 4).
- For example: 6 + 8 becomes (3 + 3) + (4 + 4) = 14.

Remedial drill and practice

Two ways to practice number combinations:

- *Flashcard warm-up* (2 minutes): The teacher shows flashcards one at a time. Cards answered correctly are placed in a correct pile. When students answer incorrectly, the teacher asks them to "count up." Students count up to produce the correct answer, but the card is placed in the incorrect pile. At 2 minutes, the number of cards answered correctly is counted, and the students graph this number on a graph.
- *Lesson-specific flashcard practice* (1 minute): Lesson-specific flashcards are the number combinations students need to know for that session's lesson. Correctly answered cards are placed in the correct pile. When students answer incorrectly, the teacher requires them to "count up," and the card is returned to the stack. After 1 minute, the number of flashcards answered correctly is counted, but the score is not graphed. On the second, third, and fourth sessions of a lesson topic, students get a chance to beat that session's lesson-specific flashcard score. The teacher reminds students of their scores from the first minute and encourages them to do better in the upcoming minute. Scoring and feedback are the same for the next minute. The teacher praises students when they beat their scores.

TABLE 8.9. Instructional Approaches for Improving Multiplication Fact Fluency

What the teacher does	What students do
1. Introduces new facts by using arrays or number lines to help students visualize the strategy *or* review previously taught strategies by using arrays or number lines.	1. Discuss the strategy taught and contrast it with previously taught strategies. Students are not required to memorize the strategies.
2. Administers 2-minute practice drills using worksheets. When the time is up, dictates answers.	2. Complete as many facts as possible in 2 minutes. Correct work by circling incorrect facts and writing the correct answers.
Various strategies include: 1. Teach the relationship between facts and extended facts (i.e., 4×2, 40×2, 400×2) using arrays of blocks or number lines.	Students' responses include: 1. Complete worksheets including 20 randomly ordered single-digit facts and extended facts without being timed.
2. Present extended facts using the partial product algorithm (e.g., 341×2 becomes 2×1, 2×40, and 2×300).	2. Complete sets of 10 problems using the algorithm.
3. Teach approximation skills by first emphasizing rounding to 10's and 100's. Use number lines to show how two-digit and three-digit numbers can be rounded to the nearest 10's or 100's.	3. Explain how to compute a multiplication problem using rounding. Complete worksheets that require rounding and computing approximate answers using extended facts.
4. Present word problems using extended facts.	4. Demonstrate how they use extended facts to find approximate answers to problems.

Building Reading Fluency

An increasing number of basal reading programs offer technology-based tools for student engagement (e.g., Earobics). However, there are also stand-alone software applications as well as websites that offer practice to develop phonological awareness, vocabulary skills, and general reading strategies. For example, Don Johnston (see *www.donjohnston.com*) has developed software applications to enhance reading fluency. *WordMaker* (see *www.donjohnston.com/resources/wordmaker___index.html*) is designed to teach phonic patterns. It does so by letting students see, hear, and spell words multiple times to aid in comprehension and retention. Each word is broken into parts and supported by audio, graphics, and simulation (where needed) to strengthen the connections between the word's orthography and phonology. Lessons progress sequentially, offering ample opportunities to practice, spell, hear, and sound out words, while data is being collected on progress. As a result, students gain in phonological awareness and their knowledge of letters and phonics.

As noted in Chapter 5, a number of text-to-speech and audio-enhanced books are increasingly available for student reading. Scholastic and similar companies sell the audio book with varied supports to enable the student to read along and listen (repeatedly if needed) to a fluent reader. Web-based resources (often free) also offer teachers and students tools to create interactive repeated reading experiencea. For example, CAST's Book Builder (see *bookbuilder.cast.org*) allows teachers, students, and parents to create, publish, share, and read digital books that embed features to support the development of proficient reading skills and offer opportunities for continued practice. Whether you build your own or select from the growing free library, the books include text, pictures, audio, text-to-speech capability, and visual and auditory prompts. Developers can select from various characters, assigning them strategic tasks to support the reader. For example, one of the characters provided (i.e., coaches) is a cute dog standing on his two hind legs. The book developer gives a name for the dog, decides the purpose of the dog (e.g., what strategy will the dog reinforce for the reader), and provides the actual text that the dog will speak and the user will see as text. Thus, as the user reads the book, the character/coach is available (via a click of the mouse) to share its thoughts on the passage, offer suggestions in how to understand the reading (e.g., comprehension strategy), and the like. For consistency, the dog would focus on the same strategy throughout the online book, offering key insight on each and every page. We should note that CAST's Book Builder offers a number of characters/coaches and allows developers to upload their own image as well. Again, the coach's thoughts, the strategy he or she emphasizes, what he or she shares on each page, and related information all comes from the book developer. Therefore, the developer, in a purposeful manner, creates a book with strategic supports for the user. Of course, multiple characters can be used simultaneously, with each developed to emphasize a particular reading strategy or to offer a particular support.

Recording your own or a student's voice offers a model for appropriate reading and further practice for the student. While Book Builder might be a preferred site, other free sites include TarHeel Reader (see *tarheelreader.org*), GenieBooks (see *www.auburn.edu/~murrag1/bookindex.html*), and Storyline Online (see *www.storylineonline.net*). For the reader who needs access to an audio reader or additional practice hearing him- or herself read, there are a number of audio recorders available for teacher and students. One of the most accessible and easy to use is Audacity (see *audacity.sourceforge.net*). Free for both the Windows and Apple platforms, Audacity allows anyone to record his or her voice digitally. For example, the teacher who wants access to audio books for the various readings she assigns could easily record these books in Audacity and save and disseminate them on a CD or as a digital audio file. Instead of a simple audio book, the teacher could add verbal prompts, suggestions, ideas about assignments affiliated with the book, and much more as he or she reads the book into Audacity. As a result, the students gain access to an audio book plus. The plus would be the added narration, the identification and definition of key vocabulary words, the emphasis of portions of the book that challenge comprehension, and the list goes on. For the busy teacher, Audacity allows students to record their own readings. They then save them to the computer or a designated place, allowing teachers and/or parents a chance to review as needed.

Building Writing Fluency

Writing is an area where a number of technology tools have infused effective approaches within a technology tool. For example, *Science Writer* (see *sciencewriter. cast.org*) incorporates thinking sheets, checklists, progress monitoring, and additional supports to aid the struggling writer. Structured around a draft, revise, and edit process in writing science reports, the web-based tool provides variable prompts including sentence starters to assist the writer in completing portions of a science report. Animated helpers walk the writer through the thought process, providing examples of how they are developing their thoughts, what they are writing, and what process they follow to complete the written assignment. Thus, Science Writer infuses multiple features of effective strategic writing instruction into its web-based tool. The Journal tool, which is part of Science Writer, even offers a forum where students can take notes, reflect on the process, revise notes, and most important, ask questions and engage a peer or his or her teacher for targeted assistance during the writing process.

Instructional prompts are increasingly integrated into word processing and technology-based writing supports to assist the troubled writer. Software similar to Don Johnston's *Co-Writer* seeks to interpret spelling and grammar mistakes and offer word suggestions (e.g., sentence starters) when needed. Dictionary and word list features individualize the application, as do linguistic predictors (e.g., learning the writer's patterns to provide appropriate spelling options for a particular word) to further support the struggling writer. Likewise, applications like *Clicker 5, Picture It*, and *Writing with Symbols* use pictures to support text whereby pictures are displayed above the words as they write. Similar to word prompts, picture prompts in the form of word lists offer students a library of pictures (words) to add to their sentence. Outcomes with word and picture prompts suggest an enhanced use of vocabulary, better spelling and grammar, improved writing fluency, and an increase in the quantity of written text. Most word prediction software works in conjunction with a number of applications (e.g., *Microsoft Word*, online browsers).

Advances in text-to-speech and speech-to-text also assist in the drafting, revising, and editing of written material. Text-to-speech engines are primarily seen as a tool for reading. However, text-to-speech engines are also applicable to the writing process, allowing the writer to review what he or she has written and listen to individual letters, words, sentences, or complete paragraphs when needed. Most text-to-speech applications feature highlighting functions providing audio as well as visual support as writers draft, edit, and revise a paper. In addition, word-processing applications often include the text-to-speech option to support the writing process. Likewise, teachers are using audio components to relay directions, offer instructional prompts within the text document, and provide regular and ongoing strategic supports as the students complete their writing. For example, demonstrating one's knowledge via a science report often challenges struggling learners. They often struggle with what to include in the various sections of the reports (e.g., introduction, results, conclusions). A science report template could embed audio directions (e.g., Inspiration and Kidspiration embed this audio recording feature) for each of the sections. The audio prompts would remind students what belongs in each section, could ask questions that need to be answered for each section, and could offer check/edit suggestions before they complete the report. Text prompts can also be available, but embedded audio prompts reinforce skill development for students that struggle to read the spoken word.

Speech-to-text is another strategic support but works in a different manner. The speech-to-text feature translates the student's speech into digital text (see *www. nuance.com*). Now, these applications demand verbal competency on the part of the user. This may limit its use for some struggling writers, but as the technology advances it will continue to offer options for students with mild disabilities.

Building Math Fluency

The drill and practice features of many technology-based solutions provide excellent outlets for fluency support, practice, and development. An example of this in mathematics instruction is Tom Snyder's *FASTT Math* (see *www.tomsnyder.com/fastt-math*). *FASTT Math* incorporates seven features to enhance math fluency including (1) identification of fluent and nonfluent facts; (2) restricted presentation of nonfluent information; (3) student generation of problem/answer pairs (e.g., students required to type each newly introduced fact connecting the two elements together, such as 3 + 9 = 12); (4) use of "challenge times"; (5) spaced presentation of nonfluent information; (6) the appropriate use of drill and practice; and (7) computer monitoring of student performance. It covers basic 0–9 and 0–12 addition, subtraction, multiplication, and division facts while offering teachers and students a baseline assessment, daily adaptive instruction focused on the student's problem facts, and independent practice where students gain fluency by practicing their learned and fluent facts.

Flashcards and other memory aides have also been enhanced via technology tools. For example, Fact Monster (see *www.factmonster.com/math/flashcards.html*) and AplusMath (see *www.aplusmath.com/flashcards*) are two of a variety of web-based flashcard sites allowing students to enhance fluency with basic math operations. These web-based flashcards offer audio, interactive images, color, and timers (to check speed); record data on accuracy; and provide other features to enhance fluency practice. Flashcard sites are also increasingly allowing teachers to customize the cards, so they can include only the facts students need to practice. Scholastic's Flash Card Maker (see *www.scholastic.com/kids/homework/flashcards.htm*) is a popular site developing both math and word flashcards. Flashcard Machine (see *www.flashcardmachine.com*) also develops flashcards for the web while allowing a download function to a student's iPod via iStudyToGo (see *www.istudytogo.com*).

In the age of computer gaming, a number of free web-based applications have been developed to support math and vocabulary fluency. One popular website is the Academics Skill Builders (see *www.academicskillbuilders.com*). The games on this website feature individual and multiplayer options in the area of multiplication, division, subtraction, addition, integers, and fractions. The games blend the features of video games with instructional research to enhance time-on-task for skill and fluency development. Students control the games via simple mouse or keyboard commands, while the games automatically track progress through items answered correctly, number of attempts, and duration of time. Like other instructional games, the intent is to provide a fun and focused repetition practice that enables fluency to be achieved more quickly through structured and rapid responding.

CHAPTER 9

Managing Inclusive Classrooms

with KRISTIN MURPHY

Study Guide Questions

- Why is classroom management essential to setting up effective learning environments?
- What contributes to students' classroom management problems?
- What are effective strategies for preventing classroom management problems?
- How can teachers intervene in more problematic behaviors?

THE CASE OF COLIN

Colin has been working on a group project during his seventh-grade social studies class. Specifically, he and his peers are developing a group project about key battles in World War II. Although Colin has a great deal of interest in this topic, his general education teacher, Ms. Adele, has noticed that he is off-task during group project time. Frequently, Colin just looks at pictures related to the project, rather than reading to gather information, or he talks and plays with peers. Ms. Adele feels frustrated and concerned about Colin's behavior

Kristin Murphy, MS, EdM, is a doctoral candidate in Special Education at the University of Florida. Her research interests focus on teacher quality and students with severe emotional and behavioral disorders.

because she realizes that it is detracting from his learning and that of other students. She also did not anticipate the problems Colin would encounter; she thought cooperative learning would be a way to accommodate students like Colin in her classroom. Feeling as if she is out of ideas, she reaches out to her special education colleague, Mr. Rios, for help.

Mr. Rios schedules a time to come and observe Colin during classroom instruction. What he notices is that Ms. Adele has strategies for helping students get started on their work and has been very clear about what she expects in the assignment. Further, Mr. Rios notices that Colin is listening and on-task until he participates in the group work. He sees that Colin is most off-task when he is supposed to be taking notes or when he has selected a text that is advanced for his grade level. Mr. Rios makes a note of this behavior, as he realizes that Colin has a great deal of difficulty with spelling and knows that taking notes would be challenging. Mr. Rios also observes that a number of students are not productive during the group project; however, they are quiet and not drawing attention to themselves. He asks Ms. Adele about the expectations she has established for the group and finds that, while she has been very clear about the assignment and her classroom rules, she has been less clear about how she expects students to contribute to the group project. Ms. Adele has not spoken with the students about behaviors expected during group project work, nor has she explicitly taught these behaviors to the students. Furthermore, she has not assigned students roles in the group, nor has she provided Colin with an alternative mechanism for expressing his ideas. Mr. Rios decides to meet with Ms. Adele to see if they can come up with a plan for making group work more productive and supportive for Colin so he can be a more successful participant.

WHY WELL-MANAGED CLASSROOMS ARE IMPORTANT FOR ALL STUDENTS

Students like Colin demonstrate discipline problems for different reasons. In Colin's case, environmental demands appear to trigger his off-task behavior. To assist Colin and other students like him, Ms. Adele needs to understand what is contributing to his discipline problems and how classroom management strategies that include academic supports can be used to help him become a productive member in his group.

Well-managed classrooms are fundamental to educating all students and particularly those with disabilities. When strong management systems are not in place, discipline problems are sure to emerge, and these problems can interfere with learning (Brophy, 1988). Discipline problems lead to off-task behaviors and reduce productive learning time, both for individual students and groups of students. Consider the classroom where the teacher spends 5 minutes getting students settled and ready to begin instruction. If she wasted 5 minutes every day, then over the course of a typical school year, she would waste over 900 minutes of instructional time. Since time spent on academic learning is essential to student learning, discipline problems that result in off-task behavior interfere with successful student learning (Seidel & Shavelson, 2007).

Effective management strategies are also important for establishing classroom communities that are calm, safe, and characterized by effective relationships among adults and students (Evertson & Weinstein, 2006). In well-managed classrooms, teachers have rules and routines that help students understand what is expected of them. Such rules and routines provide students with the sense that classroom life is predictable and safe. Additionally, when teachers are able to minimize discipline problems in their class, they are able to engage in more productive relationships with students. Teachers who have well-managed classrooms are able to interact with students in more productive and positive ways. Their attention is focused on helping students learn and reacting positively to their efforts to participate. Further, students are more likely to rate these teachers as fair, even if the teacher is demanding, and more likely to engage in productive classroom behavior that contributes to on-task learning.

In contrast, teachers who are constantly trying to curb misbehavior often resort to reprimands and punishment. Overuse of reprimands and punishment can cause anxieties in the target student and those observing the negative interactions, a situation that can result in additional disruptive behaviors (Kounin, 1970). Research demonstrates that negative and punitive teacher behavior is related to negative student responses, including withdrawal from or animosity toward the teacher, increased anxiety, or increased disruptive behavior on the part of the student or students in the class (Hyman & Snook, 1999). Students see such teachers as unfair, mean, and demanding, rather than as demanding and caring. They see these teachers as working against them rather than operating in their best interest.

Teachers with strong classroom management skills play an important role in helping students with disabilities. Many students with disabilities exhibit challenging behaviors that are the result of their learning problems or their disability. When students have experienced considerable frustration trying to learn or realize that their learning issues may expose their failings, they can engage in a variety of off-task and disruptive behaviors to avoid participating in the task at hand. For these students, learning is aversive and they will sometimes go to great lengths to avoid it. A smaller percentage of students have disabilities that result in behaviors that impede their learning. For instance, students can demonstrate attention problems, impulsive behaviors, and difficulties transitioning from one activity to another. Other students with disabilities might have problems with anxiety or aggression and can either seem withdrawn in class or overtly noncompliant. Clear expectations, well-structured tasks, sufficient academic supports, and effective behavioral interventions can go a long way toward preventing misbehavior, or helping students manage their behavior problems. Further, by setting up a well-managed classroom, teachers can engage in more positive, academically productive relationships with all of their students. By establishing positive classroom relationships, they help students with disabilities to learn more and to be viewed more favorably by their peers.

PREVENTION AND INTERVENTION

Effective classroom management depends on approaches to student behavior that involve prevention and intervention strategies (Epstein, Atkins, Cullinan, Kutash, & Weaver, 2008). Teachers must know effective strategies for both preventing student behavior problems and intervening successfully when they occur. Though we are focusing on effective classroom management strategies in this chapter, we recognize that classrooms exist in a broader school context and the quality of this school context is likely to influence the degree to which teachers can be successful. Thus, it should come as no surprise that teachers are more likely to create effective classroom environments when there are schoolwide efforts to create positive behavioral environments. In a recent research report published by the What Works Clearinghouse, U.S. Department of Education, Epstein and his colleagues (2008) found support for a schoolwide approach to managing student behavior. According to these researchers, "Positive behavior is more likely to thrive when relationships at all levels are trusting and supportive and reflect a shared commitment to establish a healthy school and community" (p. 8).

General and special education teachers working together in individual classrooms also can be more effective if they employ the following techniques for promoting positive behaviors.

- Understand inappropriate behaviors students are exhibiting and determine the antecedents or causes of those behaviors.
- Recognize that many behavior problems are preventable through setting expectations for students' behavior, establishing classroom rules and routines, employing effective instruction, and using simple management techniques.
- Use well-paced instruction and simple management strategies before more intensive strategies, such as time-out, to manage student behavior.
- Realize that other professional staff and parents can be important resources in promoting more positive behavior.

In the sections that follow, we describe what teachers need to understand and do in relationship to these techniques for improving behavior in their classrooms.

UNDERSTANDING CLASSROOM BEHAVIOR PROBLEMS

Inclusive classrooms, like all classrooms, are ecological systems. In any ecological system, the actions of any one participant are the result of events occurring in that system and the participant's response to those events (Doyle, 2006). Teachers, individual students, and peers are all participants in the classroom ecology, and each contributes to the behavior that unfolds. Discipline problems are the result of these behavioral exchanges. The first step to preventing discipline problems is to recognize what contributes to them. By recognizing contributing factors, teachers can set up learning situations and classroom environments to minimize their impact on student behavior.

How Can Teachers Contribute to Discipline Problems?

When students exhibit undesirable behaviors in a classroom, teachers must decide how they want to respond. Should they ignore the behavior, redirect the student, or reprimand the student? These responses are just a few of the available choices. What teachers must recognize is that they can minimize or contribute to discipline problems by what they say and do or fail to say and do. Consider the following scenario.

> After reviewing a new math concept, Ms. Adele asks students to start working on the problems she assigned. Most of the class has started the assignment. Colin, however, is talking to other students about the weekend and obviously ignoring Ms. Adele's second reminder that everyone needs to start their work. From across the room, Ms. Adele says, "Colin, you need to stop fooling around and get started on your work. If I have to speak to you again, you will be in danger of receiving a referral." Colin completely ignores her request and continues to talk to his friends. This time, however, his off-task behavior is even more noticeable. Also, many students in the class have stopped doing their own work to watch the unfolding exchange.

In this scenario, Ms. Adele draws negative attention to Colin and his off-task behavior. She publically reprimands Colin and threatens to punish him if he does not comply. Colin, a strong-minded student, refuses to comply by completely ignoring her and continuing to do what he wants. Both Ms. Adele and Colin are contributing to the discipline problem. Colin is making it difficult for his peers to learn by distracting them; however, Ms. Adele further disrupts the class by responding to Colin's behavior. Her reprimand causes other students to be off-task and contributes to Colin's own increased off-task behavior. Additionally, Ms. Adele may unwittingly have created other problems. If Colin's peers find humor in the situation and see his behavior as desirable, it may erode some of Ms. Adele's authority in the classroom.

What Contributes to Student Discipline Problems?

Students engage in disruptive behaviors for a variety of reasons (Levin & Nolan, 2010). Students may not understand what is expected of them in certain classroom settings. Moreover, if instruction is tedious or disorganized, students may stop paying attention or start acting silly. Other times, students are trying either to avoid situations in which they have failed or to acquire attention by acting out.

Avoiding Unpleasant Circumstances

Students, just like adults, attempt to avoid situations that are unpleasant for them (DuPaul & Barkley, 1998). Many behavior problems, such as off-task behavior or refusal to complete a task, are often the result of students' attempts to avoid tasks in which they are experiencing boredom or frustration. Particularly problematic are tasks in which students have experienced repeated failure and perhaps even ridicule from their peers for their failures. Colin's off-task behavior during the group project is the classic example of a student attempting to avoid a task that he feels incompetent to complete. No one wants to repeatedly do tasks or activities for which he or she lacks competence. Adults frequently avoid tasks they find too challenging by opting out of them or even switching careers. Students, however, cannot opt out of challenging tasks, and students with disabilities often find themselves having to complete tasks that are too challenging. In these cases, students with disabilities will demonstrate a variety of behaviors (e.g., fooling around, daydreaming, refusing to do the task, or acting out to avoid it) to escape from such unpleasant situations. Colin's off-task behavior during group work in Ms. Adele's class is the perfect example.

In other cases, students attempt to avoid a teacher or peers they view as unpleasant. They might see a teacher as unsupportive of their learning and behavioral needs. Or they might avoid peers who are teasing or intimidating them in some way. They often try to escape the situation through a variety of means, including creating a disruption, asking to see the school nurse, or going to the restroom. In these cases, students' strategies work because they get what they want: removal from the situation.

Seeking Attention or Power to Fulfill an Emotional Need

Students also engage in behaviors that seem inappropriate because they are trying to acquire something intangible, such as approval from their peers (Dreikurs, Grundwald, & Pepper, 1982). The majority of students who exhibit disruptive behavior in school are seeking attention, and they may constantly seek assistance, use excessive charm, show off, or call out. Attention-seeking students feel important when others notice them. When their needs are not met, they may resort to power to secure attention. Students who crave attention may openly challenge teachers to gain acceptance from peers. Unfortunately, such behaviors often cause teachers to feel defensive and they attempt to force the student to comply. At this point, the teacher and the student find themselves in a power struggle, a struggle that students ultimately win because they secure the approval they were seeking. Students may also exhibit inappropriate behaviors because they lack self-worth. Students with chronic behavior problems often have few ways of seeking social reinforcement. They often struggle academically and athletically and are disliked by peers, teachers, and sometimes even their parents. Their only mechanism for building up self-worth is to seek power in the classroom, usually by bothering the teacher or bullying other students.

PREVENTING CLASSROOM DISCIPLINE PROBLEMS

Teachers can prevent many discipline problems, particularly minor ones, by eliminating antecedents to common behavior problems. For instance, teachers can provide extra structure and instructional support when students are acting out in an attempt to avoid difficult tasks. These strategies are considered effective prevention strategies: (1) setting appropriate expectations for student performance and behavior; (2) developing classroom routines and rules; (3) using reinforcement and consequences appropriately; (4) designing organized, effective, and supportive instruction; (5) developing a supportive classroom context; and (6) using simple surface management techniques.

Teacher Expectations

What teachers expect from students, both academically and behaviorally, can foster learning environments that promote learning and prosocial behavior. Since the late 1960s researchers have been able to show that teachers' expectations for academic performance are tied to the amount of achievement gains students make. Students believed (by their teachers) to be academically capable often end up demonstrating greater competence than those believed to be less capable. Although teachers' expectations for performance are often accurate indicators of students' abilities (Gresham, Reschly, & Carey, 1987), the fact remains that when teachers expect students to achieve, they will.

Teachers react differently when they expect students to learn, irrespective of their disability (Jordan, Glenn, & McGhie-Richmond, 2010). Such teachers respond more proactively than teachers who believe students with disabilities cannot learn. They demonstrate self-efficacy. Although self-efficacious teachers realize that students with disabilities have limitations, they believe that they can use their knowledge and skills to assist them. Self-efficacious teachers set realistic goals, both for groups of students and individuals. Additionally, they have the needed skills to instruct students systematically and enable them to meet these realistic goals (Brophy & Good, 1974).

Less self-efficacious teachers perceive students as being limited by their disability or low achievement and unable to learn much regardless of what the teacher does. These teachers provide fewer learning opportunities to low-achieving students and students with disabilities by dismissing their responses more rather than by trying to improve their responses, criticizing their responses or rewarding inappropriate responses, interacting with these students less during instruction, and often relying on punishment more than reinforcement to change behavior (Good &

Brophy, 1987; Harris & Rosenthal, 1986). These teacher–student interactions not only diminish low-achieving students' opportunities to learn, but they also negatively impact students' sense of efficacy as learners and their behavior in the classroom. Struggling students may give up or act out to avoid academic tasks or gain the attention they cannot secure by being a successful student. In this case, the teacher becomes part of the academic and the discipline problems.

Developing Classroom Rules and Procedures

Teachers can prevent behavior problems by setting clear expectations for how students are to conduct themselves in class. Setting rules, determining consequences, and developing classroom procedures make clear expected classroom behaviors and develop group norms for interacting in a classroom.

Classroom rules provide guidance about behaviors needed for teaching and learning to take place. For rules to be effective, they must be aimed at promoting a learning environment that encourages teaching and learning, not controlling student behavior (Brophy, 1988). To develop rules, teachers should consider those behaviors that are absolutely necessary for teaching and learning to take place. Developing long lists of rules to cover every potential misbehavior is ineffective. Long lists of rules require teachers to constantly monitor behavior, leaving less time for instruction. Further, students see long lists of rules as picky and impossible to follow, and they view teachers who enforce long lists of rules as nagging and unreasonable (Levin & Nolan, 2010).

Teachers can work alone or with students to develop reasonable lists of rules that will be perceived as fair and can be adhered to without excessive monitoring (Emmer & Evertson, 2008). To develop effective classroom rules, teachers must first distinguish between general behaviors required in the classroom versus specific behaviors needed while lining up for lunch or taking a bathroom break. General behaviors are those required throughout the day to maximize engaged learning time. Specific behaviors, in contrast, are those required to perform certain tasks, such as passing out papers or lining up for lunch. When setting classroom rules, teachers must first identify key behaviors necessary for increasing academic engagement time during the day. Before meeting with their class, teachers need to consider the following question: "What are the necessary student behaviors that I need in my classroom so that student discipline problems will not occur?" (Levin & Nolan, 2010, p. 137).

Any rule that is developed must be designed to protect (1) teachers' right to teach, (2) students' right to learn, (3) students' psychological and physical safety, and (4) school and student property (Levin & Nolan, 2010). Additionally teachers need to consider the developmental needs of students when crafting rules. Young children probably cannot handle more than five rules, and for all students, rules should be stated positively in clear language. Rules should also begin with an action word. Action words communicate the behaviors needed to follow the rules (Rademacher, Callahan, & Pederson-Seelye, 1998). See Table 9.1 for examples of appropriate rules.

TABLE 9.1. Sample Rules and Associated Behaviors

Sample rule	Associated behaviors
Listen while others speak.	Look at the person talking. Acknowledge what the other person is saying by nodding or smiling. Ask questions when you do not understand. Take notes on important information. Wait until the person talking is finished before speaking or ask permission to speak.
Use appropriate language.	Avoid angry words or curse words. Use encouraging words. Give "I" messages when you are upset.

Once rules have been established, teachers must assist students in learning rules. Teachers can post the rules so that they can always refer to them; however, simply posting rules will be insufficient. Teachers need to define the behaviors associated with specific rules and then support students as they learn them (Rademacher et al., 1998). Teachers can conduct discussions with students to identify examples and nonexamples of rule-related behaviors. In Table 9.1, sample rules and associated behaviors are listed. Teachers can help students learn these rules and behaviors by reviewing what is expected of them and describing why they are important, modeling and role-playing appropriate behaviors, and reinforcing behaviors through the use of consequences. For instance, we once observed a teacher modeling how students should look when someone is speaking. First, the teacher described the behavior she expected from students: sitting up, looking, and demonstrating listening behaviors (e.g., nodding, smiling). Second, the teacher had the students show her what good attending behaviors looked like. Third, as students demonstrated appropriate behavior, she provided specific praise related to the attending behavior. Finally, she noted days when the class was doing a particularly good job of attending. Giving such feedback on behavior is an important part of teaching prosocial behaviors.

Clear classroom procedures, such as routines for passing out papers or handing in homework, also help to create well-managed classrooms. Well-designed procedures maximize on-task student behavior, as they reduce time in classroom transitions and minimize disruptions. Research shows that more effective teachers, compared to their less effective peers, spend time early in the school year explaining procedures used during learning activities and daily routines. Effective teachers, however, spend significantly less time explaining procedures after the first several months of school than their less effective colleagues (Cameron, Connor, Morrison, & Jewkes, 2008). Just as with rules, teachers have to explain and teach behaviors associated with classroom procedures. To accomplish this, teachers must consider all the essential behaviors needed for various procedures, such as lining up for lunch or recess. As an example, the following behaviors help students handle concrete manipulatives appropriately during mathematics instruction.

1. Keep all manipulatives in their appropriate container unless you are using them.
2. Only select the manipulatives you need to solve the problem.
3. Keep all manipulatives on your desk or in the container.
4. Pick up any manipulatives that fall to the floor.
5. Put manipulatives away when not in use.

Developing Consequences

Teachers must spend as much time developing consequences as they spend developing rules if they want to reinforce rule learning (Levin & Nolan, 2010). Appropriate consequences help students learn to follow rules and to develop a genuine respect for teachers, whereas the misuse of consequences, particularly punishment, can cause antagonistic, and potentially destructive, relationships to develop between students and teachers.

To develop effective consequences, teachers need to plan in advance, as doing so will help them respond in evenhanded and consistent ways when rules are broken. There are two types of consequences: natural and logical. Natural consequences are the most effective; they are events that occur, without the teachers' intervention, in response to misbehavior. For instance, a student misses an exciting activity because he was late for school, or a student falls and gets hurt because she was running down the hall. Natural consequences are believed to work because students perceive them as undesirable and occur without teacher intervention. Students realize that the consequence is the direct result of their own behavior (Dreikurs, 2004), helping them to understand the cause-and-effect nature of behavior.

As much as possible, natural consequences should be employed in classrooms; however, doing so is not always plausible. For one, teachers cannot always allow students to suffer the natural consequences of their behavior. A natural consequence may allow students to get exactly what they want. For instance, talking too much during a classroom activity may cause a student to lose his opportunity to engage in an academic activity, an outcome he desires. Two, certain natural consequences may pose safety risks to students. Teachers cannot allow students to suffer injuries during physical fights, even though getting injured in a fight would be a natural consequence for bullying another student.

Since natural consequences are not always feasible, teachers need to plan for logical consequences. Logical consequences are directly related to a behavior, but usually are the result of another person's intervention. For example, a teacher may ask students to remove themselves from a group activity because they are not following the rules or bothering other students. Logical consequences are best administered in a calm and positive manner, using an assertive tone of voice. Logical consequences may or may not involve student choice. The following two teacher statements reflect consequences that are stated clearly, without emotion. One involves student choice and the other does not.

"John, you can either work quietly with your peers, or I will remove you from
the group and you can work with me."

"Marcel, when you stop talking, we can start the game."

Teachers and other school personnel often employ punishments as a way of discouraging inappropriate student behavior. Punishments are adverse consequences with the intention of suppressing undesirable behavior. Common punishments used in schools include office referrals, moving students to another part of the room or placing them in time-out, and in-school suspension for inappropriate behavior. Although punishment can be delivered effectively, its misuse and overuse often creates behavior problems and fosters adversarial relationships between teachers and students. Often punishments are not logically related to the offending behavior; thus, its use does little to help students understand what the acceptable behavior would have been in any given situation. Moreover, students learn that it is okay to punish others, particularly when you are in a position of authority. As a result, students lose opportunities to learn more appropriate prosocial behaviors. Punishing acts do not help students examine the motivation behind their behavior or its consequences, an important connection students must make if they are to learn to self-control (Jones & Jones, 2006). Further, the overuse of punishment often leads students to resent their teachers and increases hostility toward them (Dreikurs, Grundwald, & Pepper, 1982; Jones & Jones, 2006).

Designing Effective Instruction

Well-structured, engaging instruction that fosters student success is a key ingredient in preventing behavior problems. In previous chapters, we described instructional approaches that help support the learning of students with disabilities and other struggling students. Providing effective instruction, designed to meet the needs of individual students, will prevent many classroom behavior problems. It is well documented that organized classroom instruction prevents off-task behavior, which leads to behavior problems, and improves student learning (Epstein et al., 2008). In this section, we describe strategies for maximizing student engagement.

Increasing Rates of Student Responding

When students have multiple opportunities to respond during instruction, they are more likely to be actively engaged and less likely to demonstrate off-task and unproductive behaviors (Haydon, Borders, Embury, & Clarke, 2009). Table 9.2 includes several strategies teachers can use to improve student responding.

As with any strategy, teachers must consider the degree to which different response techniques support their goals. Choral responding and errorless learning will be effective for mastering skills or improving fast retrieval of information, such as the ability to rapidly compute basic facts, but less appropriate for developing higher order thinking skills, such as the ability to summarize a paragraph.

TABLE 9.2. Strategies for Improving Student Responding

Strategy	Description
Group responding techniques	The teacher can use choral responding or some type of activity that requires all students to participate when answering a question. Choral responding involves all students verbally responding to a question. Other group participation response techniques require all students to do something in response to a teacher prompt. For instance, if a teacher asks students to spell a decodable word using their letter tiles, then all students would spell the word using the tiles.
Mixed responding techniques	The teacher can use a combination of group response techniques and calling on individuals to assess individual performance. This approach is effective because students often do not know when they will be asked to respond; thus, it keeps students on their toes during instruction.
Think–pair–share	In this technique, the teacher first poses a question or problem to students or might ask students to summarize the main points of the lesson so far. The teacher then asks students to share responses with the class. This technique helps encourage students with more fragile understandings to participate because anxieties associated with answering incorrectly are minimized.
Asking open-ended questions	When a teacher asks well-formulated open-ended questions about something students have done, he or she can promote student engagement. For instance, asking students to talk about the pictures in and title of a book before they make a prediction can engage students. Or asking students how characters in a story might have felt after an event can promote discussion.
Errorless learning	Strategies that enable the teacher to reduce incorrect responding can also help reduce disruptive behaviors. One strategy that promotes errorless learning is errorless responding. Here the teacher models the correct answer prior to asking the question. For instance, the teacher may demonstrate how to blend the word *clap* and then ask a student to blend the word. The teacher can also provide students with two choices for a response to minimize errors.

Fostering Student Interest

Students are motivated to engage in instruction that they find interesting. When students are motivated, they are more likely than their less motivated peers to be on-task and to achieve academically. Research shows that teachers can employ specific techniques to improve student motivation (Brophy, 1987). See Table 9.3 for examples of those techniques.

Well-Structured Cooperative Learning Activities

To accommodate the differentiated needs of students with disabilities in inclusive classrooms, peer-learning activities inevitably will be used. Well-structured,

TABLE 9.3. Techniques for Fostering Motivation

Motivational techniques	Definition and examples
Relating content to student interests	Students are more interested in those tasks and concepts that are relevant to them. For example, a teacher might use an interesting movie to introduce a topic.
Addressing student needs	Students are more likely to be invested in an academic task if they can meet basic needs by engaging in it. For example, a student might gain a sense of belonging by participating in classwide peer tutoring activities.
Building a strong rationale for learning	Students will try a new strategy or learn a new skill when they are aware of how it can help them (e.g., see building rationales in Chapter 7).
Introducing novelty and variety	Students can hold their attention for longer periods of time when the teacher introduces novelty and variety into his or her instruction (e.g., using a concrete activity to introduce a science concept or changing activities every 15–20 minutes).
Increasing chance of student success	Students are more motivated to try tasks when they know they will be successful and avoid those when they know they might fail. This is why principles of universal design and differentiated learning, described in Chapter 4, are so important.
Creating a feeling tone	Students work best in a class that has a moderately positive tone, one where they believe they will be rewarded for their efforts, but also expected to work hard. By using the strategies described in this chapter, the teacher should be able to create such a tone.
Providing assessment and corrective feedback	Ongoing assessment of students' academic and classroom behavior can do much to improve their motivation to learn, not to mention their skills. When the teacher uses assessment to help students set goals, monitor their progress, and determine how well they are achieving their goals, students are likely to be committed to working harder at their goals. Strategies for addressing such self-regulated learning are articulated in Chapter 7 and later in this chapter.

focused, peer-learning activities, such as those described in Chapter 8, can help students with disabilities learn. To make cooperative learning activities more productive, teachers must think carefully about behaviors they want students to demonstrate and procedures they want students to use (O'Connor & Jenkins, 1996). For instance, teachers will want students to know how to:

- Move quietly to meet peers.
- Get materials out quickly.
- Observe or listen to their peers.
- Provide feedback.
- Provide encouragement.

Teaching the language and verbal cues that provide encouragement and feedback will be very important (e.g., smiling and saying, "You did a great job, you only missed one"; "Try that word again"; "That wasn't quite right, the correct word was . . .").

In cooperative activities that involve three or more students, teachers should consider assigning roles. For instance, one student could record ideas, another could ask students to elaborate or clarify their ideas, and a third could be responsible for editing ideas. Again, students will need to learn the behaviors that will allow them to be successful in their roles, so that they can work productively.

As with teaching rules, teachers will want to provide instruction in how to work together (Johnson, Johnson, & Holubec, 1993), by explaining appropriate behaviors and procedures, modeling what to do, using role plays to practice behaviors and procedures, reinforcing cooperative behaviors, and providing corrective feedback. Teachers may want to assign points to students for working together productively, points that will contribute toward their grade. Doing so will help emphasize that the process of working together is as important as the product generated.

Surface Management Techniques for Addressing Disruptive Behaviors

Surface management techniques are nonintrusive techniques teachers can use to stop minor behavior problems and redirect students toward more appropriate behaviors, reducing the need for more structured interventions (Levin & Nolan, 2010). Many teachers use these techniques naturally; as such, we see the following list as a reminder.

1. *Change pace of classroom activities.* When students start showing signs of inattention, such as yawning or slumping in their chair, teachers know it is time to restructure the situation. Playing a game or moving to another more engaging activity might help. Well-developed lesson plans can help teachers be prepared for such changes.

2. *Remove seductive objects.* Cell phones, toys, money, magazines, or other items will be distracting to students during instruction. Teachers can minimize distractions associated with such objects by collecting them during class and promising to return them at the day's end.

3. *Interest boosting.* Sometimes students can be reengaged in tasks when teachers show interest in their work. When teachers ask students how they solved a problem, check their work, or ask them questions about their work, they communicate that they are interested in what students are doing.

4. *Redirecting student behavior.* When students are not paying attention, teachers can call on them to answer a question or do a problem to redirect their attention. When using this technique, teachers must treat students as if they were paying attention. If a student misses the answer, the teacher should ask the student to ask

a peer for help. Teachers should not ridicule students for incorrect answers because they are not paying attention.

5. *Nonpunitive time-out*. Sometimes students seem as if they are getting frustrated, angry, or fatigued in a situation, so teachers can get them out of potentially problematic situations by asking them to run an errand or get a drink, allowing them to calm down.

6. *Acknowledging appropriate behavior of other students*. Teachers can call attention to positive behaviors of surrounding peers as a reminder to students that are off-task or not doing what they are supposed to do. For instance, teachers can tell students they are glad to see that they are sitting up and ready to go.

7. *Planned ignoring*. Some behaviors, such as repeatedly tapping a pencil, will go away if teachers consciously ignore these behaviors. Although planned ignoring can work, teachers should be aware of its limitations. If students have received attention for a behavior before, they may increase its frequency in an attempt to get the teachers' attention. Also, surrounding students may attend to the inappropriate behavior, thus reinforcing it.

8. *Signal interference*. Teachers can use nonverbal cues to communicate that a behavior is inappropriate. For this technique to work, the offending student must know that the teacher is aware of what he or she is doing and expects that the inappropriate behavior will stop. Examples of signal interference include shaking one's head to tell a student not to do something or asking a student to sit down by pointing to his or her desk.

9. *Proximity interference*. Teachers can use physical proximity to stop disruptive behavior. Often just walking toward a student or standing next to him or her will stop disruptive behavior.

Developing Supportive Classroom Contexts

Prevention techniques can only be successful if they exist in supportive classroom contexts. In effective classrooms, teachers are able to foster social and behavioral norms that encourage cooperation and behaviors conducive to learning. Such social and behavioral norms positively influence the social and cognitive development of individuals and peer groups. When students are in orderly, safe, engaging, and cooperative classroom contexts that support their needs, they are more likely to demonstrate increased motivation for pursuing academic and social goals, increased academic interest and educational aspirations, and improved self-concept compared to those in classrooms that are more authoritarian, unsupportive, competitive, or chaotic (Goodenow, 1993; Harter, 1996; Wentzel, 1996; Ryan & Patrick, 2001).

By holding high, clear, and reasonable expectations for students, actively teaching rules, and ensuring that students follow rules, teachers can facilitate the development of an orderly environment that provides the basis for positive interactions (Wentzel, 1996). Additionally, teachers foster cooperation by teaching productive group behavior and effective communication skills (Johnson et al., 1993). Teachers demonstrate how to ask for help, provide feedback, and paraphrase or summarize what others have said. Additionally, teachers can provide instruction in managing conflicts that arise while working together, including learning how to criticize ideas without attacking an individual, listen to and understand diverse perspectives, extend peers' ideas, and probe to better understand different points of view. Cooperation skills can be taught by employing direct instruction principles, including modeling, role playing, continued reminders to practice skills, and feedback on skill use (e.g., noticing when students are using supportive comments or providing constructive feedback).

How teachers interact with students is also important. When teachers treat students fairly and respectfully they help develop positive norms for classroom behavior. Students perceive teachers as fair when they consistently reinforce rules, provide praise for appropriate behavior, and engage all students in class discussions. Teachers who conduct themselves in respectful ways are perceived as caring. How teachers communicate verbally and nonverbally, particularly when students are misbehaving, is critical for setting a respectful tone. Teachers should never use sarcasm or overly critical language, as doing so is hurtful and demeaning, and teaches students that they do not have to use respectful language with their peers. Teachers must also be aware of the language they use when students are not following the rules. Approaches that are not intrusive work best, as they draw minimal attention to behavior and minimize the chance that students will be embarrassed by or reinforced for negative attention. Also, calm but assertive approaches to rule compliance make undesirable behavior the focus, not the student. The following tips are helpful for approaching rule compliance in a nonemotional and respectful manner.

1. *Speak with students privately when possible.* Whispering to a student what you want him or her to start doing is often more effective than a public reprimand, as it avoids drawing attention to the student's behavior.
2. *Use an assertive stance.* When directing students to engage in certain behaviors, teachers should maintain eye contact, speak in a firm but calm manner, focus on the behavior not the student, and provide a rationale for why the behavior should stop (e.g., "John, please stop talking. You are making it hard for your peers to finish their work"). Finally, follow through with a consequence when students do not comply; doing so means that you believe the rule is important.
3. *Avoid arguing.* Students need to understand that rules are not something to be negotiated and that they cannot argue their way out of compliance. Simply tell students that they can discuss their concerns after class, but that they must stop now or a consequence will follow.

Fostering a mastery orientation to academic goals and providing support to meet those goals creates an environment where students feel cared for by their teachers. Teachers who set goals for learning based on individual needs, provide support to meet those goals, and give constructive feedback on goal progress promote motivation and adherence to classroom rules (Wentzel, 1996). In contrast, teachers who emphasize earning high grades, foster competition between students, and provide harsh and critical feedback impact students in negative ways. Students in these classrooms are often less motivated to achieve academically, less willing to adhere to classroom rules, and less likely to demonstrate more cooperative behavior (Feldlaufer, Midgley, & Eccles, 1988).

INTERVENING WITH MORE CHRONIC STUDENT BEHAVIOR ISSUES

Although prevention techniques go a long way toward avoiding and minimizing behavior problems, some students need more support in order to effectively manage their behavior. When challenging behavior persists, teachers must first reassess a student's behavior in light of current classroom prevention techniques to determine if more can be done. To do so, classroom and special education teachers would be advised to seek assistance from school psychologists to conduct a functional behavioral assessment (FBA; see Chapter 4). FBAs can help classroom teachers determine if more can be done to prevent challenging behaviors or to design interventions when necessary.

To determine appropriate interventions, general and special education teachers can examine results from the FBA. The FBA allows the classroom and special education teachers to identify the relationship between a student's behavior and the context in which it occurs. Then teachers can select an intervention and assess its success (Bach & McCracken, n.d.). There are several things for teachers to think about as they plan and execute an intervention. First, a primary goal should be to keep the child in the classroom. Second, depending on the individual student and FBA results, interventions may be selected in order to achieve all or any combination of the following teaching objectives:

1. Reinforcement of appropriate behavior and logical consequences for problematic behavior.
2. Teaching replacement behavior.
3. Helping students mediate behavior.
4. Helping students internalize behavior.

Interventions are often behavioral or cognitive by design. Behavioral interventions seek to extinguish target behaviors and teach replacement behaviors through the use of reinforcements, including rewards and consequences. Behavioral interventions are most successful when designed collaboratively by the classroom and special education teachers and student. Such collaboration helps students feel empowered and invested in changing their behavior. Although behavioral interventions are often successful in decreasing inappropriate behaviors and increasing appropriate behaviors, they are not without problems. Students can have a hard time maintaining behaviors in a setting or generalizing behaviors to other settings and situations when reinforcers are not present.

Cognitive interventions, in contrast, focus on the relationship between a student's thoughts and actions to extinguish target behaviors and develop appropriate replacement behaviors. Students who display difficult behaviors in the classroom often react impulsively in situations without utilizing logic and reasoning (Robinson, 2007). Cognitive interventions strive to teach students how to talk to themselves for the purpose of guiding their behavior (Meichenbaum, 1977). When students can self-regulate their own behavior, they can interact appropriately in the classroom environment and other settings. In the following sections, we provide information about research-based behavioral and cognitive interventions that teachers can use either in isolation or in combination with each other.

Behavior Contracts

Behavior contracts are agreements between the classroom teacher, special education teacher, and student. A behavior contract focuses on one target behavior and explicitly describes the target behavior as well as the reinforcer, or reward, to be received after demonstrating the behavior. Rewards can be tangible items (pencils, candy, small toys) or privileges (being class line leader or receiving extra time at the computer station). In designing a behavior contract, general and special education teachers should work with students to clearly define target behaviors, determine those times in which the contract will be in effect, and identify the quantity and/or quality of performance required to receive the reward.

When identifying target behaviors, teachers should help students focus on behaviors that are reasonable to attain. For instance, a student who struggles to stay on-task might need to demonstrate on-task behavior for short periods of time in order to receive reinforcement. In this case, the student could receive a positive mark or star for every 15 minutes that he or she stays on-task. These marks or stars can be traded later for the selected reinforcer. As students are able to more consistently demonstrate desired behaviors, they can work with the classroom and special education teachers to modify their contracts. By involving students in designing behavior contracts, teachers empower students to take responsibility for their own behavior.

Self-Monitoring

Students can learn to self-manage their behavior and reinforce it by learning a specific routine called "self-monitoring" (Shapiro & Cole, 1994). Self-monitoring is a specific technique students can use to assess progress toward achieving a designated target behavior. The technique involves identifying a target or goal behavior, self-assessing progress toward that goal, and self-reinforcement once the target behavior is reached.

Research suggests that self-monitoring routines can help students who want to control their behavior, but need additional guidance to do so (Levin & Nolan, 2010). Thus, self-monitoring interventions are wise choices for inclusive classrooms, as these interventions promote responsibility for one's behavior.

How to Help Students Learn to Self-Monitor

The self-monitoring process should begin by selecting a goal or target behavior. Specifically, teachers and students should focus on learning a positive behavior, such as staying in one's seat or completing class work. The motivation to change one's behavior might disappear if the self-monitoring intervention is presented as a punishment for misbehavior (Levin & Nolan, 2010). Once the target behavior is identified, the classroom and special education teachers and the student should discuss the target behavior and how learning it will be beneficial. In the beginning, one behavior should be selected. The teacher should help the student understand what the behavior looks like and provide feedback periodically. As the student succeeds, he or she can start learning to monitor several target behaviors (Reichle, Davis, Neilsen, & Duran, n.d.). This focus on positive behaviors, or what the student should be doing, is important as it helps students think more positively about their actions in the classroom.

When teachers and students are selecting target behaviors, they should also determine the reinforcement for exhibiting a target behavior. An effective reinforcement technique for self-management interventions is self-reinforcement (Shapiro & Cole, 1994). Instead of the teacher providing the reinforcement, the student selects and rewards him- or herself at the appropriate designated time.

Once a target behavior and self-reinforcer are selected, teachers help students figure out how they will self-assess their behavior using any of the following recording and assessment techniques (Reichle et al., n.d.):

1. *Frequency count*: Student keeps track of each target behavior occurrence.
2. *Interval count*: Student records a response to a question—for example, "Was I on-task?"—at specific time intervals.
3. *Rating*: The student rates a behavior on a predetermined scale at designated times of day. For example, a student might indicate a 3 if he or she finishes work and it is done well; a 2 if work is finished but sloppy, and a 1 if work is unfinished. The rating process helps the student engage in self-assessment by comparing current behavior to target behavior.

Regardless of how teachers and students decide to record and assess behavior, the tool must be simple enough to be completed independently and not disturb daily routines. When a tool is too complicated, it can cause more disruptive behaviors (Levin & Nolan, 2010). To use self-monitoring routines, classroom and special education teachers must explain how to use self-monitoring tools and model their use. For students who have difficulty with the independent nature of self-monitoring, teachers will have to provide more support. Teachers should begin the self-monitoring process by rating achievement of target behaviors and sharing findings with the student (Gureasko-Moore, DuPaul, & White, 2006). Gradually, both teacher and student independently rate target behaviors and share ratings during conference time. The student is rewarded if his or her ratings match the teacher's ratings. As student behaviors improve through the use of self-monitoring, the frequency of self-checks should be decreased, occurring between longer time intervals with the eventual goal of eliminating the use of the tool completely. This process improves responsibility for rating one's behavior and receiving a reinforcer (DuPaul et al., 2006).

School–Home Daily Report Card

The daily report card is an effective behavioral strategy for identifying, monitoring, and changing students' behavior and can improve communication between teachers and families (Chako, Fabiano, Williams, & Pelham, 2001). Using an FBA, special and general education teachers, working with the school psychologist, select approximately three target behaviors and determine the performance criterion a student must achieve to receive a reinforcer (see Figure 9.1 for an example of a school–home

	Language arts		Math		Social studies/ science		Special	
Stays on-task with three or fewer reminders	Y	N	Y	N	Y	N	Y	N
Remains in seat with one or fewer reminders	Y	N	Y	N	Y	N	Y	N
Keeps hands and feet to him- or herself at all times	Y	N	Y	N	Y	N	Y	N

Student: _____   Date: _____

Total yes:

Total no:

Percentage:

Teacher's signature: _____

Comments:

FIGURE 9.1. Example of a school–home daily report card. Based on Center for Children and Families (n.d.).

daily report card). The performance criterion must be challenging but also attainable. For instance, if a student is having trouble following classroom rules, the team might decide that the student initially must follow two rules per classroom period as opposed to all rules.

After determining the target behaviors and performance criterion, the school team meets with parents to set up a daily reinforcement schedule. Reinforcements are determined by students' ability to exhibit target behaviors in school and are delivered at home when the child shows the report card to his or her parents. To ensure buy-in, students should be involved in working with their parents and teachers to identify the rules and reinforcers.

Additionally, a menu of reinforcers, ranging from small to large, should be provided. Reinforcers must be arranged in ways to foster approximation of expected behaviors. For instance, smaller rewards are available if some, but not all, of the successful target behaviors are demonstrated during the school day. In constrast, a more substantial reward may be secured if all desired behaviors are exhibited (e.g., being released from a daily household chore). Second, in order to develop delayed gratification, reinforcers for meeting long-term goals should be built into the reinforcement schedule (e.g., earning points to engage in some favorite activity such as going to the movies). Helping students learn to delay gratification is important as it enables them to internalize more appropriate behaviors. See Table 9.4 for examples of reinforcement that can be used to address both short-term and long-term behavioral goals.

Social Skills Training

Social skills are behaviors and abilities that promote positive interactions with others (e.g., getting along with others, engaging in social conversations and cooperative play, and correctly interpreting others' behaviors and emotions) (Smith, 1995). To

TABLE 9.4. Sample Reinforcement Menu for Short-Term and Long-Term Behavioral Goals

Daily rewards	Weekly rewards	Monthly rewards
• Snack or dessert after dinner	• Play date with friend	• Trip to sports event
• Television, computer, or video game time for 30 minutes	• Special activity with parent such as going to the movies or getting ice cream	• Purchase of a video game
• Playtime outside for 30 minutes	• Day off from chores	• Sleepover with friend
• Other as suggested by child, parent, and/or teacher	• Other as suggested by child, parent, and/or teacher	• Other as suggested by child, parent, and/or teacher

Note. Based on Center for Children and Families (n.d.).

be socially competent, students must demonstrate a wide variety of social skills in different settings, including the classroom, playground, lunchroom, and hallways. Teachers must help students identify appropriate social skills for different school situations (Smith & Rivera, 1993, as cited in Smith, 1995).

Students with disabilities and other struggling learners do not always demonstrate social competence in school settings and may need assistance in developing appropriate social skills. Research demonstrates that students exhibit two kinds of social skills deficits: skill-based or performance-based (Smith, 1995). A student has a skill-based social skills deficit if he or she does not know how to perform a specific behavior. A performance-based social skills deficit exists when a student knows how to perform a specific behavior but does not do so at a desired intensity or within a specific environment.

When teaching social skills, teachers will be well served to first consider a student's current level of social skill mastery. To accomplish this, teachers must identify the social skills that a target student needs in order to be successful in a particular situation. For instance, a student may need to learn how to appropriately seek assistance from others. In this case, a teacher would consider those behaviors involved in asking help from teachers versus peers. Once target social skills are identified, the general education teacher should consult with other school professionals and the student's parent/guardian to determine if a skill-based or a performance-based deficit exists. Doing so will help the teacher determine the type of instructional supports he or she should provide to teach targeted skills. To teach the social skill, general and special education teachers must employ direct instruction techniques (see Table 9.6, page 180).

Finally, social skills are best taught in classrooms where prosocial behaviors are promoted and taught explicitly through the collaborative efforts of general and special education teachers. In such classrooms, general and special education teachers set an expectation for students to act in socially appropriate ways.

Cognitive-Behavioral Interventions

Cognitive-behavioral interventions (CBIs) are based on the assumption that when students change the way they think, they can change their actions. CBIs have been shown to benefit students with disabilities, particularly those with attention deficit disorders and emotional and behavioral disorders (Robinson, Smith, Miller, & Brownell, 1999) in learning to independently solve problems and to gain control over impulsive or aggressive behavior.

Students are taught to use verbal self-regulation (inner speech or self-talk) as a mechanism for making wise choices (Meichenbaum, 1977). For example, the student can learn to recognize how he or she feels when angry, to stop and think about choices for responding to anger, and to pick a solution that yields positive results. Such problem solving enables students to address problematic situations more appropriately and independently, reducing the need for teacher intervention and promoting acquisition of lifelong skills.

Social Problem Solving

Social problem solving is a type of CBI that focuses specifically on changing thought processes and subsequent action in social situations (Christner, Friedberg, & Sharp, 2006). For example, aggressive children often overreact or react inappropriately to social cues, resulting in poor choices (Smith & Daunic, 2006).

In social problem solving, students first learn to evaluate ways they can respond or react to a social problem. Then, they select the best course of action based on the consequences of each potential choice (Smith & Daunic, 2006). Teachers should help students understand how evaluating different choices before taking action can prevent problems.

Teachers can provide instruction in using self-statements (see Table 9.5) to guide evaluation and selection of behavior choices (Smith & Daunic, 2006). To read more about step-by-step direct instruction techniques, refer to Table 9.6 in the following section.

Direct Instruction in Social Skills Training and CBIs

As discussed in Chapter 7, direct instruction techniques are associated with successful cognitive strategy instruction. By following components of direct instruction, teachers can help students successfully develop social skills and learn CBIs. After determining a purpose for social skills training or CBI instruction, teachers gradually move from using teacher-directed techniques (modeling and guided practice) to student-led techniques (independent practice and generalization). (See Table 9.6.)

CONCLUDING THOUGHTS

Effective classroom management is essential for productively engaging students in inclusive classrooms. Prevention is the first course of action and is essential to the success of the class and a foundation for future interventions that may be needed. Preventing problematic behaviors depends on several key ideas: high-quality classroom instruction, an emotionally healthy classroom ecology, and clear expectations for appropriate and effective classroom management, including the use of clearly defined rules, procedures, and consequences.

TABLE 9.5. Examples of Self-Statements

1. *Guiding self-statements*: "Stop, think, act."
2. *Positive self-statements*: "I can solve this problem."
3. *Verbal self-instructions*: "What are all of my options to solve this problem?"
4. *Relaxation*: Breathing exercises.

TABLE 9.6 Components of Direct Instruction for Social Skills Training and Cognitive-Behavioral Interventions

Intervention component	Social skills training[a]	Cognitive-behavioral interventions[b]
Rationale	The teacher and students engage in a discussion about why learning the targeted social skill will be helpful. For example, how will learning to seek assistance help you in school?	The teacher and students engage in a discussion about why learning a strategy for managing anger or other impulsive behaviors will be helpful—for example, learning to recognize anger and develop more productive ways for coping with it.
Modeling	The teacher explains and models exactly what the student does when using a social skill. For example, in order to get a peer's attention, the student might be taught to gently tap the peer on the shoulder and ask for help. The model can include a role play in which the teacher demonstrates how to engage in the social skill with another student.	The teacher describes and demonstrates how self-statements can be used to direct thinking aloud. For example, the teacher might describe his or her anger triggers and then talk aloud about the choices for responding. The teacher may use role play to demonstrate strategy use.
Guided practice	The teacher helps students practice the targeted social skill. He or she might use a series of role plays with different students to practice. The teacher might also use peer-mediated instruction, asking students to role-play with each other.	The teacher works with students, using various role-play situations, to practice the strategy. He or she might present different anger-producing situations and prompt students to use self-statements to problem-solve.
Independent practice	Students engage in structured activities that require them to employ the targeted social skill. For instance, the teacher might observe and record times a student appropriately asks a peer for help during math class.	The teacher observes and records times during class when students can employ self-statements and records their success in doing so.
Generalization	Students are asked to record times during the day in which they employ the targeted social skill and indicate if the result is positive or negative.	Students record times during day when they felt angry or impulsive and employed the strategy. Students also indicate the outcome.
Assessment	Intervention effectiveness should be regularly reviewed and modified as necessary in response to student progress.	

[a]Based on Vaughn et al. (2003).
[b]Based on Robinson (2007).

Even when teachers exhibit effective classroom management behaviors, some students may still exhibit behavior problems. Fortunately, there are a variety of interventions to guide teachers in helping students to meet short- and long-term behavioral goals. FBAs can be used to help classroom and special education teachers evaluate a student's behavior and select an intervention plan. Once the problem behavior is identified and described and contributing factors are determined, teachers can work collaboratively with parents to implement a variety of evidence-based cognitive and behavioral strategies. To ensure successful implementation of the right strategies, teachers should regularly evaluate students' progress.

Classroom management and its evaluation is an ongoing process. As classroom and special education teachers work together to help all students succeed, they are encouraged to continuously collaborate with each other, with students and their families, and with other school professionals in order to achieve each student's goals.

CHAPTER 10

Using Evidence and Collaborative Inquiry Successfully in Inclusive Classrooms

with ELIZABETH FILIPPI

Study Guide Questions

- What should accomplished teachers understand about the collaborative process and the role that general and special educators play in that process?
- What challenges might accomplished teachers encounter and how can they make their ideas more accessible to each other?
- How can teachers build trust and manage conflict?
- How can administrators help set the context for collaboration?

Becoming an effective collaborator is an essential skill for today's inclusive educators. Throughout this book, we have emphasized how important it is for special and general education teachers to work together in analyzing and interpreting data so inclusive instruction might be both powerful and responsive to the needs of struggling learners. In earlier chapters we used case studies to illustrate the work of inclusive teachers accomplished at solving problems together, and at implementing increasingly intensive interventions to support their students with high-incidence disabilities. In this chapter we emphasize the importance of creating collaborative

---

Elizabeth Filippi, EdS, is a doctoral candidate in Special Education at the University of Florida. She has taught students, some of them with disabilities, for more than 20 years.

cultures where teachers and administrators share responsibility for the success and failure of all students and jointly deliver effective instruction to students that is responsive to their needs. We begin by looking at what is known about collaboration and by examining how inclusive educators might collaborate more effectively. We also consider ways that teachers and school leaders can improve their teamwork as they become more accomplished collaborators.

USING EVIDENCE AND COLLABORATIVE INQUIRY

MONITORING THE NEEDS OF ALL STUDENTS

At Reese Elementary School, each teacher meets with an administrative team every trimester to discuss individual student data. These "co-op meetings" are considered tremendously effective in helping classroom teachers meet the needs of all students. The team at Reese Elementary uses a matrix, which has the assessment results on one side and various interventions on the other. The teacher fills this matrix out for every child in the class in advance of this meeting. The team then makes decisions about each child. Does this student need an intervention? Is the current intervention working for this student? Does this student need more challenge? If this student is a special needs learner, what services are being provided?

The team is able to complete one co-op meeting in 30 minutes and 12 co-op meetings a day. The school principal hires a rotating substitute teacher for co-op meeting days to cover each class while the teacher meets with the administrative team. Those teachers who meet after school are able to get a half-hour of release time on another day, if they so choose. While the focus is mainly on academics, the team also discusses other barriers to the child's success, as well as available resources. The teachers appreciate these meetings because they lead to fast action rather than allowing children to slip through the cracks. The administrators value the meetings as an important accountability tool. These data-based meetings help ensure that the needs of each child are being met, whether by intervention, enrichment, or otherwise.[1]

In this case personnel at Reese Elementary School developed a team approach to supporting students with learning and behavior problems in general education classrooms. Reese faculty members drew on each others' strengths to solve complex learning problems, and school administrators provided the resources to cover classes or to compensate teachers for working extra hours beyond the school day. Often collaborative problem-solving teams such as these are used to reduce the number of students inappropriately referred for special education, but this type of collaborative inquiry can also be used to focus on students already receiving specialized services. Collaborative practice in inclusive schools takes a variety of forms from schoolwide and grade-level teams, to classroom consultation and co-teaching.

---

[1] Adapted and used with permission from WestEd, Schools Moving Up, at *www.schoolsmovingup. net/cs/smu/view/rs/13018.*

Most agree that collaboration involves working together to improve instruction in mutually beneficial and supportive ways. Teachers and administrators who work together to create conditions that support collaboration throughout the school can significantly increase the likelihood of providing high-quality inclusive instruction.

Research suggests that using evidence and collaborative inquiry successfully requires a schoolwide effort (Corcoran & Lawrence, 2003; Klingner, 2004). Specific strategies to support academic and social learning once taught by special education teachers in specialized instructional settings now have broader appeal. Classroom teachers are recognizing that most students need learning strategies such as those described in the previous chapters to become accomplished learners, and special education teachers are helping deliver content-area instruction, as well as intensive instruction to students with disabilities on key strategies, concepts, and skills (Leko & Brownell, 2009). By working together with administrators inclusive general and special educators can create learning environments in which they can readily take the following actions collaboratively:

- Select, teach, and practice key strategies for struggling students across content areas.
- Provide structures that support a continuum of explicit and intensive instruction.
- Differentiate expectations for content mastery, and teach so that special needs learners master the critical content.
- Promote high-quality strategy-based instruction throughout their schools (Lenz, 2006).

General education teachers typically have the preparation to provide informed content-area instruction that complements the more pedagogical focus of special education teachers. So it makes sense that schoolwide collaboration is recommended as a way of linking the two knowledge bases and expanding the professional capacities of special educators and general educators.

WHAT SHOULD TEACHERS KNOW ABOUT COLLABORATION?

Collaboration among colleagues can help solve complex problems and at the same time build a sense of community within a school. Now that teachers are under extreme pressure to help every student achieve higher academic standards, collaboration is no longer a luxury but a necessity (Brownell & Walther-Thomas, 2002). Inclusive educators like Desera and Kristi who teach children with learning and behavior difficulties engage in complex instructional interactions not only with their students but with each other. As we followed the interactions of these accomplished teachers and others like them throughout this book, we saw them act as careful observers who recognized the various ways struggling students learn. We also saw them act as effective communicators who provided detailed descriptions of their observations to someone else. Effective communication skills are essential to working with parents and other professionals if schools are to provide the kind of learner-centered, content-focused, assessment-driven, and community-based instruction that helps students learn (Bradford, Brown, & Cocking, 2000).

Friend and Cook, who study how special and general educators work together in teaching struggling learners, define *collaboration* as "a style for direct interaction between at least two coequal parties voluntarily engaged in shared decision making as they work toward a common goal" (Friend & Cook, 2010, p. 7). According to this definition, collaboration is an approach or a way of interacting with others that encourages ideas and participation from all relevant parties. Collaboration is essentially a voluntary decision. Teachers might be assigned to work together but whether they truly collaborate is their own personal choice. Teachers who choose to work collaboratively share resources and accountability, and their individual input is considered to be of equal value.

As collaborators, classroom teachers and special education teachers share mutual goals and equally share responsibility for decisions leading toward the achievement of those goals. They also share resources and often classroom space. Accomplished inclusive educators know that collaboration involves hard work and develops slowly over time so that matters of trust and respect, as well as team or community building, can evolve. The underlying premise of collaboration is that everyone has something to give and everyone has something to learn. Teachers' belief systems and communication skills have a bearing on their effectiveness as collaborators, and those who believe collaboration is worth the effort are more likely to have or to learn the communication skills necessary to allow it to happen (Friend, 2011). The views of teachers and principals about collaboration are shown in the survey results in Box 10.1.

Collaboration—in various forms of teaming, consultation, and co-teaching—is a relatively new way of working in schools and classrooms, and the knowledge base is still emerging. Although not yet a proven strategy, collaboration has become a standard practice in inclusive classrooms (Friend, 2011).

WHAT DOES COLLABORATION LOOK LIKE IN INCLUSIVE SCHOOLS?

Collaboration is considered to be an essential component of inclusive instruction for special needs learners and there are multiple opportunities for teachers to collaborate throughout the school day (Friend & Cook, 2010; Walther-Thomas, Korinek, & McLaughlin, 2005). Aside from informal student-centered conversations, there are also formal opportunities for special and general educators to collaborate on decision-making teams, in consultative relationships, and in co-teaching assignments. The adoption of schoolwide multitiered instructional systems, such as

---

BOX 10.1. How Teachers and Principals View Collaboration

The MetLife Survey of the American Teacher: Collaborating for Student Success examined the views of teachers, principals, and students about their collaborative roles, responsibilities, and current practices. The results are based on a national survey of 1,003 K–12 public school teachers, 500 K–12 public school principals, and 1,018 public school students in grades 3–12 conducted in fall 2009.

- Two-thirds of teachers (67%) and three-quarters of principals (78%) think that greater collaboration among teachers and school leaders would have a major impact on improving student achievement.
- On average, teachers spend 2.7 hours per week in structured collaboration with other teachers and school leaders, with 24% of teachers spending more than 3 hours per week.
- The most frequent type of collaborative activities are *teachers meeting in teams to learn what is necessary to help their students achieve at higher levels; school leaders sharing responsibility with teachers* to achieve school goals; and *beginning teachers working with more experienced teachers.* A majority of teachers and principals report that these activities occur frequently at their school.
- The least frequent type of collaborative activity is teachers observing each other in the classroom and providing feedback. Less than one-third of teachers or principals report that this frequently occurs at their school.

Source: The 2009 MetLife Survey of the American Teacher: Collaborating for Student Success, available at *eric.ed.gov/PDFS/ED509650.pdf.*

Response to Intervention models, requires teachers to plan and implement instruction based on ongoing assessment and progress monitoring. As a result special education teachers are in a position to interact with many teachers, and to truly collaborate with some.

Collaborative Teams

Support teams of all sorts—be they grade-level teams or problem-solving teams—are a popular type of formal school-based collaboration. In these teams, members typically identify with others in the group in seeking solutions to pressing problems. Educational teams usually consist of two or more people with unique skills and points of view who share a commitment to providing effective instructional programs and services (Friend, 2011). Strong relationships, team identity, clear team goals, and successful outcomes all contribute to cohesive and effective programs (Fleming & Monda-Amaya, 2001).

Some teams target decision making about how a student will be taught. For example, problem-solving teams, like those described at Reece Elementary School, decide on interventions before students are referred to special education (Bahr & Kovaleski, 2006). Decision-making teams of parents, special and general educators, and other professionals also determine whether a student is eligible to receive special services, develop an IEP, and closely monitor the student's progress toward personalized goals identified by the team members (Bateman & Linden, 2006). The Individuals with Disabilities Education Act (IDEA) requires general educators to participate on IEP teams, and the law considers parents of special needs learners to be equal partners with school personnel on teams that make decisions about their child's education.

As members of collaborative teams, teachers share responsibility with parents and other professionals in solving student-focused problems. Their effective problem solving depends on a well-researched interpersonal process of identifying problems, sharing responsibility for solutions, generating and selecting possible solutions, planning and implementing solutions, and evaluating outcomes (Friend & Cook, 2010; Knackendoffel, 2005; Prater, 2007). These steps in this collaborative problem-solving process are illustrated in Table 10.1.

It can be easy to underestimate the challenges of the collaborative problem-solving process. Each step in the process depends on concrete planning and careful implementation (Knackendoffel, 2005). The simple form in Figure 10.1 can be used by team members to implement potential solutions, and to specify and evaluate results (Prater, 2007).

TABLE 10.1. The Collaborative Problem-Solving Process

1. *Identify the problem.* Defining the problem in the first place is the most important thing team members can do. Many teams fail to find effective solutions because they fail to produce one specific problem statement (Knackendoffel, 2005).

2. *Share ownership.* Share ownership by exploring solutions together. Remember, in inclusive schools, everyone is responsible for supporting students' success.

3. *Generate solutions.* Use brainstorming techniques to identify alternative solutions. At this step, the goal is to generate ideas, not to evaluate each one. Write down each proposed solution, and briefly discuss a summary of each one before moving on.

4. *Select a solution.* Give each solution careful consideration. Consider possible benefits, costs, practicality, time, and effort. Analyze possible consequences for each solution based on the research evidence of what works best for students who struggle with learning and behavior problems. Next, rank each solution before selecting the best one.

5. *Plan and implement a solution.* Carefully plan what will be done, who will do it, and by when. Identify the criteria that will be used for evaluating success to avoid misunderstandings. Carry out the solution as planned and monitor the consistency of its implementation.

6. *Evaluate outcomes.* Use data to determine if the solution had the desired effect. Make a decision to continue using the solution, or discontinue its use because the problem is resolved or because the solution was ineffective. If the solution is only partially successful, determine why and reenter the problem-solving process at the most appropriate step. In some cases, this might be at the point of generating and selecting solutions. If the solution was ineffective, the cycle can resume from the beginning.

Student's name: _____   Date: _____   Team member: _____

Problem: _____

Potential solution: _____

Criteria for evaluating success: _____

Task/activity	Person responsible	Date to be accomplished	Outcome/results	Evaluation based on criteria

Overall outcome: _____

Next step: _____

FIGURE 10.1. Planning guide for implementing potential solutions. This form can be used to facilitate the collaborative problem-solving process. From *Teaching Strategies for Students with Mild to Moderate Disabilities*, 1st edition, by M. A. Prater (2007, p. 77). Copyright 2007. Reprinted by permission of Pearson Education, Inc., Upper Saddle River, NJ.

In addition to schoolwide teaming with parents and other professionals, general and special educators use the collaborative problem-solving process in classrooms with each other, and with paraprofessionals, using various approaches to consultation and co-teaching.

Consultation

Consultation is a way of providing indirect classroom support in which one professional voluntarily helps another to address a practical problem concerning a third party (Friend & Cook, 2010). Most often the third party is a struggling student. School psychologists and counselors have significant consultation roles as part of their responsibilities, and special education teachers frequently provide this indirect instructional support, especially when a student needs only minimal support.

THE CONSULTING TEACHER

When Kristi consults with a classroom teacher, she needs key information to work toward a possible solution. The consultation must involve evidence, observation, and conversation that follow from questions like these:

- What does the teacher see happening in the classroom?
- What evidence is there that the student is struggling?
- How is the teacher using data to inform his or her assessment?
- What does the teacher think might be the problem?

Next, Kristi, armed with the information from this inquiry, observes the student in the class. Only through data collection and analysis can she identify potential solutions that can be implemented in the classroom. Once some potential solutions are identified, Kristi and Desera select the one that seems most appropriate and decide how they will evaluate its effectiveness.

Mentoring and coaching are also common forms of consultation that provide opportunities for more experienced teachers to use their expertise. Consultation has a rich research base in the fields of business, school psychology, and education. Less is known, though, about the relationship between *collaboration* as a style that values parity among teacher colleagues, and *consultation* as a process that values some teachers' expertise over others. One of the well-known downsides of consultation is the resistance some teachers have to the process, and little is known about why some teachers resist implementing recommended practices and what to do about it when they do (Dinkmeyer & Carlson, 2001). More research is needed to understand what happens when teachers interact collaboratively as they provide consultation to their colleagues (Friend & Cook, 2010), and about the popular but unproven practice of co-teaching.

Co-Teaching

Co-teaching is considered to be the most sophisticated form of collaboration among those who work with diverse students because of the high degree of interaction this kind of partnership requires. In previous chapters we provided many illustrations of co-teaching, as special educators and classroom teachers shared the classroom when jointly teaching their diverse students. We saw case-study teachers use a variety of different co-teaching approaches.

APPROACHES TO CO-TEACHING

At times, special educator Kristi taught a lesson and Desera observed; or Desera taught and Kristi assisted, helping students fill in graphic organizers or ensuring that they were solving problems accurately. At other times they divided the responsibility for planning and teaching and set up learning stations where students could work independently, in groups, or under each teacher's supervision. To cope with large classes they found it useful to use a parallel teaching strategy, which meant they planned together but divided the class in half and delivered instruction to two smaller groups of students. Sometimes they needed to use an alternative teaching approach that allowed one of them to select a small group of students to receive different, and often more intensive, instruction for preteaching or reteaching content, or providing enrichment to students who needed something more. As Kristi and Desera became more accomplished co-teachers, they developed skills that allowed them to genuinely team-teach lessons. Teaming requires the highest level of mutual trust and commitment because both teachers share instruction for all of their students, whether that instruction is provided in large or in small groups (see Friend & Cook, 2010).

Accomplished inclusive teachers understand their roles in the collaborative process, and make decisions about what roles each will take on a day-to-day basis. Like Kristi and Desera, teachers might assume a variety of roles including *lead teacher*; *facilitator* to specific students; *adapter and creator* of instructional materials; *small group instructor*; *co-presenter*; *assessor*; and *consultant* on behavior, teaching techniques, or curricular content (Vaughn & Bos, 2009). Co-teachers might also coach one another in teaching the skills and content with which the other is less familiar. The roles co-teachers decide to play should arise from their efforts to plan and implement instruction collaboratively. For example, the decision to employ special education to facilitate students' use of a particular strategy while the general education teacher is providing whole-class instruction should be made consciously during the planning process, and both general and special education teachers should be able to articulate why they thought that particular strategy would be helpful.

In theory co-teaching has potential to draw on the mutual strengths of the general educator's content knowledge and the special educator's pedagogical skills in differentiating instruction. In reality, though, research suggests that true collaboration is an elusive goal. The most common role played by general and special educators is "the one teach, one assist" approach (Scruggs, Mastropieri, & McDuffie, 2007), but this role is only appropriate at the beginning stages of collaboration because it does not represent a shared responsibility (Friend & Cook, 2010). In some cases, special education teachers assume the role of providing more assistance to colleagues than to students. More frequently, though, special educators play inappropriately subordinate roles, sometimes because they lack knowledge of the curricular content, but more frequently because of turf issues with classroom teachers and the larger number of general rather than special education students in schools. These practices suggest that both partners need to clarify their roles and interact differently so they can create a genuine opportunity to share responsibility for substantive teaching.

The research, however, has not provided sufficient information about how special and general education co-teachers might go about clarifying their roles and interacting differently. To date, studies have focused more on the logistics than the outcomes of co-teaching, which means we know more about various models of co-teaching than we do about the ways in which these models improve teaching and raise student achievement (Friend & Cook, 2010; Scruggs et al., 2007).

TABLE 10.2 Collaborative Goals, Challenges, and Strategies

Goals	Challenges	Strategies
Sharing responsibility for students' success and failure	Student ownership	General and special education teachers work together to negotiate shared ownership for instruction.
Focusing on individual students' diverse learning needs	Student-focused versus class-focused planning and instruction	Promote a coherent vision by first determining what all students need to learn and then employ team planning, using the planning pyramid, or other strategies mentioned in Chapter 5, to determine how goals for instruction might be differentiated.
Ensuring access to the general curriculum	Curricular coverage versus mastery of important curricular concepts	Seek professional development on the use of universally designed instruction, differentiated instruction, evidence-based strategies for students with disabilities, technology, etc.
Managing caseloads and schedules	Insufficient resources and unrealistic expectations for success	Advocate for resources to support intensive instruction.
Receiving sufficient resources and administrative support	Lack of commitment from school administrators	Continue to engage in evaluation and improvement practices with colleagues even when funds are scarce and formal administrative supports are weaker than they should be.

WHAT CHALLENGES MIGHT TEACHERS ENCOUNTER?

Desera and Kristi, as accomplished collaborators, have overcome many challenges that prevent collaboration from being focused, as it should be, on individual students, centered on curriculum, and driven by assessments in supportive classroom environments. As teachers work more collaboratively, they often encounter a host of problems that can easily become sources of conflict. We next consider some common goals of collaborative practice, typical challenges encountered by teachers in inclusive classrooms, and practical strategies for effective, collaborative problem solving as illustrated in Table 10.2.

Challenge 1: Sharing Responsibility for All Students

In successful inclusive classrooms all team members share responsibility for students' success or failure in making progress toward learning goals. The struggle faced by many inclusive educators is the challenge of making joint ownership work for the benefit of the whole class as well as for individual students within it—in other words, moving beyond the concept of *my* students to the shared construct of *our* students. To make this happen, teams of general and special education teachers, therapists, and parents need strategies for developing coherent goals for instruction that can address core concepts, strategies, and skills we want all or most students to learn and then determine how individual students fit into those goals. Thinking about what students need to become accomplished (Chapter 2) and the state content standards are a good place to start, but teams also need frameworks for planning together.

The RTI framework that is being implemented in many schools across the country provides a powerful model for developing shared goals while focusing on individual students' needs. In RTI frameworks, school teams draw heavily on research about student learning in reading and mathematics, as they consider what quality instruction looks like for all students. They then use universal screening to determine students' learning strengths and needs to determine if more intensive instruction is needed, beyond that provided to all students. Such a view of instruction and assessment sets the stage for thinking about all students. Other strategies, such as UDL, mentioned in Chapter 5, also provide frameworks for promoting shared decision making.

Challenge 2: Focusing on Individual Students

Special-needs learners included within general education classes typically have academic and/or social skills that need to be recognized and intensively addressed. But a common problem in inclusive classrooms is this: students with special needs are likely to be treated in the same manner as their general education classmates, and this means no adjustment is being made for individual students who need intensive, research-based instruction to learn. For students with special needs, personalized programming is required by the IDEA. The legally proscribed special education process invites close collaboration and comprehensive planning with others in recognizing and responding to individual learning needs within and beyond the inclusive classroom (Gleckel & Koretz, 2008; Walther-Thomas et al., 2005). In Chapter 5, we talked about techniques teachers can use to facilitate collaborative planning, but the successful implementation of these techniques depends on a coherent vision for teaching and learning. To ensure student-focused teaching, all team members must share a vision about the direction instruction must take for each student who struggles to learn. Comprehensive, student-focused planning also defines the contribution each team member can make toward that end (Walther-Thomas et al., 2005).

Challenge 3: Managing Caseloads and Schedules

Most often maximizing individual learning opportunities is a challenge because there is little time to provide intensive instruction. Special education teachers often work across several general education classrooms and are only present in each one for 30 minutes per day. Caseloads for special education teachers are frequently high, and communication and cooperation between teachers may be insufficient for problem solving. In some instances poor understandings of collaboration and the role special education teachers can play in this process have reduced the special education teacher to a tutor or aide and unrealistically reduced intensive and direct instruction for special-needs learners in the content areas. Insufficient instructional time is compounded by incomplete understandings of how to teach specific content intensively and individually and by an overreliance on whole-group instructional formats. Instructional time can be maximized if teachers can engage students in using technology, reducing the need for teacher assistance, and design effective peer work that engages students in learning needed skills and concepts. Making instruction more accessible from the start will help maximize student engagement in academic tasks. To accomplish this, however, general and special education teachers need time to work together and in many schools teaching loads and schedules need to be adjusted with the support of concerned administrators.

Challenge 4: Ensuring Access to the General Curriculum

Addressing all content-area standards in one school year has become even more challenging for classroom teachers with the inclusion of special education students who often acquire content knowledge at a slower pace. When classes are taught using large-group instruction that does not attend to the principles of universal design or differentiated instruction, and students with disabilities ask few questions, respond to few teacher queries, and rarely participate, chances are their needs are not being met. Teachers who use the planning and instructional strategies described in this text can offset the impact of a student's disability and make learning the same material as other classmates a reality. So can developing in students skills such as peer mediation, self-monitoring, and self-advocacy often recommended by special education teachers.

The knowledge that teachers need to have about academic learning and behavior to help students with disabilities and other struggling learners is extensive. Participating in professional development can help inclusive teachers who need more content-area knowledge, or the foundation to implement evidence-based teaching practices in the content areas for special needs learners.

Challenge 5: Receiving Sufficient Resources and Support

The most common concern expressed by collaborating teachers is the lack of sufficient time to plan and implement instruction, and the most likely solution to this problem is securing administrative support. The building principal is the most influential person in determining whether collaboration actually takes place in a school building (Friend, 2011). Principals can nurture a culture of collaboration and can often position resources where they will assist teachers' collaborative efforts. Principals can also ensure that teachers are paired on a voluntary basis, that they share responsibility for students, and that high-quality professional development is made available. In reality sustaining the work of collaborative practice in a school is a difficult challenge, and support from administrators can dwindle over time. When this occurs having established practices of continuous evaluation and improvement in place can help ensure collaborators continue to meet on a regular basis, use practices with integrity, and provide struggling students with appropriately direct and intensive instruction (Santangelo, 2009).

BUILDING TRUST AND NEGOTIATING CONFLICT

As colleagues increasingly use collaborative inquiry to guide decisions, interpersonal conflicts are likely to occur. Conflict is inevitable whenever people perceive others as interfering with their ability to achieve their goals (Friend & Cook, 2010). Disagreements can arise easily around educational priorities for a struggling learner, scheduling and class assignments, perceived positions of power among partners, and unclear interpersonal communication. Both special education and general education teachers have traditionally taught different students and aimed for different goals. In most schools they do not have a shared history and often lack a common vocabulary that might facilitate common planning (Weiner & Murawski, 2005). Cultural norms have changed with inclusive and standards-based instruction, but general and special education teachers still often come at instruction from different points of view. Thus, the potential for viewing colleagues as cultural outsiders—"one who 'doesn't think like us' who may therefore, do the 'unthinkable'" (Tschannen-Moran, 2004, p. 49)—is great. Trust can be hard to foster, and conflict can be tough to negotiate. How teachers respond to conflict can either foster trust among colleagues or destroy it (see Table 10.3).

TABLE 10.3. Managing School-Based Conflicts

1. Parties must agree to seek solutions to the conflict. Establish an atmosphere that sets the tone for productive, respectful conversations when emotions have settled. Ensure that each person's perspective is expressed and heard by others.
2. Examine common ground. Overlapping interests form the basis for effective resolution.
3. Handle relational issues so that past problems are separated from the current conflict.
4. Decide early in the process how decisions about resolving the conflict will be made. For example, will conflict be managed by consensus or by majority rule?
5. Set ground rules for conversations about the conflict and abide by those rules.

There is no simple formula for resolving school-based conflicts, but experts suggest that the collaborative problem-solving process, described earlier in this chapter, can be used to clarify the issue at the heart of the conflict, generate and select manageable solutions, and come to an agreement that maximizes mutual gain (Bradley & Monda-Amaya, 2005; Friend & Cook, 2010; Knackendoffel, 2005; Prater, 2007).

Teachers have traditionally tended to avoid conflict, but the energy it produces can be a constructive catalyst for change (Uline, Tschannen-Moran, & Perez, 2003). Conflicts frequently result in high-quality decisions because of emotional investments made in discussing points of view and creating alternative solutions to problems. Conflicts tend to engender a strong sense of ownership for decisions and commitment to carry them forward. Conflicts can also sharpen teachers' thinking and clarify their points of view, making it easier for their ideas to be accessible to others. Those who manage conflict well tend to develop more open and trusting relationships with others, which facilitates future interactions and paves the way for collaboration. Teachers have also traditionally embraced the idea that trust matters in schools, because without it many things most deeply cherished could not be accomplished (Tschannen-Moran, 2004).

Whether teachers trust one another can significantly affect a school's climate. Cultivating a collegial atmosphere, genuine relationships, and engaging in joint decision making all contribute toward the growth of trust among coworkers, making it easier to deal with conflicts when they arise. Teacher morale is strongly related to teachers' trust in colleagues—high trust creates positive morale, and low trust creates environments where distrust is pervasive and collaboration is unlikely (Bryk & Schneider, 2002). A sense of caring forms the foundation of trust among colleagues, and honesty, openness, and reliability are contributing factors. Reliance on one another's professional competence is also a critical factor. As a result, trust among teachers is strengthened by formal supports such as certification, job qualifications, hiring practices, as well as norms and values in the school's culture. Trust is also strengthened when school administrators set the tone for teachers to trust one another by promoting cooperation and caring rather than competition and favoritism (Tschannen-Moran, 2004). Trust promotes a sense of community, and supportive communities are crucial to how people learn (Bransford et al., 2000; Vescio, Ross, & Adams, 2008).

ESTABLISHING A PROFESSIONAL COMMUNITY

Schools with an established sense of professional community report better outcomes for students and increased satisfaction and support for teachers (Center for Comprehensive School Reform and Improvement, 2007). For inclusive instruction to thrive, teachers, administrators, and other school personnel must work together to ensure administrative supports and high-quality professional development to strengthen their collaborative practice. In this way these colleagues can build professional communities where those who teach and those who learn feel a sense of "identity, belonging, and place" (Salisbury & McGregor, 2005, p. 6).

Strategies for Developing Administrative Support

Administrators in inclusive schools can play a powerful role in helping teachers reconsider their beliefs and expectations about special needs learners in the context of holding high expectations for all students. In fact, principals have tremendous influence in shaping the type of interactions and instruction that occurs in schools by supporting certain practices and expecting them to be used (Klingner, 2004). Research indicates that outcomes for students with disabilities are improved when principals focus on instruction, demonstrate support for special education, and provide quality professional development and support for teachers (DiPaola & Walther-Thomas, 2002).

Teachers should expect principals to focus on instruction by holding high expectations for achievement, exerting academic pressure, and supporting teachers' efforts to provide expert instruction (Bays & Crockett, 2007). Teachers should expect principals to support special education by requiring instruction that accounts for the unique learning needs of individual students with disabilities and advocates for their meaningful outcomes in the context of the general curriculum (Crockett, 2011). Teachers can also expect principals to provide resources for professional growth, and structural supports including adjusting schedules and personnel assignments, obtaining resources and materials, utilizing data, evaluating programs, and ensuring compliance with state and federal policies (Billingsley, 2011).

There are a variety of strategies teachers can use to help school administrators learn about their work and develop a commitment to collaboration. Table 10.4 provides examples of how teachers might keep administrators informed and encourage support for their collaborative practice (Friend & Cook, 2010).

Collaborative cultures and supportive contexts play important roles in encouraging teachers to use effective instructional practices (Hoy & Hoy, 2003). In addition to setting the direction for instruction and supporting the development of teachers' expertise, accomplished leaders also "make the organization work" for people by changing procedures in ways that enhance instruction for teachers and learners (Liethwood, Louis, Anderson, & Wohlstrom, 2004) Using strategies that encourage administrators to support collaborative inquiry can go a long way toward enhancing teachers' professional growth.

TABLE 10.4. Strategies for Developing Administrative Supports

Planning

Ask your administrator to join initial planning sessions for any collaborative initiatives in the school. Administrators can help communicate your efforts to others in the school community.

Advocating

Discuss with your principal how you use or intend to use collaboration in your program. Decide together the kinds of resources and supports you can expect.

Inviting

Invite administrators to join you in visiting another school to observe an especially good collaborative program.

Sharing articles and websites

Share journal articles, websites, and news stories on pertinent topics with your administrators. Aim to share one item each month.

Alerting

Alert your administrators to professional development activities that feature collaboration. Request permission to attend with a partner and ask the principal or assistant principal to come too.

Sharing professional development opportunities

Share handouts from conferences with your administrator. Ask if particularly relevant materials might be distributed to faculty teams or at grade-level meetings.

Updating

Take time to talk informally with your administrators about the successes and challenges of your collaborative work. Regular conversations can be more effective than summaries in getting the help you need when you need it most.

Maintaining lists

Keep a running list of topics related to your collaborative practice to discuss with administrators. Prioritize the items and discuss one or two when you meet.

Presenting

Invite your principal to make presentations with you about your school's collaborative efforts. Presenting together at other schools and districts can provide you both with a professional boost.

Note. Adapted from *Interactions: Collaborative Skills for School Professionals*, 6th edition, by M. Friend and L. Cook (2010, p. 331). Copyright 2010. Adapted by permission of Pearson Education, Inc., Upper Saddle River, NJ.

Receiving Quality Professional Development

Most teachers who work in inclusive classrooms both want and need to improve the way they teach so that special-needs learners will be successful in school. Depending on preparation and experience, teachers vary in their content and pedagogical knowledge. In some studies, for example, special educators have demonstrated stronger-than-average classroom management skills, but average to below-average practices in teaching reading (Brownell et al., 2010). To accomplish their goals special educators need to know how to assist general educators in delivering content instruction and how to provide direct and explicit instruction to special-needs learners on key strategies, concepts, and skills (Leko & Brownell, 2009). Classroom teachers, in contrast, often lack preparation in working collaboratively and in targeting content-area instruction to students with special needs (Griffin, Kilgore, Winn, & Otis-Wilborn, 2008). Inclusive teachers should expect to participate in professional development differentiated to address their wide-ranging knowledge and skills, and relevant to their roles in improving achievement for special-needs learners in the broad school context.

School leaders and inclusive teachers can collaborate in crafting professional development that meets the following criteria for effectiveness (see Leko & Brownell, 2009):

- Effective professional development is highly relevant and coherent with teachers' goals and needs and with standards-based accountability.
- Effective professional development is content-focused. In fact, focusing on content may be the most important component for changing teaching practices.
- Effective professional development is active and situated in settings where teachers can easily apply their learning to classroom practice.
- Effective professional development is collaborative and focused on student data.

Collaborative inquiry aims to improve student achievement. As a result, teachers should work closely with school leaders to ensure opportunities to mutually discuss and apply what they are learning, and to analyze, using data, whether new practices are making a difference for their students. Analysis of student data and collaborative discussions around that data hold strong potential for strengthening students' gains in academics and behavior.

Learning Together and Focusing on Data

Research suggests that teachers who participate in collaborative professional development make stronger gains in student achievement in both reading and mathematics than colleagues who do not participate (Baker & Smith, 2001; Gersten & Dimino, 2001). Teachers in schools with an exemplary capacity to collaborate typically take advantage of every available technology to connect with colleagues for mentoring and coaching on specific practices (Canon & McLaughlin, 2002). Collaborative discussion between general and special educators helps both make decisions about using limited instructional time to incorporate intervention strategies learned in professional development sessions into their inclusive classrooms (Leko & Brownell, 2009). In Chapter 5, we also provided some ways professionals could use technology to accommodate time constraints in schools.

Although professional development designed to enhance collaborative teaching is important, school leaders need to understand that special educators have instructional needs that differ from general education teachers, and these must be addressed for collaboration to be successful. Special educators, for example, find it helpful to talk with each other about how "they design intensive instruction, as opposed to how they might help their general education colleagues improve classwide instruction" (Leko & Brownell, 2009, p. 69). Working with school leaders to facilitate connections among special education teachers on this point is critical, given that classroom-focused, rather than student-focused, conversations are a common pitfall of collaborative teaching. When teachers and school leaders collaborate effectively, conditions can be set for productive student learning, and teachers can be provided with appropriate professional support.

CONCLUDING THOUGHTS

Becoming an accomplished collaborator—a teacher who uses evidence and collaborative inquiry successfully—is essential for helping students with high-incidence disabilities become more accomplished learners in the competitive and inclusive context of today's schools. Throughout this chapter and book, we emphasized that special and general education teachers need to work together in a variety of ways to analyze and interpret student data if inclusive instruction is to be both responsive and powerful. We highlighted the work of inclusive teachers, who are accomplished at solving problems together and at implementing increasingly intensive, research-based interventions to help struggling learners master academic content. In closing, we emphasize that recognizing and responding to students' needs depends on the use of research-based interventions and collaborative inquiry—on the careful, challenging, and collaborative work of professionals reflecting collectively on student progress to design and evaluate instruction.

References

Alexander, P. A. (2003). The development of expertise: The journey from acclimation to proficiency. *Educational Researcher, 32*, 10–14.

Alexander, P. A., & Judy, J. E. (1988). The interaction of domain-specific and strategic knowledge in academic performance. *Review of Educational Research, 58*, 375–404.

Arbaugh, F., Herbel-Eisenmann, B., Ramirez, N., Knuth, E., Kranendonk, H. M., & Quander, J. R. (2010). Linking research and practice: The NCTM research agenda conference report. Reston, VA: National Council of Teachers of Mathematics.

Bach, P., & McCracken, S. G. (n.d.). Best practice guidelines for behavioral interventions. Bloomington, IL: Author. Retrieved from *www.bhrm.org/guidelines/bach-mccraken.pdf*

Bahr, M. W., & Kovaleski, J. F. (2006). The need for problem-solving teams. *Remedial and Special Education, 27*, 2–5.

Baker, S., Gersten, R., Haager, D., & Dingle, M. (2006). Teaching practice and the reading growth of first-grade English learners: Validation of an observation instrument. *Elementary School Journal, 107*, 199–221.

Baker, S., Simmons, D. C., & Kame'enui, E. J. (1998). Vocabulary acquisition: Instructional and curricular basics and implications. In D. C. Simmons & E. J. Kame'enui (Eds.), *What reading research tells us about children with diverse learning needs: Bases and basics* (pp. 183–217). Mahwah, NJ: Erlbaum.

Baker, S., & Smith, S. (2001). Linking school assessments to research-based practices in beginning reading: Improving programs and outcomes for students with and without disabilities. *Teacher Education and Special Education, 24*, 315–332.

Bateman, B. D., & Linden, M. A. (2006). *Better IEPs: How to develop legally correct and educationally useful programs* (4th ed.). Champaign, IL: Research Press.

Batsche, G. M. (2007). Response To Intervention: Overview and research-based impact on overrepresentation. *Florida RTI Update, 1*(1), 1–2, 5. Retrieved September 25, 2007, from *floridarti.usf.edu/resources/newsletters/2007/summer2007.pdf.*

Bauer, A. M., & Shea, T. M. (2003). *Parents and schools: Creating a successful partnership for students with special needs.* Upper Saddle River, NJ: Merrill Prentice Hall.

Bays, D. A., & Crockett, J. B. (2007). Investigating instructional leadership for special education. *Exceptionality. 15*, 143–161.

201

Beck, I. L., & McKeown, M. G. (2007). Increasing young low-income children's oral vocabulary repertoires through rich and focused instruction. *Elementary School Journal, 107*, 251–271.

Beck, I. L., McKeown, M. G., & Kucan, L. (2002). *Bringing words to life*. New York, NY: Guilford Press.

Beck, I. L., McKeown, M. G., & Omanson, R. C. (1987). The effects and uses of diverse vocabulary instructional techniques. In M. G. McKeown & M. E. Curtis (Eds.), *The nature of vocabulary acquisition* (pp. 147–163). Hillsdale, NJ: Erlbaum.

Billingsley, B. (2011). Factors influencing special education teacher quality and effectiveness. In J. M. Kauffman & D. P. Hallahan (Eds.), *Handbook of special education* (pp. 391–405). New York: Routledge.

Binder, C., Haughton, E., & Bateman, B. (2002). *Fluency: Achieving true mastery in the learning process*. Retrieved December 20, 2010, from *special.edschool.virginia.edu/papers*.

Bishop, A. G., Brownell, M. T., Klingner, J. K., Menon, S., Galman, S., & Leko, M. (2010). Understanding the influence of personal attributes, preparation, and school environment on beginning special education teachers' classroom practices during reading instruction. *Learning Disability Quarterly, 33*, 75–93.

Boardman, A. G., & Vaughn, S. (2007). Response to Intervention as a framework for the prevention and identification of learning disabilities: Which comes first, identification or intervention? In J. Crockett, M. M. Gerber, & T. J. Landrum (Eds.), *Achieving the radical reform of special education: Essays in honor of James M. Kauffman*, pp. 15–35. New York: Lawrence Erlbaum.

Bos, C. S., & Anders, P. L. (1990). Effects of interactive vocabulary instruction on the vocabulary learning and reading comprehension of junior-high learning disabled students, *Learning Disability Quarterly, 13*, 31–42.

Bradley, J. F., & Monda-Amaya, L. E. (2005). Conflict resolution: Preparing preservice special educators to work in collaborative settings. *Teacher Education and Special Education, 28*, 171–184.

Bradley, R., Danielson, L., & Doolittle, J. (2007). Responsiveness to intervention: 1997 to 2007. *Teaching Exceptional Children, 39*(5), 8–12.

Bransford, J. D., Brown, A. L., & Cocking, R. R. (Eds.). (2000). *How people learn: Brain, mind, experience, and school*. Washington, DC: National Academy Press.

Brophy, J. E. (1987). Synthesis of strategies for motivating students to learn. *Educational Leadership 45*, 40–48.

Brophy, J. E. (1988). Educating teachers about managing classrooms and students. *Teaching and Teacher Education, 4*, 1–18.

Brophy, J. E., & Good, T. (1974). *Teacher–student relationships: Causes and consequences*. New York: Holt, Rinehart & Winston.

Brownell, M. T., Adams, A., Sindelar, P., Waldron, N., & vanHover, S. (2006). Learning from collaboration: The role of teacher qualities. *Exceptional Children, 72*, 169–187.

Brownell, M. T., Bishop, A. G., Gersten, R., Klinger, J. K., Penfield, R. D., Dimino, J., et al. (2009). The role of domain expertise in beginning special education teacher quality. *Exceptional Children, 75*, 391–411.

Brownell, M. T., Haager, D., Bishop, A. G., Klingner, J. K., Menon, S., Penfield, R., et al. (2007, April). *Teacher quality in special education: The role of knowledge, classroom practice, and school environment*. Paper presented at the annual meeting of the American Education Research Association, Chicago, IL.

Brownell, M. T., Sindelar, P. T., Kiely, M. T., & Danielson, L. C. (2010). Special education teacher quality and preparation: Exposing foundations, constructing a new model. *Exceptional Children, 76*, 357–377.

Brownell, M., & Walther-Thomas, C. (2002, March). An interview with . . . Dr. Marilyn Friend. *Intervention in School and Clinic*, pp. 223–228.

Bruner, J. (1966). *Toward a theory of instruction*. Cambridge, MA: Harvard University Press.

Bryk, A. S., &, Schneider, B. (2002). *Trust in schools: A core resource for school improvement*. New York: Russell Sage Foundation.

Bulgren, J. A., Deshler, D. D., Schumaker, J. B., & Lenz, B. K. (2000). The use and effectiveness of analogical instruction in diverse secondary content classrooms. *Journal of Educational Psychology, 92*(3), 426–441.

Bulgren, J. A., Deshler, D., & Lenz, K. (2007). Engaging adolescents with LD in higher order thinking about history concepts using integrated content enhancement routines. *Journal of Learning Disabilities, 40,* 121–133.

Bulgren, J. A., Deshler, D. D., & Schumaker, J. B. (1993). *The concept mastery routine.* Lawrence, KS: Edge.

Bulgren, J. A., Lenz, B. K., Deshler, D. D., & Schumaker, J. B. (1995). *The concept comparison routine.* Lawrence, KS: Edge Enterprises.

Butler, F. M., Miller, S. P., Crehan, K., Babbitt, B., & Pierce, T. (2003). Fraction instruction for students with mathematics disabilities: Comparing two teaching sequences. *Learning Disabilities Research and Practice, 18*(2), 99–111.

Cameron, C. E., Connor, C. M., Morrison, F. J., & Jewkes, A. M. (2008). Effects of classroom organization on letter–word reading in first grade. *Journal of School Psychology, 46,* 173–192.

Canon, E. A., & McLaughlin, M. J. (2002). Indicators of Beacons of Excellence schools: What do they tell us about collaborative practices? *Journal of Educational and Psychological Consultation, 13,* 285–313.

Carlisle, J. F. (2004). Morphological processes that influence learning to read. In C. A. Stone, E. R. Silliman, B. J. Ehren, & K. Apel (Eds.), *Handbook of language and literacy: Development and disorders* (pp. 318–339). New York: Guilford Press.

Carter, N., Prater, M. N., Jackson, A., & Marchant, M. (2009). Educators' perceptions of collaborative planning processes for students with disabilities. *Teaching Exceptional Children, 54*(1), 60–70.

Catts, H. W., Fey, M. E., Tomblin, J. B., & Zhang, X. (2002). A longitudinal investigation of reading outcomes in children with language impairments. *Journal of Speech, Language, and Hearing Research, 45,* 1142–1157.

Center for Children and Families. (n.d.). *How to establish a daily report card (school–home note).* Retrieved from *ccf.buffalo.edu/resources_downloads.php.*

Center for Comprehensive School Reform and Improvement. (2006). Characteristics of improved school districts: What are the factors that can improve school districts? Washington, DC: Author. Retrieved May 21, 2010, from *www.centerforcsri.org/files/Center_RB_dec06_C.pdf.*

Chacko, A., Fabiano, G. A., Williams, A., & Pelham, W. E. (2001). Comprehensive treatments for children with ADHD. In B. T. Rogers, T. R. Montgomery, T. M. Locke, & P. J. Accardo (Eds.), *Attention deficit hyperactivity disorder: The clinical spectrum* (Vol. 5, pp. 147–174). Timonium, MD: York Press.

Chard, D. J., Pikulski, J. J., & McDonagh, S. H. (2006). Fluency: The link between decoding and comprehension for struggling readers. In T. Rasinski, C. L. Blachowicz, & K. Lems (Eds.), *Fluency instruction: Research-based best practices* (pp. 39–61). New York: Guilford Press.

Chard, D. J., Vaughn, S., & Tyler, B. (2002). A synthesis of research on effective interventions for building reading fluency with elementary students with learning disabilities. *Journal of Learning Disabilities, 35*(5), 386–406.

Christner, R. W., Friedberg, R. D., & Sharp, L. (2006). Working with angry and aggressive youth. In R. B. Mennuti, A. Freeman, & R. W. Christner (Eds.), *Cognitive-behavioral interventions in educational settings: A handbook for practice* (pp. 138–161). New York: Routledge.

Clark, C. M., & Yinger, R. J. (1987). Teacher planning. In J. Calderhead (Ed.), *Exploring teachers' thinking* (pp. 104–124). London: Cassell.

Coleman, R. A., Buysee, V., & Neitzel, J. (2006). *Recognition & Response, an early intervening system for young children at risk for learning disabilities: Research synthesis and recommendations.* Full report. Chapel Hill: The University of North Carolina at Chapel Hill, FPG Child Development Institute.

Conderman, G., & Johnston-Rodriguez, S. (2009). Beginning teachers' views of their collaborative roles. *Preventing School Failure, 53*, 235–244.

Cook, B. G. (2001). A comparison of teachers' attitudes toward their included students with mild and severe disabilities. *Journal of Special Education, 34*, 203–213.

Cook, B. G., Landrum, T. J., Cook, L., & Tankersley, M. (2008). Introduction to the special issue: Evidence-based practices in special education. *Intervention in School and Clinic, 44*, 67–68.

Corcoran, T., & Lawrence, N. (2003). *Changing district culture and capacity: The impact of the Merck Institute for Science Education Partnership* (CPRE Research Report Series RR-054). Madison, WI: Consortium of Policy Research in Education.

Crockett, J. B. (2002). Special education's role in preparing responsive leaders for inclusive schools. *Remedial and Special Education, 23*, 157–168.

Crockett, J. B. (2004). Taking stock of science in the schoolhouse: Four ideas to foster effective instruction for students with learning disabilities. *Journal of Learning Disabilities, 37*, 189–199.

Crockett, J. B. (2011). Conceptual models for leading and administrating special education. In J. M. Kauffman & D. P. Hallahan (Eds.), *Handbook of special education* (pp. 351–362). New York: Routledge.

Crockett, J. B., & Kauffman, J. M. (1999). *The least restrictive environment: Its origins and interpretations in special education.* Mahwah, NJ: Erlbaum.

Crockett, J. B., & Yell, M. (2008). Without data all we have are assumptions: Revisiting the meaning of a free appropriate public education. *Journal of Law and Education, 37*, 381–392.

Crutch, S. J., & Warrington, E. K. (2005). Abstract and concrete concepts have structurally different representational frameworks. *Brain, 128*, 615–627.

Dalton, B., Morocco, C. C., Tivnan, T., & Rawson-Mead, P. (1997). Supported inquiry science: Teaching for conceptual change in urban and suburban science classrooms. *Journal of Learning Disabilities, 30*, 670–684.

Daniels, V., & Vaughn, S. (1999). A tool to encourage "best practice" in full inclusion. *Teaching Exceptional Children, 31*, 48–55.

De La Paz, S. (2005). Effects of historical reasoning instruction and writing strategy mastery in culturally and academically diverse middle school classrooms. *Journal of Educational Psychology, 97*, 137–156.

De La Paz, S., & MacArthur, C. (2003). Knowing the how and why of history: Expectations for secondary students with and without learning disabilities. *Learning Disability Quarterly, 26*, 142–154.

Deno, S. L. (1985). Curriculum-based measurement: The emerging alternative. *Exceptional Children, 52*, 219–232.

Deshler, D., Ellis, E. S., & Lenz, B. K. (1996). *Teaching adolescents with learning disabilities: Strategies and methods.* Denver: Love.

Deshler, D., Schumaker, J., Bulgren, J., Lenz, K., Jantzen, J.-E., Adams, G., et al. (2001). Making learning easier: Connecting new knowledge to things students already know. *Teaching Exceptional Children, 33*(4), 82–85.

Deshler, D., & Tollefson, J. M. (2006). Strategic interventions. *School Administrator, 63*(4), 24–29.

DiCecco, V. M., & Gleason, M. M. (2002). Using graphic organizers to attain relational knowledge from expository text. *Journal of Learning Disabilities, 34*(4), 306–321.

Dinkmeyer, D., & Carlson, J. (2001). *Consultation: Creating school-based interventions.* Philadelphia: Brunner-Routledge.

DiPaola, M. F., & Walther-Thomas, C. (2002). *Principals and special education: The critical role of school leaders.* (COPSSE Document No. IB-7). Gainesville, FL: University of Florida, Center on Personnel Studies in Special Education.

Division for Learning Disabilities. (2007). *Thinking about Response to Intervention and learning disabilities: A teacher's guide.* Arlington, VA: Author.

Dreikurs, R. (2004). *Discipline without tears: How to reduce conflict and establish cooperation in the classroom.* New York: Wiley.

Dreikurs, R., Grundwald, B., & Pepper, F. (1998). *Maintaining sanity in the classroom: Classroom management techniques* (2nd ed.). Philadelphia: Taylor & Francis.

Doyle, W. (2006). Ecological approaches to classroom management. In C. M. Evertson & C. S. Weinstein (Eds.), *Handbook of classroom management* (pp. 97–126). Mahwah, NJ: Erlbaum.

Duke, N. K., & Pearson, P. (2002). Effective practices for developing reading comprehension. In A. E. Farstrup & S. Samuels (Eds.), *What research has to say about reading instruction* (pp. 205–242). Newark, DE: International Reading Association.

DuPaul, G. J., & Barkley, R. A. (1998). Attention-deficit hyperactivity disorder. In R. J. Morris & T. R. Kratochwill (Eds.), *The practice of child therapy* (3rd ed., pp. 132–166). Boston: Allyn & Bacon.

Edyburn, D. (2010). Would you recognize universal design for learning if you saw it? *Learning Disability Quarterly, 33,* 33–41.

Ehri, L. C., & Snowling, M. J. (2004). Developmental variation in word recognition. In C. A. Stone, E. R. Silliman, B. J. Ehren, & K. Apel (Eds.), *Handbook of language and literacy: Development and disorders* (pp. 433–480). New York: Guilford Press.

Elbaum, B. (2002). The self-concept of students with learning disabilities: A meta-analysis of comparisons across different placements. *Learning Disabilities Research and Practice, 17,* 216–226.

Emmer, E. T., & Evertson, C. M. (2008). *Classroom management for secondary teachers* (8th ed.). Boston: Allyn & Bacon.

Englert, C. S., & Mariage, T. V. (1991). Making students partners in the comprehension process: Organizing the reading "POSSE." *Learning Disability Quarterly, 14,* 123–138.

Epstein, M., Atkins, M., Cullinan, D., Kutash, K., & Weaver, R. (2008). Reducing behavior problems in the elementary school classroom (Practice guide report # NCEE 2008-012). Washington, DC: U.S. Department of Education, What Works Clearinghouse.

Evertson, C. M., & Weinstein, C. S. (2006). Classroom management as a field of inquiry. In C. M. Evertson & C. S. Weinstein (Eds.), *Handbook of classroom management* (pp. 3–16). Mahwah, NJ: Erlbaum.

Feldlaufer, H., Midgley, C., & Eccles, J. S. (1988). Student, teacher, and observer perceptions of the classroom environment before and after the transition to junior high school. *The Journal of Early Adolescence, 8,* 133–156.

Ferretti, R. P., MacArthur, C. D., & Okolo, C. M. (2001). Teaching for historical understanding in inclusive classrooms. *Learning Disability Quarterly, 24,* 59–71.

Ferretti, R. P., MacArthur, C. D., & Okolo, C. M. (2007). Students' misconceptions about U.S. westward migration. *Learning Disability Quarterly, 40,* 145–153.

Fleming, J. L., & Monda-Amaya, L. E. (2001). Process variables critical for team effectiveness. *Remedial and Special Education, 22,* 158–171.

Flesner, D. M. (2007). *Experiences of co-teaching: Crafting the relationship.* Unpublished PhD dissertation. College of Education, University of Florida.

Fletcher, J., Francis, D. J., O'Malley, K., Copeland, K., Mehta, P., Kalinowski, S., et al. (2009). Effects of a bundled accommodations package on high-stakes testing for middle school students with reading disabilities. *Exceptional Children, 75,* 447–463.

Flores, M. M. (2006). Universal design in elementary and middle school: Designing classrooms and instructional practices to ensure access to learning for all students. *Childhood Education, 84,* 224–230.

Friend, M. (2011). *Special education: Contemporary perspectives for school professionals.* Boston: Pearson.

Friend, M., & Cook, L. (2010). *Interactions: Collaboration skills for school professionals.* Columbus, OH: Merrill.

Friend, M., & Pope, K. L. (2005). Creating schools in which all students can succeed. *Kappa Delta Pi Record, 41*(2), 56–61.

Fuchs, D., & Deshler, D. D. (2007). What we need to know about Responsiveness to Intervention (and shouldn't be afraid to ask). *Learning Disabilities Research and Practice, 22*, 129–136.

Fuchs, L. S., Fuchs, D., Powell, S. R., Seethaler, P. M., Cirino, P. T., & Fletcher, J. M. (2008). Intensive intervention for students with mathematics disabilities: Seven principles of effective practice. *Learning Disability Quarterly, 31*, 79–92.

Fuchs, L. S., Powell, S. R., Seethaler, P. M., Fuchs, D., Hamlett, C. L., Cirino, P. T., & Fletcher, J. M. (2010). A framework for remediating number combination deficits. *Exceptional Children, 76*, 135–156.

Gaskins, I. W. (2005). *Success with struggling readers: The Benchmark School Approach.* New York: Guilford Press.

Geary, D. C. (2004). Mathematics and learning disabilities. *Journal of Learning Disabilities, 37*, 4–15.

Gersten, R., Beckman, S., Clarke, B., Foegen, A., Marsh, L., Star, J., et al. (2009). Assisting students struggling with mathematics: Response to intervention (RtI) for elementary and middle schools. Retrieved July 18, 2009, from *ies.ed.gov/ncee/wwc/publications/practiceguides.*

Gersten, R., Chard, D.J., Jayanthi, M., Baker, S.K., Morphy, P., & Flojo, J. (2009). Mathematics instruction for students with learning disabilities: A meta-analysis of instructional components. *Review of Educational Research, 79*, 1202–1242.

Gersten, R., & Dimino, J. (2001). The realities of translating research into classroom practice. *Learning Disabilities Research and Practice 16*, 120–130.

Gersten, R., Fuchs, L. S., Williams, J. P., & Baker, S. (2001). Teaching reading comprehension strategies to students with learning disabilities: A review of research. *Review of Educational Research, 71*, 279–320.

Gilbert, J., & Graham, S. (2010). Teaching writing to elementary students in grades 4–6: A national survey. *Elementary School Journal, 110*, 494–518.

Gleckel, E. K., & Koretz, E. S. (2008). *Collaborative individualized education process.* Upper Saddle River, NJ: Pearson.

Good, T. L., & Brophy, J. E. (1987). *Looking in classrooms* (4th ed.). New York: Harper & Row.

Goodenow, C. (1993). The psychological sense of school membership among adolescents: Scale development and educational correlates. *Psychology in the Schools, 30*, 79–90.

Graham, S., Berninger, V., Abbott, R., Abbott, S., & Whitaker, D. (1997). The role of mechanics in composing of elementary school students: A new methodological approach. *Journal of Educational Psychology, 89*, 170–182.

Graham, S., & Harris, K. R. (2000). The role of self-regulation and transcription skills in writing and writing development. *Educational Psychologist, 35*, 3–12.

Graham, S., & Harris, K. R. (2003). Students with learning disabilities and the process of writing: A meta-analysis of SRSD studies. In L. H. Swanson, K. R. Harris, & S. Graham (Eds.), *Handbook of learning disabilities* (pp. 323–344). New York: Guilford Press.

Graham, S., & Harris, K. R. (2005). *Writing better: Effective strategies for teaching students with learning difficulties.* Baltimore: Brookes.

Graham, S., & Harris, K. R. (2009). Almost 30 years of writing research: Making sense of it all with the Wrath of Khan. *Learning disabilities research and practice, 24*, 58–68.

Graham, S., Harris, K. R., & Chorzempa, B. F. (2002). Contribution of spelling instruction to the spelling, writing, and reading of poor spellers. *Journal of Educational Psychology, 94*, 669–686.

Graham, S., Harris, K. R., & Fink, B. (2000). Is handwriting causally related to learning to write?: Treatment of handwriting problems in beginning writers. *Journal of Educational Psychology, 92*, 620–633.

Graham, S., Harris, K. R., & Loynachan, C. (1993). The basic spelling vocabulary list. *The Journal of Educational Research, 86*(6), 363–368.

Graham, S., & Perin, D. (2007). *Writing Next: Effective strategies to improve writing of adolescents in middle and high school.* Report for the Carnegie Foundation. Retrieved February 1, 2010, at *carnegie.org/publications/search-publications/?word=Writing+Next&types=&programs=.*

Gresham F., Reschly, D., & Carey, M. (1987). Teachers as tests: Classification accuracy and concurrent validation in the identification of learning disabled children. *School Psychology Review, 16*, 543–553.

Griffin, C. C., Jitendra, A. K., & League, M. B. (2009). Novice special educators' instructional practices, communication patterns, and content knowledge for teaching mathematics. *Teacher Education and Special Education, 32*, 319–336.

Griffin, C. C., Kilgore, K. L., Winn, J. A., & Otis-Wilborn, A. (2008). First-year special educators' relationships with their general education colleagues. *Teacher Education Quarterly, 35*, 141–157.

Gureasko-Moore, S., DuPaul, J. & White, G. P. (2006). The effects of self-management in general education classrooms on the organizational skills of adolescents with ADHD. *Behavior Modification, 30*, 159–183.

Haager, D., & Klingner, J. (2005). *Differentiating instruction in inclusive classrooms: The special educator's guide.* Boston: Pearson.

Harris, M. J., & Rosenthal, R. (1986). Counselor and client personality as determinants of counselor expectancy effects. *Journal of Personality and Social Psychology, 50*, 362–369.

Harris, K. R., Graham, S., Zutell, J., & Gentry, R. (1998). *Spell It-Write: Helping beginning writers.* Columbus, Ohio: Zaner Bloser.

Hart, B., & Risley, T. (1995). *Meaningful differences in the everyday experience of young American children.* Belmont, CA: Wadsworth.

Harter, S. (1996). Teacher and classmate influences on scholastic motivation, self-esteem, and level of voice in adolescents. In J. Juvenon & K. Wentzel (Eds.), *Social motivation: Understanding children's adjustment* (pp. 11–42.) New York: Cambridge University Press.

Hasbrouck, J., & Tindal, G. A. (2006). Oral reading fluency norms: A valuable assessment tool for reading teachers. *The Reading Teacher, 59*, 636–644.

Haydon, T., Borders, C., Embury, D., & Clarke, L. (2009). Using effective instructional delivery as a classwide management tool. *Beyond Behavior, 15*, 1–6.

Hehir, T. (2005). *New directions in special education: Eliminating ableism in policy and practice.* Cambridge, MA: Harvard Education Press.

Heward, W. L. (2009). *Exceptional children: An introduction to special education* (9th ed.). Upper Saddle River, NJ: Merrill/Pearson.

Hill, H. C., Blunk, M. L., Charalambos, C. Y., Lewis, J. M., Phelps, G. C., Sleep, L., et al. (2008). Mathematical knowledge for teaching and the mathematical quality of instruction: An exploratory study. *Cognition and Instruction, 26*, 1–81.

Hoy, A. W., & Hoy, W. K. (2003). *Instructional leadership: A learning-centered guide.* Boston: Allyn & Bacon.

Hudson, R. F., Lane, H. B., & Pullen, P. C. (2005). Reading fluency assessment and instruction: What, why, and how? *The Reading Teacher, 58*, 702–714.

Hudson, P., & Miller, S.P. (2006). *Designing and implementing mathematics instruction for students with diverse learning needs.* Boston: Allyn & Bacon.

Hudson, R. F., Pullen, P. C., Lane, H. B., & Torgesen, J. K. (2009). The complex nature of reading fluency: A multidimensional view. *Reading & Writing Quarterly, 25*(1), 4–32.

Hyman, I. A., & Snook, P. A. (1999). *Dangerous schools: What we can do about the physical and emotional abuse of our children.* San Francisco: Jossey-Bass.

Individuals with Disabilities Education Act (2004). 20 U.S.C. § 1400 et. seq.

Interstate New Teacher Assessment and Support Consortium. (1992). *Model standards for beginning teacher licensing, assessment and development: A resource for state dialogue.* Washington, DC: Council of Chief State School Officers. Retrieved October 11, 2010, from *www.ccsso.org/Resources/Programs/Interstate_Teacher_Assessment_Consortium_(InTASC).html.*

Jitendra, A. K., Edwards, L. L., Sacks, G., & Jacobson, L. A. (2004). What research says about vocabulary instruction for students with learning disabilities. *Exceptional Children, 70*, 299–322.

Johnson, D. W., Johnson, R. T., & Holubec, E. J. (1993). *Cooperation in the classroom* (6th ed.). Edina, MN: Interaction Book Company.

Jones, V. F., & Jones, L. S. (2006). *Comprehensive classroom management: Creating communities of support and solving problems* (8th ed.). Boston: Allyn & Bacon.

Jordan, A., Glenn, C., & McGhie-Richmond, D. (2010). The Supporting Effective Teaching (SET) project: The relationship of inclusive teaching practices to teachers' beliefs about disability and ability, and about their roles as teachers. *Teaching and Teacher Education, 26,* 259–266.

Jordan, A., & Stanovich, P. J. (2003). Teachers' personal epistemological beliefs about students with disabilities as indicators of effective teaching practices. *Journal of Research in Special Educational Needs, 3.* Available online at *www.nasen.org.uk.*

Joyce, B. R., Weil, M., & Calhoun, E. (2004). *Models of teaching* (7th ed.). Boston: Allyn & Bacon.

Kauffman, J. M., & Hallahan, D. P. (2005). *Special education: What it is and why we need it.* Boston: Pearson Education.

Kame'enui, E. J., Carnine, D. W., Dixon, R., Simmons, D., & Coyne, M. (2002). *Effective teaching strategies that accommodate diverse learners.* Columbus, OH: Merrill-Prentice Hall.

Kame'enui, E. J., Dixon, D. W., & Carnine, D. (1987). Issues in the design of vocabulary instruction. In M. G. McKeown & M. E. Curtis (Eds.), *The nature of vocabulary acquisition* (pp. 129–145). Hillsdale, NJ: Erlbaum.

Kim, A., Vaughn, S., Wanzek, J., & Wei, S. (2004). Graphic organizers and their effect on the reading comprehension of students with LD: A synthesis of research. *Journal of Learning Disabilities, 37,* 105–118.

Klingner, J. K. (2004). The science of professional development. *Journal of Learning Disabilities, 37,* 248–255.

Klingner, J. K., & Vaughn, S. (1999). Promoting reading comprehension, content learning, and English acquisition through collaborative strategic reading (CSR). *Reading Teacher, 52,* 738–747.

Knackendoffel, E. A. (2005). Collaborative teaming in the secondary school. *Focus on Exceptional Children, 37,* 1–16.

Kounin, J. S. (1970). *Discipline and group management in classrooms.* New York: Holt, Rinehart, & Winston.

Kroesbergen, E. H., & Van Luit, J. E. H. (2003). Mathematical interventions for children with special educational needs. *Remedial and Special Education, 24,* 97–114.

Kucan, L., & Beck, I. L. (1997). Thinking aloud and reading comprehension research: Inquiry, instruction and social interaction. *Review of Educational Research, 67,* 271–299.

Leithwood, K., Louis, K. S., Anderson, S., & Wahlstrom, K. (2004). *How leadership influences student learning.* Minneapolis: University of Minnesota, Center for Applied Research and Educational Improvement/Toronto, Canada: Ontario Institute for Studies in Education at the University of Toronto.

Leko, M. M., & Brownell, M. T. (2009). Crafting quality professional development for special educators: What school leaders should know. *Teaching Exceptional Children, 42,* 64–70.

Lenz, B. K. (2006). Creating school-wide conditions for high-quality learning strategy classroom instruction. *Intervention in School and Clinic, 41,* 261–266.

Lenz, B. K., Bulgren, J., Schumaker, J., Deshler, D., & Boudah, D. (2006). *The unit organizer routine.* Lawrence, KS: Edge Enterprises, Inc.

Lenz, B. K., & Deshler, D. D. (2004). *Teaching content to all: Evidence-based inclusive practices in middle and secondary schools.* Boston, MA: Pearson Education.

Lenz, B. K., Marrs, R. W., Schumaker, J. B., & Deshler, D. D. (1993). *The lesson organizer routine.* Lawrence, KS: Edge Enterprises.

Lerner, J., & Johns, B. (2009). *Learning disabilities and related mild disabilities: Characteristics, teaching strategies, and new directions* (11th ed.). Boston: Houghton Mifflin Harcourt.

Levin, J., & Nolan, J. F. (2010). *Principles of classroom management* (6th ed.). Upper Saddle River, NJ: Pearson.

Levine, M. D. (1998). *Developmental variation and learning disorders* (2nd ed.). Cambridge, MA: Educators Publishing Service.

Lovett, M. W., Lacerenza, L., and Borden, S. L. (2000). Putting struggling readers on the PHAST track: A program to integrate phonological and strategy-based remedial reading instruction and maximize outcomes. *Journal of Learning Disabilities, 33*(5), 458–476.

Maheady, L., Harper, G. F., & Mallette, B. (2003). Classwide peer tutoring: Go for it. *Current Practice Alerts, 8*, 1–4. Retrieved from *www.TeachingLD.org.*

Maheady, L., Mallette, B., & Harper, G. F. (2006). Four classwide peer tutoring models: Similarities, differences, and implications for research and practice. *Reading & Writing Quarterly, 22*(1), 65–89.

Marshall, S. P. (1995). *Schemas in problem solving.* New York: Cambridge University Press.

Marzano, R. J. (2004). Building background knowledge for academic achievement: Research on what works in schools. Alexandra, VA: ASCD.

Mastropieri, M. A., & Scruggs, T. E. (2007). *The inclusive classroom: Strategies for effective instruction.* Upper Saddle River, NJ: Pearson.

McCarthy, C. B. (2005). Effects of thematic-based, hands-on science teaching versus a textbook approach for students with disabilities. *Journal of Research in Science Teaching, 42*(3), 245–263.

McGregor, K. K. (2004). Developmental dependencies between lexical semantics and reading. In C. A. Stone, E. R. Silliman, B. J. Ehren, & K. Apel (Eds.), *Handbook of language and literacy development and disorders* (pp. 302–317). New York: Guilford Press.

McGuire, J. M., Scott, S. S., & Shaw, S. F. (2006). Universal design and its applications in educational environments. *Remedial and Special Education, 27*, 166–175.

McMaster, K., & Espin, C. (2007). Technical features of curriculum-based measurement in writing: A literature review. *Journal of Special Education, 41*, 68–84.

Meichenbaum, D. (1977). *Cognitive behavior modification: An integrative approach.* New York: Plenum Press.

Meo, G. (2008). Curriculum planning for all learners: Applying universal design for learning (UDL) to high school reading comprehension program. *Preventing School Failure, 52*(2), 21–30.

Miller, S. P., & Hudson, P. J. (2007). Using evidence-based practices to build mathematics competence related to conceptual, procedural, and declarative knowledge. *Learning Disabilities Research and Practice, 22*, 47–57.

Miller, S. P., & Mercer, C. D. (1993). Using data to learn about concrete–semiconcrete–abstract instruction for students with math disabilities. *Learning Disabilities Research and Practice, 8*, 89–96.

Muller, D., Sharma, M., & Reimann, P. (2008). Raising cognitive load with linear multimedia to promote conceptual change. *Science Education, 92*, 278–296.

Nagy, W. E., & Scott, J. A. (2000). Vocabulary processes. In M. L. Kamil, P. Mosenthal, P. D. Pearson, & R. Barr (Eds.), *Handbook of reading research* (Vol. 3, pp. 269–284). Mahwah, NJ: Erlbaum.

National Assessment of Education Progress (2000). *2000 Reading Assessments.* Washington, DC: National Center for Education Statistics.

National Assessment of Education Progress (2001). *2001 Reading Assessments.* Washington, DC: National Center for Education Statistics.

National Center for Education Statistics. National Assessment of Educational Progress (NAEP). (1995). *Reading Assessments.* Washington, DC: U. S. Department of Education, Institute of Education Sciences.

National Council of Teachers of Mathematics. (2000). *Principles and standards for school mathematics.* Reston, VA: Author.

National Mathematics Advisory Panel. (2008). *Foundations for Success: The final report for the National Mathematics Panel.* Washington, DC: U.S. Department of Education.

National Research Council. (2001). *Adding it up: Helping children learn mathematics.* Washington, DC: National Academies Press.

Nelson, R. J., Benner, G. J., & Mooney, P. (2008). *Practices for students with behavior disorders: Strategies for reading, writing, and math.* New York: Guilford Press.

Nevin, A. I., Cramer, E., Voigt, J., & Salazar, L. (2008). Instructional modifications, adaptations, and accommodations of coteachers who loop: A descriptive case study. *Teacher Education and Special Education, 31,* 283, 297.

O'Connor, R. E. (2007). *Teaching word recognition: Effective strategies for students with learning difficulties.* New York: Guilford Press.

O'Connor, R. E., Bell, K. M., Harty, K. R., Larkin, L. K., Sackor, S., & Zigmond, N. (2002). Teaching reading to poor readers in the intermediate grades: A comparison of text difficulty. *Journal of Educational Psychology, 94,* 474–485.

O'Connor, R. E., & Jenkins, J. R. (1996). Cooperative learning as an inclusion strategy: A closer look. *Exceptionality, 6,* 29–51.

Okolo, C. M., & Ferretti, R. P. (1996). Knowledge acquisition and multi-media design in the social studies for children with learning disabilities. *Journal of Special Education Technology, 13*(2), 91–103.

Overton, T. (2004). Promoting academic success through environmental assessment. *Intervention in School and Clinic, 39*(3), 147–153.

Overton, T. (2009). *Assessing learners with special needs: An applied approach* (6th ed.). Upper Saddle River, NJ: Pearson Merrill/Prentice Hall.

Owens, R. E. (2004). *Language disorders: A functional approach to assessment and intervention.* Boston: Pearson.

Palinscar, A. S., Magnusson, S. J., Collins, K. M., & Cutter, J. (2001). Making science accessible to all: Results of a design experiment in inclusive classrooms. *Learning Disability Quarterly, 25,* 15–32.

Parker, B. (2006). Instructional adaptations for students with learning disabilities: An action research project. *Intervention in School and Clinic, 42*(1), 56–58.

Pellegrino, J. W., & Goldman, S. R. (1987). Information processing and elementary mathematics. *Journal of Learning Disabilities, 20,* 23–32.

Perfetti, C. A. (1985). *Reading ability.* New York: Oxford University Press.

Pintrich, P. R., Anderman, E. M., & Klobucar, C. (1994). Intraindividual differences in motivation and cognition in students with and without learning disabilities. *Journal of Learning Disabilities, 27,* 360–370.

Prater, M. A. (2007). *Teaching strategies for students with mild to moderate disabilities.* Boston: Allyn & Bacon.

Rademacher, J. A., Callahan, K., & Pederson-Seelye, V. A. (1998). How do your classroom rules measure up? *Intervention in School and Clinic, 33,* 284–289.

Rayner, K., Foorman, B. R., Perfeti, C. A., Pesetsky, D., & Seidenberg, M. S. (2001). How psychological science informs the teaching of reading. *Psychological Science in the Public Interest, 2*(Suppl.), 31–74.

Reed, S. K. (1999). *Word problems: Research and curriculum reform.* Philadelphia: Erlbaum.

Reichle, J., Davis, C., Neilsen, S., & Duran, L. (n.d.). Addressing the needs of children who engage in challenging behaviors. Minneapolis, MN: Author. Retrieved from *www.education.umn. edu/ceed/publications.*

Reid, R., & Lienemann, T. O. (2006). *Strategy instruction for students with learning disabilities.* New York: Guilford Press.

Robinson, T. R. (2007). Cognitive behavioral interventions: Strategies to help students make wise behavioral choices. *Beyond Behavior, 17,* 7–13.

Robinson, T. R., Smith, S. W., Miller, M. D., & Brownell, M. T. (1999). Cognitive behavior modification of hyperactivity–impulsivity and aggression: A meta-analysis of school-based studies. *Journal of Educational Psychology, 91,* 195–203.

Royer, J. M., Tronsky, L. N., Chan, Y., Jackson, S. J., & Merchant, H. (1999). Math fact retrieval as the cognitive mechanism underlying gender differences in math test performance. *Contemporary Educational Psychology, 24,* 181–266.

Ryan, A. M., & Patrick, H. (2001). The classroom social environment and changes in adolescents' motivation and engagement during middle school. *American Educational Research Journal, 38,* 437–460.

Saddler, B., & Graham, S. (2005). The effects of peer-assisted sentence combining instruction on the writing instruction of more and less skilled young writers. *Journal of Educational Psychology, 97*, 43–54.

Salahu-Din, D., Persky, H., & Miller, J. (2008). The Nation's Report Card: Writing 2007 (NCES 2008-468). Washington, DC: National Center for Education Statistics, U.S. Department of Education.

Salend, S. J. (2008). *Creating inclusive classrooms: Effective and reflective practices.* Upper Saddle River, NJ: Pearson.

Salisbury, C., & McGregor, G. (2005). Principals of inclusive schools: National Insitute for Urban School Improvement. Retrieved from *www.urbanschools.org/pdf/principals.inclusive.LETTER. pdf.*

Santangelo, T. (2009). Collaborative problem solving effectively implemented, but not sustained: A case for aligning the sun, the moon, and the stars. *Exceptional Children, 75*, 185–209.

Schumaker, J. B., Deshler, D. D., Alley, G. R.,Warner, M. M., Clark, F. L., & Nolan, S. (1982). Error monitoring: A learning strategy for improving adolescent academic performance. In W. M. Cruickshank & J. W. Lerner (Eds.), *Coming of age: Vol. 3. The best of ACLD* (pp. 170–183). Syracuse, NY: Syracuse University Press.

Schumaker, J. B., Deshler, D. D., & Denton, P. (1984). *The learning strategies curriculum: The paraphrasing strategy.* Lawrence: University of Kansas.

Schumaker, J. B., & Sheldon, J. (1985). *The sentence writing strategy.* Lawrence: University of Kansas.

Schumm, J. S., Vaughn, S., & Harris, J. (1997). Pyramid power for collaborative planning for content area instruction. *Teaching Exceptional Children, 29*, 62–66.

Scigliano, D., & Hipsky, S. (2010). 3 ring circus of differentiated instruction. *Kappa Delta Pi Record, 46*, 82–86.

Scott, C. M. (2004). Syntactic contributions to literacy learning. In C. A. Stone, E. R. Silliman, B. J. Ehren, & K. Apel (Eds.), *Handbook of language and literacy: Developmental disorders* (pp. 340–362). New York: Guilford Press.

Scott, T. M., Alter, P. J., & McQuillan, K. (2010). Functional behavior assessment in classroom settings: Scaling down to scale up. *Intervention in School and Clinic, 46*, 87–94.

Scruggs, T. E., & Mastropieri, M. A. (2004a). Science and schooling for students with LD: A discussion of the symposium. *Journal of Learning Disabilities, 37*, 270–276.

Scruggs, T. E., & Mastropieri, M. A. (2004b). Recent research in secondary content area instruction for students with learning and behavioral disabilities. In T. E. Scruggs & M. A. Mastropieri (Eds.), *Research in secondary schools: Advances in learning and behavioral disabilities* (Vol. 17, pp. 243–263). Oxford, UK: Elsevier Science/JAI Press.

Scruggs, T. E., Mastropieri, M. A., & McDuffie, K. A. (2007). Co-teaching in inclusive classrooms: A meta-synthesis of qualitative research. *Exceptional Children, 73*, 393–416.

Seidel, T., & Shavelson, R. (2007). Teaching effectiveness research in the past decade: The role of theory and research design in disentangling meta-analytic results. *Review of Educational Research, 77*, 454–499.

Seo, S. (2006). *Special education reading teachers' understandings and enactment of motivational teaching for elementary students with learning disabilities.* Unpublished dissertation, University of Florida.

Seo, S., Brownell, M. T., Bishop, A. G., & Dingle, M. (2008). Beginning special education teachers' classroom reading instruction: Practices that engage elementary students with learning disabilities. *Exceptional Children, 75*, 97–122.

Shapiro, E. S., & Cole, C. L. (1994). *Change in the classroom: Self management interventions.* New York: Guilford Press.

Smith, J. O. (1995). *Behavior management: Getting to the bottom of social skills deficits.* Presented at the Calumet LD Forum, Purdue University, West Lafayette, IN. Retrieved from *www.ldonline. org/article/6165.*

Smith, S. W., & Daunic, A. P. (2006). *Modifying difficult behaviors through problem-solving instruction: Strategies for the elementary classroom.* Boston: Pearson Allyn and Bacon.

Snow, C. E. (2002). *Reading for understanding: Toward a research and development program in reading comprehension.* Pittsburgh, PA: RAND.

Spooner, F., Baker, J. N., Harris, A. A., Ahlgrim-Delzell, L., & Browder, D. (2007). Effects of training in universal design for learning on lesson plan development. *Remedial and Special Education, 28,* 108–116.

Stanovich, K. E. (1986). Matthew effects in reading: Some consequences of individual differences in the acquisition of literacy. *Reading Research Quarterly, 21,* 360–406.

Sternberg, R. J., & Ben-Zeev, T. (2001). *Complex cognition: The psychology of human thought.* Cambridge, UK: Cambridge University Press.

Stichter, J. P., Conroy, M. A., & Kauffman, J. M. (2008). *An introduction to students with high incidence disabilities.* Upper Saddle River, NJ: Prentice Hall.

Stough, L. M., & Palmer, D. J. (2003). Special thinking in special settings: A qualitative study of expert special educators. *Journal of Special Education, 36,* 206–222.

Stuart, S. K., & Rinaldi, C. (2009). A collaborative planning framework for teachers implementing tiered instruction. *Teaching Exceptional Children, 42,* 52–57.

Swanson, H. L. (1999). Reading comprehension and working memory in learning-disabled readers: Is the phonological loop more important than the executive system? *Journal of Experimental Child Psychology, 72,* 1–31.

Swanson, H. L. (2000). What instruction works for students with learning disabilities?: Summarizing the results from a meta-analysis of intervention studies. In R. Gersten, E. P. Schiller, & S. Vaughn (Eds.), *Contemporary special education research: Syntheses of the knowledge base on critical instructional issues* (pp. 1–30). Mahwah, NJ: Erlbaum.

Swanson, H. L., & Deshler, D. (2003). Instructing adolescents with learning disabilities: Converting a meta-analysis to practice. *Journal of Learning Disabilities, 36,* 124–135.

Swanson, H. L., Hoskyn, M., & Lee, C. (1999). *Interventions for students with learning disabilities: A meta-analysis of treatment outcomes.* New York: Guilford Press.

Tabassam, W., & Grainger, J. (2002). Self-concept, attributional style and self-efficacy beliefs of students with learning disabilities with and without attention deficit hyperactivity disorder. *Learning Disabilities Quarterly, 25,* 141–151.

Taylor, B. M., Pearson, P. D., Peterson, D. S., & Rodriquez, M. (2005). Reading growth in high poverty classrooms: The influence of teacher practices that encourage cognitive engagement in literacy learning. *Elementary School Journal, 104,* 3–18.

Tomlinson, C. A. (2008). The goals of differentiation. *Educational Leadership, 66*(3), 26–30.

Tomlinson, C. A. (2009). Intersections between differentiation and literacy instruction: Shared principles worth sharing. *New England Reading Association Journal, 45,* 28–33.

Tomlinson, C. A., & Edison, C. C. (2003). *Differentiate in practice: A resource guide for differentiating curriculum.* Alexandria, VA: Association for Supervision and Curriculum Development.

Torgesen, J. K. (2007). *Using an RTI model to guide early reading instruction: Effects on identification rates for students with learning disabilities.* FL: Florida Center for Reading Research at Florida State University. Retrieved September 24, 2007, from *www.fcrr.org/newsletter/Two-Column/august.htm#highlight.*

Torgesen, J. K., Rashotte, C. A., & Alexander, A. (2001). Principles of fluency instruction in reading: Relationships with established empirical outcomes. In M. Wolf (Ed.), *Dyslexia, fluency, and the brain* (pp. 333–356). Parkton, MD: New York Press.

Torgesen, J. K., Rashotte, C., Alexander, A., Alexander, J., & MacPhee, K. (2003). Progress towards understanding the instructional conditions necessary for remediating reading difficulties in older children. In B. Foorman (Ed.), *Preventing and remediating reading difficulties: Bringing science to scale* (pp. 275–298). Baltimore: York Press.

Troia, G. (2004). Phonological processing and its influence on literacy learning. In C. A. Stone, E. R. Silliman, B. J. Ehren, & K. Apel (Eds.), *Handbook of language and literacy* (pp. 271–301). New York: Guilford Press.

Tschannen-Moran, M. (2004). *Trust matters: Leadership for successful schools.* San Francisco: Jossey-Bass.

Uline, C., Tschannen-Moran, M., & Perez, L. (2003). Constructive conflict: How controversy can contribute to school improvement. *Teachers College Record, 105*, 782–815.

U.S. Department of Education. (2010). *29th Annual (2007) Report to Congress on the Implementation of the Individuals with Disabilities Education Act* (Vol. 1). Washington, DC: Office of Special Education and Rehabilitative Services, Office of Special Education Programs.

Vaughn, S., & Bos, C. S. (2009). *Strategies for teaching students with learning and behavior problems* (7th ed.). Upper Saddle River, NJ: Pearson.

Vaughn, S., Bos, C., & Schumm, J. (2007). *Teaching students who are exceptional, diverse, and at risk in the general education classroom*. Boston: Pearson.

Vaughn, S., Kim, A.-H., Morris Sloan, C. V., Hughes, M. T., Elbaum, B., & Sridhar, D. (2003). Social skills interventions for young children with disabilities. *Remedial and Special Education 24*, 2–15.

Vaughn, S., & Linan-Thompson, S. (2003). What is special about special education for students with learning disabilities? *Journal of Special Education, 37*, 140–147.

Vescio, V., Ross, D., & Adams, A. (2008). A review of research on the impact of professional learning communities on teaching practice and student learning. *Teaching and Teacher Education: An International Journal of Research and Studies, 24*, 80–91.

Walther-Thomas, C., & DiPaola, M. F. (2003). What instructional leaders need to know about special education. In W. Owings & L. Kaplan (Eds.), *Best practices, best thinking, and emerging issues in school leadership* (pp. 125–136). Thousand Oaks, CA: Corwin Press.

Walther-Thomas, C., Korinek, L., & McLaughlin, V. L. (2005). Collaboration to support students' success. In T. M. Skrtic, K. R. Harris, & J. G. Shriner (eds.), *Special education policy and practice: Accountability, instruction, and social challenges* (pp. 182–211). Denver, CO: Love Publishing.

Weiner, I., & Murawski, W. (2005). Schools attuned: A model for collaborative intervention. *Intervention in School and Clinic, 40*, 284–290.

Welch, M. (1992). The PLEASE strategy: A metacognitive learning strategy for improving the paragraph writing of students with mild disabilities. *Learning Disability Quarterly, 15*, 119–128.

Wentzel, K. R. (1996). Social and academic motivation in middle school: Concurrent and long-term relations to academic effort. *Journal of Early Adolescence, 16*, 390–406.

Wiggins, G., & McTighe, J. (1998). *Understanding by design*. Alexandria, VA: Association for Supervision and Curriculum Development.

Witzel, B. S., Mercer, C. D., & Miller, M. D. (2003). Teaching algebra to students with learning difficulties: An investigation of an explicit instruction model. *Learning Disabilities Research and Practice, 18*, 121–131.

Wolf, M., Barzillai, M., Gottwald, S., Miller, L., Spencer, K., Norton, E., Lovett, M., & Morris, R. (2009). The RAVE-O intervention: Connecting neuroscience to the classroom. *Mind, Brain, and Education, 3*, 84–93.

Wolf, M., Miller, L., & Donnelly, K. (2000). Retrieval, automaticity, vocabulary elaboration, orthography (RAVE-O): A comprehensive fluency-based reading intervention program. *Journal of Learning Disabilities, 33*, 375–386.

Woodward, J. (2006). Developing automaticity in multiplication facts: Integrating strategy instruction with timed practice drills. *Learning Disability Quarterly, 29*, 269–289.

Woodward, J., & Baxter, J. (1997). The effects of an innovative approach to mathematics on academically low-achieving students in inclusive settings. *Exceptional Children, 63*, 373–388.

Xin, Y. P., & Jitendra, A. K. (1999). The effects of instruction in solving mathematical word problems for students with learning problems: A meta-analysis. *Journal of Special Education, 32*, 207–225.

Yell, M. L. (2010). *The law and special education*. Upper Saddle River, NJ: Pearson.

Zentall, S. S., & Ferkis, M. A. (1993). Mathematical problem-solving for youth with ADHD, with and without learning disabilities. *Learning Disability Quarterly, 16*, 6–18.

Zigmond, N. (2003). Where should students with disabilities receive special education services?: Is one place better than another? *Journal of Special Education, 37*, 193–199.

Index

Page numbers followed by t or f indicate tables or figures.